The Book of Mormon:

Jacob Through Words of Mormon,

To LEARN With JOY

RELIGIOUS STUDIES CENTER PUBLICATIONS

BOOK OF MORMON SYMPOSIUM SERIES

The Book of Mormon: The
Keystone Scripture
The Book of Mormon: First
Nephi, the Doctrinal
Foundation

The Book of Mormon: Second
Nephi, the Doctrinal Structure
The Book of Mormon: Jacob
Through Words of Mormon,
To Learn with Joy

MONOGRAPH SERIES

Nibley on the Timely and the
Timeless
Deity and Death
The Glory of God Is
Intelligence
Reflections on Mormonism
Literature of Belief
The Words of Joseph Smith
Book of Mormon Authorship
Mormons and Muslims
The Temple in Antiquity

Isaiah and the Prophets
Scriptures for the Modern World
The Joseph Smith Translation:
The Restoration of Plain and
Precious Things
Apocryphal Writings and the
Latter-day Saints
The Pearl of Great Price:
Revelations From God
The Lectures on Faith in
Historical Perspective

SPECIALIZED MONOGRAPH SERIES

Supporting Saints: Life Stories
of Nineteenth-Century
Mormons
The Call of Zion: The Story of
the First Welsh Mormon
Emigration
The Religion and Family
Connection: Social Science
Perspectives

Welsh Mormon Writings
from 1844 to 1862: A
Historical Bibliography
Peter and the Popes
John Lyon: The Life of a
Pioneer Poet

OCCASIONAL PAPERS SERIES

Excavations at Seila, Egypt

The Book of Mormon:

Jacob Through Words of Mormon,

To LEARN With JOY

Papers from the Fourth Annual Book of Mormon Symposium, 1988

Edited by Monte S. Nyman and Charles D. Tate, Jr.

Religious Studies Center
Brigham Young University
Provo, Utah

Library of Congress Catalog Card Number: 90-60015

ISBN 0-88494-734-3

First Printing, 1990

Distributed by BOOKCRAFT, INC.
Salt Lake City, Utah

Printed in the United States of America

Contents

"The Law and the Light"   1

Elder Boyd K. Packer

My title is taken from 3 Nephi 15:9:

Behold, I am the law, and the light. Look unto me, and endure to the end, and ye shall live; for unto him that endureth to the end will I give eternal life.

Introduction

W hat I shall present is a personal conviction for which I am willing to take full personal responsibility. I ask for your forbearance if I speak longer than is my practice.

The Book of Mormon records generations of contention between the Nephites and the Lamanites; it then describes one

---

Elder Boyd K. Packer is a member of the Quorum of the Twelve Apostles of The Church of Jesus Christ of Latter-day Saints.

time when peace and righteousness prevailed. "There was no contention in the land." There were no "manner of -ites; but they were in one, the children of Christ" (4 Nephi 1:15, 17). That is worth keeping in mind as we open a discussion on the origin of man, a subject which often leads defenders of opposing views to controversy and to label one another. In the spirit of the Book of Mormon, please, may we drop all labels, all of the "ites," and "isms," and "ists"? Let there be no "evolution*ists*" nor "creation-*ists*" nor any manner of "ists"; just seekers after truth.

One need not be labeled a creationist to accept the hand of God in a separate creation of man. And I surely will not qualify as an evolutionist notwithstanding I believe that many things evolve, for I believe that many other things do not. Views can change, evolve, if you will, toward the truth. I declare the gospel to be both true and inclusive of every true element of any philosophy, indeed the gospel is a fulness of the truth in all of them. Those who defend opposing views on the origin of man use the same words but sometimes attach very different meanings to them. I will define some words in the hope that you will understand what I mean.

The Law

The first word is *law*. A law is an invariably consistent rule, independent and irrevocable in its existence. Consequences always follow the observance of, the breaking of, even the ignoring of a law. Laws govern the physical universe with such constancy and precision that once man has discovered them, he can demonstrate their existence, generally by their effect, with unfailing accuracy. Laws do not change. A law, like truth, "abideth and hath no end" (D&C 88:66). A theory is tentative, subject to change, and may or may not be true. A theory is a means to an end, not the end in itself.

The point of my presentation is this: There are moral and spiritual laws pertaining to values, good and evil, right and wrong;

laws as constant, precise, and valid as those which govern the physical universe. If there is a crucial point of divergence between views on the origin of man, it is whether law governs *both* the physical, or temporal, and the moral, or spiritual, in the universe. If you reject the premise that unchangeable law governs both, I shall have great difficulty communicating my view as to how man came to be. I am counting on Latter-day Saints agreeing that laws governing spiritual things were irrevocably decreed in heaven before the foundation of the earth (D&C 130:20). More often it is students of the physical universe who fail to accept moral and spiritual laws as valid and authoritative because such laws are not measured by methods they have been accustomed to use in their studies. Physical or natural laws are generally more visible and therefore much easier to demonstrate.

These students tend to gather endless examples of the effects of *natural law* to support their theory on the origin of man. But all their examples put together—compelling or not, true or not, whether they prove natural laws or not—cannot disprove the existence of *moral* and *spiritual* laws. To study mankind and his beginnings by analyzing his physical body and environment only is to study but half of him. Regardless of how much physical truth is discovered, it is but half the truth.

Man is a dual being, "For man is spirit. The elements are eternal, and spirit and element, inseparably connected, receive a fulness of joy" (D&C 93:33).

Conscience

We are separated from animals by more than upright posture, an articulated thumb, and the size of our brain. We are separated by a conscience.

Conscience is a most interesting word. It is made up of the prefix *con*, meaning "with," and the word *science*, meaning "to know." The *Oxford English Dictionary* says it comes from the Latin *conscientia*, meaning "knowledge [knowing] within oneself." The first definition listed there is "inward knowledge, consciousness, inmost thought, mind." The second one is "consciousness of right and wrong," or in just two words, "moral sense."

Our conscience might be described as a memory, a residual awareness of who we really are, of our true identity. It is perhaps the best example of the fact that we can become aware of truths because we *feel* them rather than by knowing them because we perceive them through the physical senses.

The scriptures teach us of the light of Christ, "the light which is in all things, which giveth life to all things, which is the *law* by which all things are governed" (D&C 88:13; emphasis added; compare John 1:9; D&C 84:45-47; 88:6), and the "Spirit of Jesus Christ . . . [which] giveth light to *every* man that cometh into the world" (D&C 84:45-46; emphasis added; compare D&C 88:1-13; John 1:9; Moroni 7:15-19). This is of profound importance. As Lehi taught, "Men are instructed sufficiently that they *know* good from evil. And the *law* is given unto men" (2 Nephi 2:5; emphasis added).

Whether this inner light, this knowledge of right and wrong, is called the light of Christ, moral sense, or conscience, it moderates our actions unless, that is, we subdue it or destroy it. It is an ingredient which has no counterpart in animals. Conscience affirms the reality of the Spirit of Christ in man with sensitivities that animals do not possess. It affirms, as well, the reality of good and evil, justice, mercy, honor, courage, faith, love, and virtue, as well as their necessary opposites, hatred, greed, brutality, and jealousy (2 Nephi 2:11, 16). Such values, though intangible, respond to laws, with cause and effect relationships as certain as any resulting from physical laws.

A Simple Example of Moral Law

I shall state a simple moral law from the Book of Mormon by way of example. "Wickedness never was happiness" (Alma 41:10). That is as demonstrable as a physical law but by methods different from those used to study the physical universe. However different the method, the effects are no less certain. Our own experiences, lives recorded in history, the observed behavior of individuals in society, even the interaction of characters in the literature of every civilization, testify that wickedness never was happiness.

If conscience is the only thing which sets us apart from animals, it sets us a very long way apart indeed.

The many similarities between the human body and the physical bodies of animals do not, in my mind, confirm a common ancestor. Not at all! It confirms the sovereignty of physical laws. If a hip joint in the human body is of the same design as that in animals, it simply means that the ball and socket conforms to physical laws which govern space, stress, strength, motion, and articulation. If you want articulation, that design works in the flesh and bone of either man or animal, or for that matter in machines.

It is on the premise that law controls both the moral and spiritual, and the physical natures of man that I have established my conviction on his origin. All laws, even those devised by man, are established under the assumption that violation of them carries penalties. If man is no more than a highly specialized animal, there are substantial questions as to whether moral laws can apply to him.

If there is no moral law, there is no sin. The New Testament makes that clear (see Rom 5:13; Heb 10:26; 1 John 3:4), and Lehi said:

> If ye shall say there is no *law*, ye shall also say there is no sin. If ye shall say there is no sin, ye shall also say there is no righteousness. And if there be no righteousness there be no happiness. And if there be no righteousness nor happiness there be no punishment nor misery. And if these things are not there is no God. And if there is no God we are not, neither the earth; for there could have been no creation of things, neither to act nor to be acted upon; wherefore, all things must have vanished away (2 Nephi 2:13; emphasis added).

Moral law assumes accountability; no accountability, no penalties! Moral law will self-destruct if enforced against those not accountable. It is *not moral* to do so.

One of the strongest statements in all scripture speaks to those who would make little children accountable.

> Behold I say unto you, that he that supposeth that little children need baptism is in the gall of bitterness and in the bonds of iniquity; for he hath neither faith, hope, nor charity; wherefore, should he be cut off while in the thought, he must go down to hell (Moroni 8:14; compare D&C 18:42; 29:46-49; 68:25; 137:10).

Those who mentally remain children are likewise innocent (D&C 29:50).

Animals cannot be responsible for breaking moral laws. If man is but an animal, he cannot morally be made accountable for restraints governing reproduction, social relationships, power, wealth, life, and death. The laws of morality themselves tell us that. "Where there is no law given there is no punishment; and where there is no punishment," Nephi said, "there is no condemnation" (2 Nephi 9:25). Alma, in his remarkable counsel to his son Corianton on the subject of repentance, said:

> Now, how could a man repent except he should sin? How could he sin if there was no law? How could there be a law save there was a punishment? Now, there was a punishment affixed, and a just law given, which brought remorse of conscience unto man (Alma 42:17-18).

There is that word *conscience* again, that obvious part of human nature not found in animals.

Moral law regulates the behavior of human beings and sets man apart from, and above, the animal kingdom. If moral law is *not* an issue, then organic evolution is no problem. If moral law is an issue, then organic evolution as the explanation for the origin of man is *the* problem.

The Effect Upon Society

The comprehension of man as no more than a specialized animal cannot help but affect how one behaves. A conviction that man did evolve from animals fosters the mentality that man is not responsible for moral conduct. Animals are controlled to a very large extent by physical urges. Promiscuity is a common pattern in the reproduction of animals. In many subtle ways, the perception that man is an animal and likewise controlled by urges invites that kind of behavior so apparent in society today. A self-image in which we regard ourselves as children of God sponsors one kind of behavior. A conclusion which equates man to animals fosters another kind of behavior entirely. Consequences which spring from that single false premise account for much of what society now suffers. I do not speak in theoretical terms; it matters very much in practical ways. The word *abortion* should suffice as an example.

Will you accept, for the moment, the governance of law in *both* the physical and the spiritual, or, at least, understand that I accept it? The Book of Mormon speaks the truth. "Wickedness never was happiness" (Alma 41:10)! It might be otherwise if we did not have a conscience.

Many Church members are entirely unaware that fundamental doctrines cannot co-exist with a belief that man evolved from lower forms of life. From the scriptures I will briefly review fundamental doctrines on the Creation, the Fall, and the Atonement. Before doing so, however, let me tell you how I feel about you who study or teach or work in the fields of science.

The Sciences

I envy your opportunity to work in fields of scientific discovery: anthropology, paleontology, geology, physics, biology, physiology, chemistry, medicine, engineering and many others. Just think of the opportunity to study the laws of the physical universe and harness the power inherent in obeying them for the good of mankind. It gives me feelings of wonder, of reverence.

No Latter-day Saint should be hesitant to pursue any true science as a career, a hobby, or an interest, or to accept *any truth* established through those means of discovery. Nor need one become a scientist at the expense of being a Latter-day Saint of faith and spiritual maturity.

Science is seeking; science is discovery. Man finds *joy* in discovery. If all things were known, man's creativity would be stifled. There could be no further discovery, no growth, nothing to decide—no agency. All things not only *are not* known but *must not* be so convincingly clear as to eliminate the need for faith. That would nullify agency and defeat the purpose of the plan of salvation. Tests of faith are growing experiences. We all have unanswered questions. Seeking and questioning, periods of doubt, in an effort to find answers, are part of the process of discovery. The kind of doubt which is spiritually dangerous does not relate to *questions* so much as to *answers*. For that and other reasons, it is my conviction that a full knowledge of the origin of man must await further discovery, further revelation.

Latter-day Saints may safely follow an interest in science and pursue it with commitment, dedication, and with inspiration. Laws which govern *both* the temporal and the spiritual are ordained of God. After all of the tomorrows have passed and after all things have been revealed, we will know that those laws are not in conflict, but are in harmony. The Lord said that not at any time has he given either a law or a commandment which is temporal (D&C 29:34-35). Of course he has not! Temporal means *temporary* and, whether they govern the physical or the spiritual, his laws are eternal!

Physical Knowledge Cumulative

Know this: Knowledge of the physical universe and of the laws which govern it is cumulative. Thus each generation builds upon and expands the knowledge gained from discoveries of the past. Contributions to scientific and practical knowledge are gathered from one generation to the next. As greater light and knowledge are discovered, tentative theories of the past are replaced.

Unlike knowledge of the physical universe, the moral knowledge of each generation begins where the previous began rather than where they *left off*. For example, the remedy for an infection in the physical body has changed dramatically over the centuries; the remedy for infidelity, not at all. Morality is not so easily conveyed from one generation to the next. It is acquired more from example, ideally in the home.

This apparent imbalance in accumulating knowledge can easily contribute to a spirit of arrogance in students of the physical world, especially in so-called intellectuals. They may feel they have inherited the larger and more valuable legacy of knowledge.

The Book of Mormon warns of "the vainness, and the frailties, and the foolishness of men! When they are learned they think they are wise, and they hearken not unto the counsel of God, for they set it aside, supposing they know of themselves, where-fore, their wisdom is foolishness and it profiteth them not. And they shall perish. But to be learned is good, *if they hearken unto the counsels of God*" (2 Nephi 9:28-29; emphasis and comma added; see also 2 Nephi 9:42, 28:15; Alma 32:23; D&C 58:10).

Clergy

For generations, the clergy of the Christian churches (including ours) have been labeled as bumbling and naive because they rejected the theory of evolution and believed in a separate creation of man. Those who have only the Bible have just enough in the Old and New Testaments about men as the children of God, about law and sin, to enforce their belief that man is accountable for his conduct, that accountability requires a special status, a special creation. Confronted by the sophisticated arguments of articulate scientists with impressive visual evidence to support the theory of organic evolution, the clergy could but quote scriptures or testify of inner feelings. This meant little or nothing to the scientist.

Do not despise those who over the years defended these doctrines in spite of intellectual mocking. Do not belittle their efforts. However foolish they may have appeared to some, there is substance to the position they have defended. I say, God bless them!

You should not be hesitant to pursue knowledge; indeed you should excel in fields of scientific inquiry. I repeat, if you respect the truths of moral and spiritual law, you are in little danger for your soul in any field of study. You may safely study the adaptation of living things to the environment. Study "things both in heaven and in the earth, and under the earth," fossils of plants and fishes and reptiles and animals; "things which have been," dinosaurs, mastodons and mammoths, saber-tooth tigers, and, as a bird watcher, I must add pterodactyls. You may safely study "things which are," quasars and quarks, and specimens of every kind of living thing; "things which are at home, things which are abroad" (see D&C 88:79; 101:32-34). Study to your heart's content any worthy field of inquiry, just remember that all knowledge is not equal in value. You may then discover "things most precious, things that are above, and things that are beneath, things that are in the earth, and upon the earth, and in heaven" (D&C 101:34).

"Seek learning, even by study and also by *faith!*" (D&C 88:118; emphasis added). Cultivate faith, that one ingredient essential to spiritual discovery. Then you will understand the *meaning* of what you see through microscopes or telescopes or any other scopes. Your knowledge will expand, even to a knowledge of "things which must shortly come to pass" (D&C 88:79). That is the spirit of prophecy. Do not mortgage your testimony for an unproved theory on how man was created. Have faith *in* the revelations; *leave man in the place the revelations have put him!*

The Creation

Now, about the Creation. What is said in the revelations about the Creation, though brief, is repeated in Genesis, in the Book of Mormon, in Moses, in Abraham, and in the endowment. We are told it is figurative insofar as the man and the woman are concerned. We could hardly understand the Creation at all if we did not have the Book of Mormon: Another Testament of Jesus Christ, and the Doctrine and Covenants, and the Pearl of Great Price.

Who was the Creator?

The scriptures tell us *who* created the earth. Christ, who was the principal creator under the Father, said, "Worlds without number have *I* created; and *I* also created them for mine own purpose" (Moses 1:33; emphasis added).

We know the purpose for the Creation, "For behold, this is my work and my glory—to bring to pass the immortality [that is, resurrection] and eternal life [or, exaltation] of man" (Moses 1:39).

The scriptures say only this about *how* the earth was created:

> And *by the word of my power* have I created them, which is mine Only Begotten Son, who is full of grace and truth. . . . And by the Son I created them, which is mine Only Begotten (Moses 1:32-33; emphasis added).

Purpose

The scriptures use the words "organize" and "form" when discussing the Creation (Abr 4:1, 12, 15, 25, 30). The earth was created or formed of imperishable substance, for the revelations tell us that "the elements are eternal" (D&C 93:33). Matter already existed, but it was "without form, and void" (see Gen 1:2; Moses 2:2).

That word *beginning* applies only if *create* is defined as *form* or *organize*. There was no beginning and there shall be no end to matter. This is also said of intelligence, that spiritual part of man. "Intelligence, or the light of truth, was not created or made, neither indeed can be" (D&C 93:29).

This Earth Is But One of Many

We know from the revelations also that this earth is but one of an innumerable host of worlds.

> And the Lord God spake unto Moses, saying: "The heavens, they are many, and they cannot be numbered unto man; but they are numbered unto me, for they are mine. And as one earth shall pass away, and the heavens thereof even so shall another come; and there is no end to my works, neither to my words" (Moses 1:37-38).
> *But only an account of this earth, and the inhabitants thereof, give I unto you.* For behold, there are many worlds that have passed away by the word of my power. And there are many that now stand, and innumerable are they unto man; but all things are numbered unto me, for they are mine and I know them (Moses 1:35; emphasis added).

When man was created, there was no need for trial and error, or chance. Think! Pray! Open your minds to the majestic vision of the universe unfolded in the revelations! How the earth was made, I do not know! I do know that even that will be revealed (see D&C 101:32-34).

The Sequence Is Given!

All things were created spiritually before they were naturally upon the face of the earth (see Moses 3:5). And we are told, and this is crucial, the sequence of the creation. We know it from Genesis, from Moses, from Abraham, and from the endowment. We know it from the Book of Mormon.

The Spirit of God "moved upon the face of the water" (Gen 1:2). The water was divided. Light was divided from darkness. In turn came grass and herbs, and trees yielding seed and fruit. Then came fishes and fowl, beasts and creeping things. All things which were created, each in its *separate* kind, were commanded to multiply each *after its own kind* (see Gen 1-2; Moses 2-3; Abr 4-5).

How long this took, I do not know. How it was done, I do not know. This I do know: After it was declared to be good, it was not yet complete, for man was not yet found upon the earth. Man was created separately and last.

In the Image of God

However brief the information on the creation of man, one point is emphasized by repetition above all others—man, his physical body, was created, in the very beginning when it was created, in the image of God (see Abr 4:26-27). "In the *day* that God created man, in the likeness of God made he him" (Moses 6:8; emphasis added).

When the brother of Jared appealed for light for their vessels, he saw the finger of the Lord and was overcome. The Lord bade him to arise and said, "Sawest thou more than this?" Imagine his courage when the brother of Jared answered, "Nay; Lord, show thyself unto me" (Ether 3:9-10). The Lord revealed himself and said: "Seest thou that ye are created after mine own image? Yea, even *all* men were created *in the beginning* after mine own image. Behold this body, which ye now behold, is the body of my spirit; and man have I created after the body of my spirit; and even as I appear unto thee in the spirit will I appear unto my people in the flesh" (Ether 3:16; emphasis added). Oh, were there but time to say more of that interview. After the Creation came the fall of man.

The Fall

It is easier for me to understand the word *fall* in the scriptures if I think both in terms of *location* and *condition*. The word *fall* means to descend to a lower place.

Knowledge and agency were given to man in the Garden of Eden—on the day of creation (see Moses 7:32). Choice can not exist unless both good and evil are options. The fall of man was a move from the presence of God to mortal life on earth. That move down to a lower place came as a consequence for breaking a *law.*

Whatever else happened in Eden, in his supreme moment Adam made a choice. He had his agency, he had knowledge of the law, was given a commandment with consequences, was accountable. "Adam fell that men might be; and men are, that they might have joy" (2 Nephi 2:25).

Fall may also describe a change in *condition.* For instance, one can *fall* in reputation, or from prominence. The word *fall* describes well what transpired when Adam and Eve were driven from the garden. A transformation took place which made them "a little lower than the angels." (In the Hebrew text, the word "angel" is given as "gods," see Ps 8:5, Heb 2:7-9.) The bodies formed for mankind became temporal or physical bodies. The scriptures say "the life of all flesh is in the blood thereof" (Lev 17:11-13; Deut 12:23; *Teachings of the Prophet Joseph Smith* 199-200, 367 Kimball 5-6).

After the transformation caused by the Fall, bodies of flesh and bone and *blood* (unlike our spirit bodies), would not endure forever. Somehow the ingredient blood carried with it a limit to life. It was as though a clock were set and a time given. Thereafter, all living things moved inexorably toward mortal or temporal death. Temporal, I repeat, means temporary.

Mortal death, the penalty imposed upon Adam and his posterity, is in fact a mechanism of rescue. It is the process by which we may return to the presence of God. Man *must* be released from mortality lest he live forever in his sins. Without mortal death, the plan of happiness would not just be disturbed or delayed, it would be destroyed! Alma was right when he said, "Now behold, it was not expedient that man should be reclaimed from this temporal death, for that would destroy the great plan of happiness" (Alma 42:8).

How the transformation of the Fall occurred, I do not know. I do know it resulted from choice, and law, and accountability, and consequence. The separate creation of man in the image of God and his subsequent fall were essential if the condition of mortality were to exist and the plan proceed.

If man is but an animal, then logic favors freedom without accountability or consequence. Had man evolved from animals, there could have been no fall, no law broken, no penalty, no need for a mediator. The ordinance of baptism would be an empty gesture since it is for a remission of sins. Many who perceive organic evolution to be law rather than theory do not realize they forsake the Atonement in the process.

The Atonement

If you do not accept spiritual laws to be as fixed as the laws which govern nature, I know of no way to explain what the word *atonement* means in the scriptures. While justice required that the broken law be satisfied, that same justice required that man be punished for his own sins and not for Adam's transgression. The Atonement was a vicarious act of the Messiah. Through the Atonement, all mankind *will* be redeemed from mortal death by resurrection: and, through obedience to the laws and ordinances of the gospel, all mankind *may* be redeemed from spiritual death, if they repent. The events from the creation to the final winding-up scene, all governed by law, are not based on *chance*; they are based on *choice*! It was planned that way from before the world was.

The Laws of Nature

Would you be surprised that natural law exerts a very positive influence on my testimony? I believe that temporal laws have profound *spiritual* value. In their own way, physical laws attest to a durable interdependence between the physical and the spiritual in man.

The scriptures tell us that:

All kingdoms have a law given; And there are many kingdoms; for there is no space in the which there is no kingdom; and there is no kingdom in which there is no space, either a greater or a lesser kingdom. And unto every kingdom is given a law; and unto every law there are certain bounds also and conditions (D&C 88:36-38).

They also say that *"the spirit and the body are the soul of man"* (D&C 88:15; emphasis added), and that combined—*combined*—"they might receive a fulness of joy," and are subject to *both* natural and physical law (D&C 93:33; 138:17).

The tenderest spiritual and emotional feelings of the human heart respond to manifestations of the physical universe as seemingly unspiritual as formulae of mathematics or physics. For instance, our perception of beauty is activated by abstract, cold, and impersonal physical law. That which gives beauty and variety to the face of the land and stirs the very soul of mankind conforms to rigid and inflexible laws which at once provide absolutely limitless variations.

Music

Man discovered that a cord stretched and plucked will vibrate and make a sound; if cut in half, that sound is exactly one octave higher. Divide that half, and the phenomenon recurs. If the string is three-quarters as long, the sound is one-fourth higher; if two-thirds as long, one-fifth higher. Cords arranged in lengths and intervals according to precise mathematical formulas will resonate, or vibrate, in harmonious response. Adjust the spelling of *cord* (c-o-r-d) and you have *chord* (c-h-o-r-d).

When vibrations are produced on the strings of a harp, or piano, or on an organ or horn, or on a drum, an infinite variety of sounds can be composed in endless combinations to form music; all kinds of music. There can be no end of the combinations possible—all within order and law.

New words were invented to describe what happened: resonance, harmony, symmetry, and rhythm, *acc*ord, or *dis*cord. That resonance, or vibration in response, could calm or excite the feelings and emotions of man. The spirit, the very soul of man, can respond in sympathetic resonance, in *acc*ord or in *dis*cord.

Those rigid formulas of mathematics or geometry were found everywhere in nature and connected the spirit of man with what he could see as well as what he could *hear*.

The Visible

I want to present a short lesson in geometry. It would be infinitely easier if I had a surface upon which to draw simple diagrams, a square, and a compass. But I must use words alone. I hope I do not lose you, for I assure you there is a very important point at the other end of it.

If a simple rectangle is formed so that the short side has the same proportional relationship to the long side as the long side does to both sides put together, it has a precise mathematical ratio of 1.618. Without knowing that figure, you can draw that rectangle easily and very accurately with nothing more than a square and a compass.

The relationship of those two segments to one another was known anciently as the golden segment, and is referred to in literature as the "divine proportion," for it embodies qualities of both precision and beauty. When offered a selection of many rectangles, invariably most people will choose one of this proportion simply because it pleases them most.

Draw a vertical line through the rectangle so that one division is a square, the other will be a rectangle of exactly the same proportion as the larger one. You can divide the small rectangle to form a square and yet a smaller rectangle. Repeat that process until they become invisibly small. Each rectangle, though smaller in size, has exactly the same proportion. That would be true if you made them larger. It is an infinite proportional relationship, which continues forever, much as the mirrors in the sealing room of the temple form a corridor of diminishing images which goes out of sight and on into infinity.

Somehow this proportion activates that part of human nature which responds to beauty. "Beauty is in the eye of the beholder" (Hungerford). There is something in that eye, that human eye, which is pleased with shapes which embody that proportion. Whether angular, spherical, conical, or of spiral dimension, it is *felt* to be beautiful. The musical words *harmony, symmetry, rhythm,* and *balance* are used to describe paintings and statues and also buildings and creations of every kind which embody this proportion. They are regarded as beautiful. Why? Because there is some interconnection between the perception of man and that mathematical proportion.

Scribe an arc through the square formed inside the rectangle, continue it in the next smaller one and the next and you form a spiral, a logarithmic spiral with precise mathematical proportions of the golden segment and quite remarkable properties. The logarithmic spiral is found everywhere in nature. It appears in sea shells. It allows the horns of animals to grow, each horn spiraling in an opposite direction. It appears in the arrangement of seeds on flowers, in the arrangement of limbs on a tree, in their height from one another, and in the way they are arranged on the stem at just the right angle to catch the most light. Spirals of one kind or another are found from the smallest virus to the largest galaxy. Where living things must change size but maintain the same shape, the logarithmic spiral appears.

Actually, you need look no farther than your own physical body to find an application of the golden segment. An example is as close as your own hand. Whether you are short or tall, slim or stout, the second and third bones in your finger equal the length of the other, longer one—the golden segment 1.618. That is just the beginning. This body of ours embodies that golden segment in a dozen ways and more. With billions of us on the earth, no two of us are exactly alike. But measure a number of us, each different, and the proportion emerges with mathematical precision. All that variety conforms to law—fixed, rigid law—which at once allows an infinite variety.

That golden segment embodied order and precision with such practical application that painters and designers, sculptors, musicians, masons and especially architects were guided by it. Architecture, which embodies it, has been described as "frozen music." I have but touched on the subject, but a professor of physics or mathematics, or art or music could dazzle you with examples of how these and other laws are expressed in the universe about us.

There is a testament to law right under our feet. The very mud upon which we walk, when dried, cracks into three angles—each 120 degrees. Together that adds up to 360 degrees—a perfect circle, a compass. The examples are everywhere, some as small as the double helix of DNA, others as large as the orbits of celestial bodies. I know that Dr. Hugh Nibley could impress you with examples in the writing of the ancients.

The Ancients

Anciently, alchemists, astrologers, and magicians supposed that they had discovered the secrets of the universe, and could prove them with mathematical precision. Beginning with Pythagoras and his Pythagoreans, societies and orders of many descriptions were formed to contemplate these so-called secrets of the universe. Others claiming to be sorcerers found it easy to astonish the superstitious with marvels that were simple evidence that the universe is ruled by order and law. And always (and of course, as the Book of Mormon warns us) there have been those whose works are works of darkness, for those who worship the evil one adopted some of these geometric designs as symbols of their wicked mischief.

Now what do I make of all of this? Nothing more nor less than that there is *law* and *order* and *precision* in the universe that is awesome! What is physical interconnects with the spiritual; what is spiritual, or eternal, or moral resonates with the physical. We respond in our very souls to the order in the universe. How we respect those interconnections will have profound effect upon our happiness or sorrow.

Statement of Charles Darwin

In support of this, I will quote from one who must be regarded as an expert witness of the subject. It was written in the later years of his life:

> I have said that in one respect my mind has changed during the last twenty or thirty years. Up to the age of thirty, or beyond it, poetry of many kinds, such as the works of Milton, Gray, Byron, Wordsworth, Coleridge, and Shelley, gave me great pleasure, and even as a school-boy I took intense delight in Shakespeare, especially in the historical plays. I have also said that formerly pictures gave me considerable, and music very great delight. But now for many years I cannot endure to read a line of poetry: I have tried lately to read Shakespeare, and found it so intolerably dull that it nauseated me. I have also almost lost any taste for pictures or music.—Music generally set me thinking too energetically on what I have been at work on, instead of giving me pleasure. I retain some taste for fine scenery, but it does not cause me the exquisite delight which it formerly did.

Our writer continues:

> This curious and lamentable loss of the higher aesthetic tastes is all the odder, as books on history, biographies and travels (independently of any scientific facts which they may contain), and essays on all sorts of subjects interest me as much as ever they did. My mind seems to have become a kind of machine for grinding general laws out of large collections of facts, but why this should have caused the atrophy of that part of the brain alone, on which the *higher tastes*, depend, I cannot conceive. A man with a mind more highly organized or better constituted than mine, would not I suppose have thus suffered; and if I had to live my life again I would have made a rule to read some poetry and listen to some music at least once every week; for perhaps the parts of my brain now atrophied could thus have been kept active through use. The loss of these tastes is a loss of *happiness*, and may possibly be injurious to the intellect, and more probably to the moral character, by enfeebling the emotional part of our nature (emphasis in the original).

Let me repeat that last sentence, "The loss of these tastes is a loss of *happiness*, and may possibly be injurious to the intellect, and more probably to the moral character, by enfeebling the emotional part of our nature." That remarkable confession is from the autobiography of Charles Darwin, who conceived the theory of organic evolution (138-9).

There are too many interconnections uniting the physical and the spiritual in man to suppose that they came at random or by chance—not in a billion years or a billion times a billion years! It is against the law! What law? The law of common sense!

Declaration of Conviction—Conclusion

Now in conclusion: It is my conviction that to the degree the theory of evolution asserts that man is the product of an evolutionary process, the offspring of animals—it is false! What application the evolutionary theory has to animals gives me no concern. That is another question entirely, one to be pursued by science. But remember, the scriptures speak of the spirit in animals and other living things, and of each multiplying after its own kind (D&C 77:2; 2 Nephi 2:22; Moses 3:9; Abr 4:11-12, 24).

And I am sorry to say, the so-called theistic evolution, the theory that God used an evolutionary process to prepare a physical body for the spirit of man, is equally false. I say I am sorry because I know it is a view commonly held by good and thoughtful people who search for an acceptable resolution to an apparent conflict between the theory of evolution and the doctrines of the gospel.

I give six reasons for my conviction:

Reason 1

The revelations from God. The revelations testify of the separate creation of man in the image of God—this after the rest of creation was finished. When the revelations do not fully explain something (and there is purpose in their not doing so), there is safety in clinging to whatever they do reveal. The creation of man and his introduction into mortality by the Fall as revealed in the scriptures conform to eternal laws governing *both* body and spirit.

If the theory of evolution applies to man, there was no Fall and therefore no need for an atonement, nor a gospel of redemption, nor a redeemer.

Reason 2

An understanding of the sealing authority. The sealing authority with its binding of the generations into eternal families cannot admit to ancestral blood lines to beasts. Let me repeat: *An understanding of the sealing authority with its binding of the generations into eternal families cannot admit to ancestral blood lines to beasts.* That should be reason enough for any endowed and sealed Latter-day Saint!

Reason 3

Statements of the prophets and apostles. When the First Presidency speaks, we can safely accept their word.

> And if my people will hearken unto my voice, and unto the voice of my servants whom I have appointed to lead my people, behold, verily I say unto you, they shall not be moved out of their place. But if they will not hearken to my voice, nor unto the voice of these men whom I have appointed, they shall not be blest (D&C 124:45-46).

Twice the First Presidency has declared the position of the Church on organic evolution. The first, a statement published in 1909 entitled "The Origin of Man" (75-81), was signed by Presidents Joseph F. Smith, John R. Winder, and Anthon H. Lund. The other, entitled " 'Mormon' View of Evolution," signed by Presidents Heber J. Grant, Anthony W. Ivins, and Charles W. Nibley, was published in 1929 (1090-91). It follows very closely the first statement, indeed quotes directly from it. The doctrines in both statements are consistent and have not changed. One paragraph from the first will give you a feeling for their content.

> It is held by some that Adam was not the first man upon this earth, and that the original human being was a development from lower orders of the animal creation. These, however, are the theories of men. The word of the Lord declares that Adam was "the first man of all men" (Moses 1:34), and we are therefore in duty bound to regard him as the primal

parent of our race. It was shown to the brother of Jared that all men were created in the beginning after the image of God; and whether we take this to mean the spirit or the body, or both, it commits us to the same conclusion: Man began life as a human being, in the likeness of our heavenly Father ("The Origin of Man" 80; see the full texts of both statements in Appendix A below).

Statements have been made by other presidents of the Church and members of the Quorum of the Twelve Apostles which corroborate these official declarations by the First Presidency.

I should take note of one letter signed by a president of the Church addressed to a private individual. It includes a sentence which, taken out of context, reads, "On the subject of organic evolution the church has officially taken no position." For some reasons the addressee passed this letter about. For years it has appeared each time this subject is debated.

Letters to individuals are *not* the channel for announcing the policy of the Church. For several important reasons, this letter itself is not a declaration of the position of the Church, as some have interpreted it to be. Do not anchor your position on this major issue to that one sentence! It is in conflict with the two official declarations, each signed by all members of the First Presidency. Remember the revelation in the Doctrine and Covenants, "Every decision made by . . . [the First Presidency] must be by the unanimous voice of the same; that is, every member . . . must be agreed to its decisions. . . . Unless this is the case, their decisions are not entitled to the same blessings which the decisions of a quorum of three presidents were anciently, who were ordained after the order of Melchizedek, and were righteous and holy men" (D&C 107:27, 29).

Reason 4

Moral laws of force and validity. If the laws of genetics alone governed the reproduction and adaptation of living things, then the theory of evolution might convincingly apply to man. But they do not. There are moral laws of force and validity which govern that spiritual part of man, the power to reason, the conscience, which animals do not possess.

Can you not see how careful, how clever, the adversary is? He need not even challenge the *existence* of moral laws; simply convince us that, as animals, we are not accountable and are therefore exempt from them. To regard myself as but an animal would cost me my agency, my accountability; I would forfeit justice, mercy, love, faith, the *Atonement*—all that endures beyond mortality—values more dear than life itself. I will not do it!

Reason 5

The word *beauty*. Beauty itself cannot be imagined as having come by accident. The precision, harmony, and symmetry of the physical universe and the compelling interrelationship of natural laws with the spirit and emotion of mankind attest to an order directed by divine intelligence.

Unanswered Questions

Those reasons leave questions yet unanswered. How old is the earth? I do not know! But I do know that matter is eternal. How long a time has man been upon the earth? I do not know! But I do know that man did not evolve from animals.

Both questions have to do with time. Time is a medium for measurement, perhaps no more than that. Occasionally I wonder if time exists at all. Quantum physicists are now beginning to say strange things like that. "Time" comes from the word "tempus"; so do temporal and temporary. The revelations say that the day will come when "there shall be time no longer" (Rev 10:6; D&C 84:100). In any case, they say "time only is measured unto men" (Alma 40:8).

What Can I Offer You?

What help can I offer as you face persuasive advocates with visible evidence supporting their premise that man evolved from animals when you have little visible evidence to the contrary? Faith!

> Faith is not to have a *perfect knowledge* of things; therefore if ye have faith ye hope for things which are *not seen*, which are true (Alma 32:21; emphasis added).

Again:

> Now faith is the substance of things hoped for, the evidence of things *not seen* (Heb 11:1; emphasis added).

Notice that both scriptural definitions of faith include the words "not seen." All the answers as to how man was created have not been discovered by scientists; neither has God revealed them, but he has promised that he will reveal them.

> Yea, verily I say unto you, in that day when the Lord shall come, he shall reveal all things—Things which have passed, and *hidden things* which *no man knew*, things of the *earth*, *by which it was made*, and *the purpose* and *the end* thereof—Things most precious, things that are above, and things that are beneath, things that are in the earth, and upon the earth, and in heaven (D&C 101:32-34; emphasis added).

When confronted by evidence in the rocks below, rely on the witness of the heavens above. Do not be contentious. Speak of conscience, values, moral law. Perhaps others will also see the spiritual side to man and his creation. From that may come a humility and a willingness to see together in faith. You will not be left alone. God has promised a comforter, "Even the Spirit of truth; whom the world . . . seeth . . . not, neither knoweth" (John 14:17).

Reason 6

The Light. I said I would give six reasons for my conviction, and I have listed only five. The sixth is *personal revelation.*

Most of you know how to receive revelation. "Study it out in your mind; then . . . ask" (D&C 9:8).

Man is the child of God, formed in the divine image and endowed with divine attributes, and even as the infant son of an earthly father and mother is capable in due time of becoming a man, so the undeveloped offspring of celestial parentage is capable, by experience through ages and aeons, of evolving into a God.

> If thou shalt ask, thou shalt receive revelation upon revelation, knowledge upon knowledge, that thou mayest know the mysteries and peaceable things—that which bringeth joy, that which bringeth life eternal (D&C 42:61).

Here we are, spirit children of God, clothed in flesh, sojourning in mortality for a season. Know that your body is the instrument of your mind, and the foundation of your character. Do not mortgage your soul for unproved theories; ask, simply ask! I have asked, but not how man was created; I have asked if the scriptures are true. And I have a witness and a testimony, and I give it unto you: That Jesus is The Christ, the Son of God; that he is our Redeemer and our Messiah; that there was the fall of man; and that he is our Mediator and our Redeemer; that he wrought the Atonement; that he is our Lord. I know him. I bear to you a witness of him, a special witness of him.

Remember what he told the Nephites:

> Behold, I am the law, and the light. Look unto me, and endure to the end, and ye shall live; for unto him that endureth to the end will I give eternal life (3 Nephi 15:9).

BIBLIOGRAPHY

Darwin, Charles. *The Autobiography of Charles Darwin.* Ed. Nora Barlow. London: Colline, 1958.

Hungerford, Margaret Wolfe. *Molly Bawn.* New York: A. L. Burt, n.d.

Kimball, Spencer W. "Absolute Truth." *Ensign* (Sep 1978) 8:3-8.

"'Mormon' View of Evolution." *Improvement Era* (Sep 1925) 28:1090-91.

"The Origin of Man: by the First Presidency of the Church." *Improvement Era* (Nov 1909) 13:75-81.

Teachings of the Prophet Joseph Smith. Comp. Joseph Fielding Smith. Salt Lake City: Deseret Book, 1976.

APPENDIX

"The Origin of Man"

... It is held by some that Adam was not the first man upon this earth, and that the original human being was a development from lower orders of the animal creation. These, however, are the theories of men. The word of the Lord declares that Adam was "the first man of all men" (Moses 1:34), and we are therefore in duty bound to regard him as the primal parent of our race. It was shown to the brother of Jared that all men were created in the *beginning* after the image of God; and whether we take this to mean the spirit or the body, or both, it commits us to the same conclusion: Man began life as a human being, in the likeness of our heavenly Father.

True it is that the body of man enters upon its career as a tiny germ or embryo, which becomes an infant, quickened at a certain stage by the spirit whose tabernacle it is, and the child, after being born, develops into a man. There is nothing in this, however, to indicate that the original man, the first of our race, began life as anything less than a man, or less than the human germ or embryo that becomes a man.

Man, by searching, cannot find out God. Never, unaided, will he discover the truth about the beginning of human life. The Lord must reveal Himself, or remain unrevealed; and the same is true of the facts relating to the origin of Adam's race—God alone can reveal them. Some of these facts, however, are already known, and what has been made known it is our duty to receive and retain.

The Church of Jesus Christ of Latter-day Saints, basing its belief on divine revelation, ancient and modern, proclaims man to be the direct and lineal offspring of Deity. God Himself is an exalted man, perfected, enthroned, and supreme. By His almighty power He organized the earth, and all that it contains, from spirit and element, which exist co-eternally with Himself. He formed every plant that grows, and every animal that breathes, each after its own kind, spiritually and temporally—"that which is spiritual being in the likeness of that which is temporal, and that which is temporal in the likeness of that which is spiritual." He made the tadpole and the ape, the lion and the elephant; but He did not make them in His own image, nor endow them with Godlike reason and intelligence. Nevertheless, the whole animal creation will be perfected and perpetuated in the Hereafter, each class in its "distinct order or sphere," and will enjoy "eternal felicity." That fact has been made plain in this dispensation (Doctrine and Covenants, 77:3).

Man is the child of God, formed in the divine image and endowed with divine attributes, and even as the infant son of an earthly father and mother is capable in due time of becoming a man, so the undeveloped offspring of celestial parentage is capable, by experience through ages and æons, of evolving into a God.

> JOSEPH F. SMITH,
> JOHN R. WINDER,
> ANTHON H. LUND,
> First Presidency of The Church of
> Jesus Christ of Latter-day Saints

> (*Improvement Era* [Nov 1909] 13:80-81)

"'Mormon' View of Evolution"

"God created man in his own image, in the image of God created he him; male and female created he them."

In these plain and pointed words the inspired author of the book of Genesis made known to the world the truth concerning the origin of the human family. Moses, the prophet-historian, who was "learned" we are told, "in all the wisdom of the Egyptians," when making this important announcement, was not voicing a mere opinion. He was speaking as the mouthpiece of God, and his solemn declaration was for all time and for all people. No subsequent revelator of the truth has contradicted the great leader and law-giver of Israel. All who have since spoken by divine authority upon this theme have confirmed his simple and sublime proclamation. Nor could it be otherwise. Truth has but one source, and all revelations from heaven are harmonious one with the other.

Jesus Christ, the Son of God, is "the express image" of his Father's person (Hebrews 1:3). He walked the earth as a human being, as a perfect man, and said, in answer to a question put to him: "He that hath seen me hath seen the Father" (John 14:9). This alone ought to solve the problem to the satisfaction of every thoughtful, reverent mind. It was in this form that the Father and the Son, as two distinct personages, appeared to Joseph Smith, when, as a boy of fourteen years, he received his first vision.

The Father of Jesus Christ is our Father also. Jesus himself taught this truth, when he instructed his disciples how to pray: "Our Father which art in heaven," etc. Jesus, however, is the first born among all the sons of God—the first begotten in the spirit, and the only begotten in the flesh. He is our elder brother, and we, like him, are in the image of God. All men and women are in the similitude of the universal Father and Mother, and are literally sons and daughters of Deity.

Adam, our great progenitor, "the first man," was, like Christ, a pre-existent spirit, and, like Christ, he took upon him an appropriate body, the body of a man, and so became a "living soul." The doctrine of pre-existence pours [a] wonderful flood of light upon the otherwise mysterious problem of man's origin. It shows that man, as a spirit, was begotten and born of heavenly parents, and reared to maturity in the eternal mansions of the Father, prior to coming upon the earth in a temporal body to undergo an experience in mortality.

The Church of Jesus Christ of Latter-day Saints, basing its belief on divine revelation, ancient and modern, proclaims man to be the direct and lineal offspring of Deity. By his Almighty power God organized the earth, and all that it contains, from spirit and element, which exist co-eternally with himself.

Man is the child of God, formed in the divine image and endowed with divine attributes, and even as the infant son of an earthly father and mother is capable in due time of becoming a man, so the undeveloped offspring of celestial parentage is capable, by experience through ages and aeons, of evolving into a God.

HEBER J. GRANT,
ANTHONY W. IVINS,
CHARLES W. NIBLEY,
First Presidency.

(*Improvement Era* [Sep 1925] 28:1090-91)

Jacob: Prophet, Theologian, Historian

2

Robert J. Matthews

Introduction

I am pleased to have the opportunity to write about Jacob, the son of Lehi. My emphasis in my study and teaching has usually been doctrinal, so to become biographical is a bit of a change, but I am happy to do so because I believe Jacob is unsurpassed as a doctrinal teacher. Since all the doctrines that have ever been revealed since Adam have been communicated to us through the teachings of one prophet or another, I am honored and eager to present a paper on the life of one of the greatest of these, the prophet Jacob. It is easy to get excited telling about one so great and I pray I may have the Spirit so I can do it properly. There have been few people in history who have possessed the combination of spirituality, intellectual capacity, judgment, literary ability, parentage, faith, and seership that Jacob did. He exhibited an inherent desire for righteousness. He was a plain-spoken man, but used very descriptive language. With all these natural endowments, what an opportunity and advantage it was for him to have Lehi as a father and Nephi as an older brother to get him started right.

Our sources about Jacob consist of 31 pages in the Book of Mormon of Jacob's own words (13 in 2 Nephi; 18 in the book

Robert J. Matthews is professor of Ancient Scripture and dean of Religious Education at Brigham Young University.

of Jacob), plus eleven brief references to him by Nephi, Lehi, Enos, Alma, and Mormon (1 Nephi 18:7; 18:19; 2 Nephi 2:1-4; 5:6; 5:26; 11:1; 11:3; 31:1; Enos 1:1-3; Alma 3:6; WofM 1:3).

There have been but few writings in the Church giving biographical references to Jacob. In 1891 Elder George Reynolds offered a brief biographical sketch in his *Dictionary of the Book of Mormon* (156-57). In 1966 I included a half-page entry on Jacob and a biographical note in my *Who's Who in the Book of Mormon* (25, 82). In October 1976, the *Ensign* magazine carried a short but informative article by C. Terry Warner. And in 1981, the index to the new edition of the Book of Mormon offered a list of 26 well-documented statements about Jacob. I have benefited from each of these publications and have endeavored to include all that these previous works have offered. But beyond their separate contributions, I have tried to make this paper the most complete recitation on Jacob that I could, by basing it on the text of the Book of Mormon itself, and by avoiding unreasonable speculation. I have admired Jacob for more than 40 years, and that admiration has increased with this study.

Overview of Jacob's Life

Jacob is first mentioned in 1 Nephi 18:7 when Lehi's group was about to enter the ship on the Arabian coast to sail to the promised land. Nephi introduces Jacob in this manner: "And now, my father had begat two sons in the wilderness; the elder was called Jacob and the younger Joseph."

These two sons were born during the eight years Lehi's family journeyed in the wilderness (1 Nephi 17:4). We do not know the exact date of Jacob's birth, but we know it had to be within the first seven years of their journey in the wilderness, since Joseph was born after Jacob and was also born within the eight-year period. Since Lehi left Jerusalem in 600 BC, Jacob had to have been born between 600 and 593 BC.

Lehi's group spent an undetermined length of time at Bountiful while the ship was being built. This would likely take a year or two. If the ship set sail at about 590 BC, and arrived in the promised land about 589 BC, the boy Jacob could be not less than three nor more than ten years old at that time. There is, however, additional information that has a bearing on the date of Jacob's birth.

Nephi's record of his family's travels in the wilderness and of the rebellions of Laman, Lemuel, and Ishmael's sons while voyaging at sea, tells us that his "parents being stricken in years, and having suffered much grief because of their children . . . were brought down, yea, even upon their sickbeds" (1 Nephi 18:17). Nephi said Lehi and Sariah's sorrow was so great that it almost caused their deaths, and that "Jacob and Joseph also, being young, having need of much nourishment, were grieved because of the afflictions of their mother" (1 Nephi 18:18-19).

Lehi, recalling these trying times, especially those in the wilderness, said to Joseph, "Thou wast born in the wilderness of mine afflictions; yea, in the days of my greatest sorrow did thy mother bear thee" (2 Nephi 3:1). And to Jacob he said: "Thou art my first-born in the days of my tribulation in the wilderness. And behold, in thy childhood thou hast suffered afflictions and much sorrow, because of the rudeness of thy brethren. Nevertheless, Jacob, my firstborn in the wilderness, thou knowest the greatness of God; and he shall consecrate thine afflictions for thy gain" (2 Nephi 2:1-2).

The tone of these verses suggests that certainly Jacob and possibly Joseph were old enough to remember their parents' suffering, the rebellion of Laman and Lemuel, and the goodness of Nephi while they were in the wilderness. Hence they would not have been mere infants at the time all of this was happening. Such evidence argues for Jacob's having been born during the early part of the wilderness journey, and therefore being at least seven and possibly as many as ten years old when they arrived in the promised land.

Lehi no doubt named his son Jacob in memory of the patriarch Jacob, father of the twelve tribes of Israel. It may well be that Lehi and Sariah, having recently obtained the plates of brass, a record of the house of Israel, and embarking on a journey toward a new promised land, were impressed to name their new son after their great ancestor. In like manner we conclude that Lehi's next son, Joseph, was named in honor of Joseph of Egypt, who was also their direct ancestor and would have been spoken of often in the plates of brass (see 2 Nephi 3:3, 4, 22).

All that we know about Jacob's life we have gleaned from the writings on the small plates of Nephi—the religious record. More detailed information would probably be found on the large plates of Nephi and also in Lehi's record (1 Nephi 19:1-2; see also 1 Nephi 1:16-17; 6:1; 9:1-5), which Nephi says contains genealogical information "and the more part of all our proceedings in the wilderness." I thus presume that the 116 pages of lost manuscript, which were a translation of Mormon's abridgement of the "Book of Lehi" (see heading of D&C 3), would contain considerably more about the boyhood of Jacob than does our present record.

After the death of father Lehi in the promised land, the Lord warned Nephi to separate himself from the families of his elder brethren and to take those people with him who believed in the revelations of God. Nephi speaks of this event: "Wherefore, it came to pass that I, Nephi, did take my family, and also Zoram and his family, and Sam, mine elder brother and his family, and Jacob and Joseph, my younger brethren, and also my sisters, and all those who would go with me. And all those who would go with me were those who believed in the warnings and the revelations of God" (2 Nephi 5:6).

We know from an earlier passage (1 Nephi 16:7) that Laman, Lemuel, Sam, Nephi, and Zoram had each married daughters of Ishmael, and it is interesting that now, a decade or so later, each of them is said to have "his family," but Jacob and Joseph are referred to only in the singular with no mention of a family. We know but little about when Jacob was married, to whom, or the manner of his family. We are informed that he did indeed have a family and that he taught them many times in the "nurture and admonition of the Lord" (Enos 1:1) and often spoke to them of "eternal life and the joy of the saints" (Enos 1:3). We also know that he had a righteous son named Enos (Jacob 7:27; Enos 1:1-3). A posterity is also shown in the prophetic instruction to Jacob that the small plates would be handed down through his seed from generation to generation (Jacob 1:3).

As to how old he got or when he eventually died, we do not have much detail. The only certain date we have in the mature years of Jacob's life is found in Jacob 1:1, where he indicates that fifty-five "years had passed away from the time that Lehi left Jerusalem." This would be 545 BC and is near the beginning of the time when Jacob became the keeper of the records and the spiritual leader of his people. This seems to be very near the time of Nephi's death (Jacob 1:9-12; 2:1). Jacob would have been at least fifty years old at the time. All the events recorded in the book of Jacob happened after that, which as we will see took a number of years. When Jacob died he was therefore "some years" (see Jacob 7:1) past fifty.

Writing the Book of Jacob

Nephi had been both the spiritual and secular leader. But Jacob informs us that when Nephi became old he separated the responsibilities of the Church and the secular government and conferred each upon a different person. To Jacob he gave the sacred records known as the small plates. Although the report does not specifically say it, I assume that Jacob was also appointed at that time to succeed Nephi as the spiritual leader. Nephi conferred the responsibility of the civil government upon a man who became known among the people as second Nephi (see Jacob 1:1-11).

Nephi instructed Jacob that he should write upon the small plates only those things that were "most precious" such as "preaching which was sacred, or revelation which was great, or prophesying," and that he should touch but lightly on the history of the people (Jacob 1:2-4). That type of commandment required that Jacob wait for a while before writing upon the plates, since it calls for time to make comparisons and gain perspective. We can discern that Jacob waited for some length of time after he was given the records before he began writing, for in his first chapter he speaks of the "reigns of the kings" after Nephi, and also tells us that the successors to Nephi had taken the title of second, and then third Nephi, and so forth (see Jacob 1:9-11; see also 3:13). He would not have been able to make such a glance into the past had he written immediately.

The book of Jacob consists of three main sections. The first is Jacob 1:1 through 3:14, which contains a lengthy sermon by Jacob against the materialistic influence of riches and pride, and against the grosser crime of immorality. This portion of the book of Jacob concludes with these words: "These plates are called the plates of Jacob, and they were made by the hand of Nephi. And I make an end of speaking these words" (Jacob 3:14).

The second section is Jacob 4-6, and includes the marvelous allegory of Zenos. This section concludes with Jacob's farewell to his people until they meet at the "pleasing bar of God" (Jacob 6:13). It seems that Jacob had intended this "farewell" to be the end of his book.

The third and final section, Jacob 7, was written "some years" (v 1) later than the other two parts and tells of a man named Sherem, who was an anti-Christ. Apparently Jacob's encounter with Sherem was so important that he added it to his record, even though it was "some years" (v 1) after he had thought it was finished. Jacob concludes with an observation that his writing "has been small" (Jacob 7:27), which probably means small in comparison to the longer books of 1 and 2 Nephi.

The closing words of Jacob are these:

> And it came to pass that I, Jacob, began to be old; and the record of this people being kept on the other plates of Nephi, wherefore, I conclude this record, declaring that I have written according to the best of my knowledge, by saying that the time passed away with us, and also our lives passed away like as it were unto us a dream, we being a lonesome and a solemn people, wanderers, cast out from Jerusalem, born in tribulation, in a wilderness, and hated of our brethren, which caused wars and contentions; wherefore, we did mourn out our days.

And I, Jacob, saw that I must soon go down to my grave; wherefore, I said unto my son Enos: Take these plates. And I told him the things which my brother Nephi had commanded me, and he promised obedience unto the commands. And I make an end of my writing upon these plates, which writing has been small; and to the reader I bid farewell, hoping that many of my brethren may read my words. Brethren, adieu (Jacob 7:26-27).

Multiple Writings and Copies

Understanding that Jacob wrote on the small plates over a period of years with great care and selection leads to another important conclusion about his writing pattern and probably that of other Nephite prophets. A casual reader may think that what they engraved on the plates was all the writing the prophets did. However, Jacob makes an observation about the difficulty of engraving on metal compared to writing on other material. We read in Jacob 4:1-3:

Now behold, it came to pass that I, Jacob, having ministered much unto my people in word, (and I cannot write but a little of my words, because of the difficulty of engraving our words upon plates) and we know that the things which we write upon plates must remain; but whatsoever things we write upon anything save it be upon plates must perish and vanish away; but we can write a few words upon plates, which will give our children, and also our beloved brethren, a small degree of knowledge concerning us, or concerning their fathers—Now in this thing we do rejoice; and we labor diligently to engraven these words upon plates, hoping that our beloved brethren and our children will receive them with thankful hearts.

We see from this explanation that the Nephites did write upon other materials, probably leather or paper. I would conclude therefore that what Jacob finally engraved on metal plates would rarely, if ever, be his first draft of a document.

Jacob's Ministry

When Jacob became the chief spiritual leader of the Nephites, or in other words their prophet, at about 545 BC, he had already been tried, tested and proven worthy, and for 20-30 years had been a vigorous preacher of righteousness under Nephi's leadership. At an early age Jacob had a vision of the Savior. In Lehi's blessing to Jacob, recorded in 2 Nephi 2, we read: "Wherefore, thy soul shall be blessed . . . and thy days shall be spent in the service of thy God. Wherefore, I know that thou art redeemed, because of the righteousness of thy Redeemer . . . and thou hast beheld in thy youth his glory; wherefore, thou art blessed even as they unto whom he shall minister in the flesh" (vv 3-4).

Relatively early in his lifetime, Jacob was consecrated "a priest and a teacher over the land of my people" by his brother Nephi (2 Nephi 5:26; see also 6:2; Jacob 1:18). That he "came in at the gate" (see D&C 43:7), and was properly and regularly called to the work in the established order of the kingdom of God, is shown by Jacob's own statement about his call to the ministry: "I, Jacob, [have] been called of God, and ordained after the manner of his holy order, and [have] been consecrated by my brother Nephi" (2 Nephi 6:2).

The Priesthood and the Law of Moses

It is necessary that I say something about Jacob's being consecrated as "a priest and teacher." The faithful Nephites from Lehi to the time of Christ were diligent in performing the requirements of the law of Moses. It is true that they also had the gospel in its fulness and the Melchizedek Priesthood; yet they understood that it was necessary to obey the ordinances of the law of Moses until that law was fulfilled (see 2 Nephi 25:24-30; Jacob 4:5; Mosiah 13:30).

As originally established in Israel under the law of Moses, the Aaronic Priesthood was a hereditary office, and the priests were selected only from the family of Aaron. The Lord designated that the lesser priesthood was to be conferred on men called from the tribe of Levi, that within the tribe the direct descendants of Aaron should be designated as the priests (the highest office within the Levitical or Aaronic Priesthood), and that the presiding priests (high priest or "bishop") should be called only from the firstborn among the descendants of Aaron (see Ex 30:30-31; 40:15; D&C 68:16-19; 84:18; and 107:13-17). The Prophet Joseph Smith had this to say about the established order: "The Levitical Priesthood is forever hereditary—fixed on the head of Aaron and his sons forever, and was in active operation down to Zacharias the father of John" (*Teachings of the Prophet Joseph Smith* 319).

There were no descendants of Levi or Aaron among the Nephites because Lehi's family was of Joseph (1 Nephi 6:2), rather than Levi. Therefore, the Nephites could not be regularly called to officiate in the ordinances of the law of Moses and Aaronic Priesthood. However, since the Melchizedek Priesthood encompasses all the powers and authority of the Aaronic, worthy men among the Nephites, such as Jacob and Joseph, could be consecrated as priests and teachers and could function in the ordinances of the law of Moses, as well as the gospel, by virtue of the Melchizedek Priesthood (see D&C 68:18-20). These were not the offices of priest and teacher as we know them today in the Aaronic Priesthood. It should be clear to us that the Nephites did not have an established order of priests and Levites such as that found in ancient Israel, because there were no Levites among them. Yet, there is strong evidence that the Nephite leaders held the Melchizedek Priesthood, since they performed the ordinances of the law of Moses, which they could not have done unless they had priesthood authority. Since they were not of the lineage to hold the Aaronic Priesthood, they must have held this Melchizedek Priesthood, which has no limitations on tribal lineage.

After the law of Moses was fulfilled by the atonement of Jesus Christ, the stipulations pertaining to the lineage of Levi and Aaron were no longer in effect. Hence after the coming of Christ, the Nephites could ordain non-Levite men to all of the Aaronic Priesthood offices even as we do today in the Church. However, in the restoration of all things, Aaron's lineage shall yet again be given a special assignment (see Smith 3:91-94; McConkie 10, 598-99).

Jacob's Colorful Methods

We will now return to the account of Jacob's ministry. In 2 Nephi 6-10, Nephi included a lengthy sermon that Jacob had delivered to the people. We are not informed what the occasion was, but we can discern that it was a conference or a special gathering, because Nephi appointed Jacob to speak and requested that his topic include those parts of Isaiah we call chapters 49 through 52. Although the written account of this sermon occupies 13 pages in 2 Nephi, it is only a portion of what Jacob said at the time. The discourse was so long that it took Jacob two days to deliver it. Nephi was so pleased with the discourse that he recorded part of it on the small plates and then commented: "And now, Jacob spake many more things to my people at that time; nevertheless only these things [2 Nephi 6-10] have I caused to be written" (2 Nephi 11:1). The words "at that time" further suggest that this was a particular occasion or conference. And there can be no missing the fact that Nephi recognized that his younger brother had a special ability to declare the word of the Lord and teach the people.

At the beginning of this sermon, Jacob says a few things that are useful to us in learning about him as a person and as a teacher. First, he states his authority as his having been "called of God, and ordained after the manner of his holy order," and "consecrated" by Nephi. He then informs his hearers that he has already spoken to them of "exceedingly many things," but wants to speak again, for he is "desirous for the welfare of" their souls and has great anxiety for his people. He has previously exhorted them with "all diligence," and taught "the words of [his] father," and has "spoken unto [them] concerning all things which are written, from the creation of the world" (2 Nephi 6:2-3). He then explains:

> And now, behold, I would speak unto you concerning things which are, and which are to come; wherefore, I will read you the words of Isaiah. And they are the words which my brother has desired that I should speak unto you. And I speak unto you for your sakes, that ye may learn and glorify the name of your God. And now, the words which I shall

read are they which Isaiah spake concerning all the house of Israel; wherefore, they may be likened unto you, for ye are of the house of Israel. And there are many things which have been spoken by Isaiah which may be likened unto you, because ye are of the house of Israel (vv 4-5).

It is clear that Jacob was lively and energetic in his ministry, a preacher of the gospel, a student of the holy scriptures and an exhorter to righteousness. Nephi respected him and approved of his preaching and his doctrine. Nephi even tells us that one of the reasons he likes Jacob so much is that Jacob is a personal eye witness of the Redeemer and therefore has something important to say. Nephi places Jacob alongside Isaiah and himself:

And now I, Nephi, write more of the words of Isaiah, for my soul delighteth in his words. For I will liken his words unto my people, and I will send them forth unto all my children, for he verily saw my Redeemer, even as I have seen him. And my brother, Jacob, also has seen him as I have seen him; wherefore, I will send their words forth unto my children to prove unto them that my words are true. Wherefore, by the words of three, God hath said, I will establish my word (2 Nephi 11:2-3).

The records show that early in life Jacob had exhibited those traits of stability, spiritual capacity, and doctrinal clarity that make him one of the outstanding Book of Mormon prophets.

Jacob not only covers a multitude of subjects, "all things which are written, from the creation of the world" (2 Nephi 6:3), but he demonstrates his sincerity and illustrates his seriousness in a number of ways. He is descriptive in his language, using a large number of adjectives and metaphors. In addition he is blunt and forceful in his message. He expresses great love for the people, but was not of the opinion that he must always maintain a positive image or say only nice things. Without being crude, he is nevertheless devastatingly direct in reminding the people of their sins.

He must have been animated as a speaker, for on at least one occasion as he stood before the people he literally shook their sins from his garments. His words are so graphic we need to read them to feel the impact:

> O, my beloved brethren, remember my words. Behold, I take off my garments, and I shake them before you; I pray the God of my salvation that he view me with his all-searching eye; wherefore, ye shall know at the last day, when all men shall be judged of their works, that the God of Israel did witness that I shook your iniquities from my soul, and that I stand with brightness before him, and am rid of your blood (2 Nephi 9:44).

There is no way Jacob could have shaken his garments in that manner without attracting considerable attention. It is significant that he did this while he was a relatively young man serving under the leadership of Nephi. He was not the prophet at that time, but he was a prophet in the making. From the record, we learn that Jacob taught by the Spirit and was a bold, charismatic expounder of the gospel of Jesus Christ. By reading his words I developed a mental image of him illustrated by terms such as stalwart, strong, courageous, compassionate, deliberate, forthright, meek, dignified, appropriate, reflective, poetic, sensitive, and kind.

It is noteworthy that in the 31 pages of the Book of Mormon containing firsthand material given us from Jacob's mouth and pen, he says little about himself. When he does, he usually focuses on his ministry, his call, his preaching, visits from an angel, and so forth. His interest is in the sacred word and the doctrine. Although that leaves us without personal details, it nevertheless tells us something about him.

Subject Matter of Jacob's Teachings

We have already mentioned that Jacob taught the words of his father and that he taught "all things from the creation" (2 Nephi 6:3) from the scriptures. We have also noted that he enjoyed using the words of Isaiah. Following is a discussion about some of Jacob's prominent teachings, specifically noting what we owe to him, or learn specifically from him, in the Book of Mormon. These are doctrines that we would not otherwise have in such clarity were it not for his teachings. In making this selection I chose topics on which I turn to Jacob for help in teaching. That is, I chose things for which Jacob is sometimes the only source, or in some instances the best source, and always a very good source.

The Scattering and Gathering of Israel

Although Jacob is only one of several Book of Mormon writers who discuss the scattering and gathering of Israel, he is probably the most prolific on the subject. I don't think anyone has revealed more about this subject than he has, unless possibly Nephi. Jacob informs us that he knows whereof he speaks because it was told him by an angel (see 2 Nephi 6:9, 11), or he read of it from the writings of Isaiah or Zenos, or he was taught it by the Spirit (Jacob 4:15). He speaks in detail of the destruction of Jerusalem by the Babylonians and also of a second destruction and scattering of the Jews after the time of Christ (2 Nephi 6:8-15; 9:1-2; 10:1-22). His great interest in the worldwide scattering and gathering of Israel and their eventual acceptance of the Lord Jesus Christ led him to quote the lengthy allegory of Zenos found in Jacob 5. We are ever grateful to Jacob for including this marvelous excerpt from the plates of brass, which is the most comprehensive statement we have on the scattering and gathering anywhere in scripture.

What if There Were No Atonement?

In 2 Nephi 9 Jacob presents a most informative explanation of the fall of Adam and the Savior's atonement. In this chapter Jacob explains that the great Creator himself is the Holy One of Israel, who will come and die for all mankind and provide an infinite atonement (2 Nephi 9:5-7). This statement by Jacob is the first use of the phrase "infinite atonement" in the Book of Mormon. What would have been the consequences if there had been no atonement by Jesus Christ? Do you know the answer? Jacob knew. He declares that because of the fall of Adam, which has passed upon all mankind, if there were not an infinite atonement the fleshly bodies of all mankind would return to the earth never to receive a resurrection, and the spirits of mankind would all become devils, forever miserable, and be forever subject to the devil. "And our spirits must have become like unto him, and we become devils, angels to a devil . . . in misery, like unto himself" (2 Nephi 9:9). This declaration about what would have been the fate of mankind, especially of man's spirit, if there were no Savior, is plainer than is found in any other passage of scripture, and is one of the greatest testimonies of the benefit mankind receives from the atonement of our Redeemer. If you want to see how little this is known, and thus how important this information is, test it on your family or friends. Ask them what the condition of our spirits would be if there had been no atonement. Few will understand this without the help of Jacob. We find ourselves turning to 2 Nephi 9:7-9 again and again in teaching the atonement of Jesus Christ.

Jacob's Vivid Use of Language

Jacob continues his discourse by speaking of death, hell, the grave, paradise, resurrection, judgment, spiritual death, redemption, happiness, misery, obedience, disobedience, and other topics that belong to the plan of salvation. But Jacob doesn't call it simply the plan of salvation, he labels it the "merciful plan of the great Creator" (2 Nephi 9:6), or the "great plan of our God" (v 13), or the "way of deliverance of our God" (v 11). Likewise, the work of the devil is "that cunning plan of the evil one" (v 28).

Furthermore, Jacob does not simply speak of "death," but of "the slumber of death" (Jacob 3:11) and three times he speaks of death as an "awful monster" (2 Nephi 9:10, 19, 26). If a person neglects to keep the commandments he is not merely disobedient, he "wasteth the days of his probation, [and] awful is his state" (2 Nephi 9:27). He doesn't say that mankind is under the eye of God, but that man is under "the all-searching eye of God" (2 Nephi 9:44). In one breath Jacob speaks of "awful fear," "awful guilt," "awful misery," and "awful reality" awaiting the ungodly (2 Nephi 9:46-47).

In describing the futility of mortal man's rebellion against God, Jacob mentions, "the piercing eye of Almighty God" (Jacob 2:10), and exclaims, "O that he would show you that he can pierce you, and with one glance of his eye he can smite you to the dust" (Jacob 2:15). To illustrate the scope of the Lord's knowledge, he proclaims, "How unsearchable are the depths of the mysteries of him . . . it is impossible that man should find out all his ways" (Jacob 4:8), and "he knoweth all things, and there is not anything save he knows it" (2 Nephi 9:20). Jacob likes adjectives to accompany his nouns, so he speaks of the "great Creator" (2 Nephi 9:5), the "merciful plan" (2 Nephi 9:6), the "infinite atonement" (2 Nephi 9:7), "captive bodies" in the grave, and "captive spirits" in hell (2 Nephi 9:13). He speaks of uncleanness, nakedness, guilt, and perfect knowledge (2 Nephi 9:14). Jacob glories in the majesty of God, and when he speaks of him he exults with phrases such as, "O, the greatness and the justice of our God" (2 Nephi 9:17), "O the greatness of the mercy of our God" (2 Nephi 9:19), "O how great the holiness of our God" (2 Nephi 9:20). We do not have anything else equal to Jacob's preaching. The Book of Mormon mentions "the gift of preaching" (Alma 9:21), and Jacob had such a gift.

Riches, Pride, and Unchastity

One of Jacob's strongest discourses is centered on the curse of trusting in material riches, the problem of harboring pride, and the damning effects of immorality. His teachings on these subjects are among the best we have in the scriptures, not only for their content, but also for the directness of his message and the beauty and power of his language. In speaking of these subjects Jacob talks of "the pleasing word of God" (Jacob 2:8) and says that "the hand of providence hath smiled upon [the people] most pleasingly" so that they have become rich in material things (Jacob 2:13), but as a consequence they have also become proud. He rebukes the men who have been untrue to their marriage vows, saying they have "broken the hearts of their tender wives and lost the confidence of their children, because of their bad examples before them," and therefore "many hearts died, pierced with deep wounds" (Jacob 2:35). Jacob says this situation is like "daggers placed to pierce their souls and wound their delicate minds" (Jacob 2:9).

The Name "Christ"

Although the Book of Mormon speaks of the Savior a great many times, beginning in the very first chapter, it does not introduce the words *Jesus* or *Christ* until 78 pages into the book. For example, the book of 1 Nephi makes 150 references to the Savior, using 23 different names, but it never uses the name *Jesus* or *Christ*. The first use of the name *Christ* in the Book of Mormon is in 2 Nephi 10:3, in Jacob's lengthy two-day sermon. It appears, from the way Jacob says it, that this is a new term among them: "Wherefore, as I said unto you, it must needs be expedient that Christ—for in the last night the angel spake unto me that this should be his name—should come among the Jews."

It is significant that Jacob emphasized his words by declaring that an angel had given him this new name just the night before. I am not surprised that this specific information was made known through this unusual and excellent prophet Jacob. The Nephites already knew of the Atonement and they had many different names for the Savior, but Jacob seems to have given them the very word and pronunciation of the name *Christ*.

The Power of Faith

Jacob's entire life is a reflection of his faith in the Lord Jesus Christ. He explains that when Sherem the anti-Christ sought him out it was in the "hope to shake me from the faith," because Sherem knew that "I, Jacob had faith in Christ who should come" (Jacob 7:3-5). However, Jacob had had "many revelations," and had "truly seen angels" and had "heard the voice of the Lord speaking unto [him] in very word, from time to time; wherefore [he] could not be shaken" (Jacob 7:5).

In Jacob 4:6 he relates some of the miraculous things which accompany the kind of faith that he and the other prophets possessed: "Wherefore, we search the prophets, and we have many revelations and the spirit of prophecy; and having all these witnesses we obtain a hope, and our faith becometh unshaken, insomuch that we truly can command in the name of Jesus and the very trees obey us, or the mountains, or the waves of the sea" (Jacob 4:6).

We do not have an account of Jacob's commanding the mountains, the waves, or the trees to obey, but he seems to be familiar with such miracles. He reasons with the reader that it should not be surprising that God can give a man power to command the elements and that the elements will obey, since God created the world in the first place by the "power of his word." So why would God not be able to command the earth, "according to his will and pleasure?" (Jacob 4:7-9).

Obtaining a Hope in Christ

Closely associated with having faith is what Jacob calls "obtaining a hope in Christ" (see Jacob 2:19; 4:6). All the prophets speak of "hope," but Jacob is unique in the way he uses the word. His phrase of "obtaining *a* hope" is more than just having "hope" and seems to be the assurance or testimony that one has reached a particular state or spiritual condition and a special relationship with the Lord. Here are some of Jacob's words on the subject. "Before ye seek for riches, seek ye for the kingdom of God. And after ye have obtained a hope in Christ ye shall obtain riches, if ye seek them; and ye will seek them for the intent to do good" (Jacob 2:18-19). And also: "We knew of Christ, and we had a hope of his glory many hundred years before his coming" (Jacob 4:4). And again: "We search the prophets, and we have many revelations and the spirit of prophecy; and having all these witnesses we obtain a hope, and our faith becometh unshaken" (Jacob 4:6). Jacob urges his hearers to have faith and to be reconciled to God through the atonement of Christ, having "obtained a good hope of glory ... before he manifesteth himself in the flesh" (Jacob 4:11).

The phrase "a hope" is used two other times in the Book of Mormon by Alma the Younger (Alma 13:29; 25:16), but the context of each shows that it is used differently than Jacob uses it. In all, the word *hope* appears 50 times in the Book of Mormon and is used by eight different prophets. Jacob, however, is unique in using it in the sense of obtaining "a hope," which is an achievement of something beyond simply "hoping."

All the Prophets Knew of Christ

That all the prophets knew of and testified of the coming of Christ is a fundamental gospel concept. The Old Testament in its present condition is not at all clear on this matter, so we look to latter-day revelation for evidence. There are numerous passages in the Book of Mormon that can be used to teach this concept, but none better than two passages in the book of Jacob. When I want a scripture that is clear and to the point on this subject I cite the following from Jacob: "We knew of Christ, and we had a hope of his glory many hundred years before his coming; and not only we ourselves had a hope of his glory, but also all the holy prophets which were before us. Behold, they believed in Christ and worshiped the Father in his name, and also we worship the Father in his name" (Jacob 4:4-5). And also: "Behold, I say unto you that none of the prophets have written, nor prophesied, save they have spoken concerning this Christ" (Jacob 7:11). Language cannot be plainer than that.

A Definition of Truth

To formulate a definition of "truth" has taxed the mental and philosophical resources of the world's thinkers. Pilate asked Jesus, "What is truth?" (John 18:38); as if he were saying, "Who knows what truth is?" Furthermore, we ask in one of our hymns, "O Say, What is Truth?" (*Hymns* #272). Jacob helps to provide an answer to these queries by defining what truth is and telling how we can learn it. These are his words: "The Spirit speaketh the truth and lieth not. Wherefore, it speaketh of things as they really are, and things as they really will be" (Jacob 4:13). In other words, Jacob says that truth is reality, learned through the Spirit.

The Lord further defined truth as "knowledge of things as they are, and as they were, and as they are to come" (D&C 93:24). The hymn, "O Say, What is Truth?" identifies truth as "the sum of existence," and in Doctrine and Covenants 91:4 the Lord says that "the Spirit manifesteth truth." Jacob's definition is in harmony with that in the Doctrine and Covenants and in the hymn, and is especially meaningful to us, because it indicates that ultimate truth is known through the voice of the Spirit. As we know, some truths are available to mortals in no other way but by the ministration of the Holy Spirit.

To Be Learned is Good

An oft-quoted verse from the Book of Mormon, at least in a university setting, comes from Jacob as recorded in 2 Nephi 9:29. But as recorded in verse 28, Jacob had just spoken of the cunning plan of the devil to deceive mankind and to cause men to trust vainly and foolishly in their own learning and "set aside" the "counsel of God," "supposing they know of themselves." Jacob doesn't say there is any particular blessedness in being ignorant. He knows that it is not the learning, but the pride and vanity men place in their learning that is a problem, so to set the matter straight he says: "But to be learned is good if they hearken unto the counsels of God" (2 Nephi 9:29). However, we should take note from Jacob's caution that many who are learned struggle with their faith.

A Perfect Knowledge of Christ

We have mentioned twice in this paper that Jacob was an eyewitness of Jesus Christ, and that even in his youth he had seen the Redeemer. Jacob himself tells us that he had seen angels, had received ministration from them, and "had heard the voice of the

Lord speaking [to him] in very word" (Jacob 7:5). He also speaks
of what he calls "a perfect knowledge" of Christ (Jacob 4:12).
He does not define exactly what a perfect knowledge is, but the
context suggests to me that he is saying there is more to the gospel
than merely learning doctrines and principles. Important as these
are, we have the opportunity to go even further and receive a
perfect knowledge of Christ. Here is the passage: "And now,
beloved, marvel not that I tell you these things: for why not speak
of the atonement of Christ, and attain to a perfect knowledge of
him, as to attain to the knowledge of a resurrection and the world
to come?"

What is a perfect knowledge over and beyond knowing the
written concepts and the principles and having a testimony? I
think it is being an eyewitness to the Redeemer. Who would
know this better than Jacob?

Conclusion

Jacob is one of the greatest doctrinal teachers and theologians of the Book of Mormon, and thus of all scripture. He
demonstrates a philosophical grasp of the gospel and offers
unique and valuable insights into important doctrinal matters.
Father Lehi was of a similar disposition. It is no coincidence that
among all of Lehi's blessings to his sons, the blessing he gave to
Jacob is the most doctrinal (see 2 Nephi 2). The content of that
blessing has captured the attention of most Book of Mormon
students because of its statements about the Creation, the Fall,
Adam's condition before and after the Fall, man's agency, and the
idea of opposition in all things. While the blessing is in the words
of Lehi, I find it significant that it was to the youthful Jacob that
he said these things. The blessing fits his mind and spirituality.

I have not included every detail about Jacob, but have
brought together enough to demonstrate the nature of the man.
There is a tone in his teachings and writings that reveals the heart
of "a just and holy man" (Alma 3:6) who was close to the Lord.
He was a special witness of the Lord Jesus Christ, a man with a

perfect knowledge of Christ, a man who knew Christ. He was a diligent advocate and teacher, a prophet, theologian, historian, father, and man of God. In the name of Jesus Christ, Amen.

BIBLIOGRAPHY

Hymns. Salt Lake City: The Church of Jesus Christ of Latter-day Saints, 1985.

Matthews, Robert J. *Who's Who in the Book of Mormon.* 3rd ed. Provo, UT: Brigham Young Univ, 1969.

McConkie, Bruce R. *Mormon Doctrine.* 1st ed. Salt Lake City: Bookcraft, 1958.

Reynolds, George. *A Dictionary of the Book of Mormon.* Salt Lake City: Parry, 1891.

Smith, Joseph Fielding. *Doctrines of Salvation.* Comp. Bruce R. McConkie. 3 vols. Salt Lake City: Bookcraft, 1956.

Teachings of the Prophet Joseph Smith. Comp. Joseph Fielding Smith. Salt Lake City: Deseret Book, 1976.

Warner, C. Terry. "Jacob." *Ensign* (Oct 1976) 6:24-30.

"I Speak Somewhat ConcerningThat Which I Have Written"

3

Cheryl Brown

*A*t the beginning of the Words of Mormon, written in approximately AD 385, Mormon tells us that he is about to turn the record he has been making over to his son Moroni. He points out that he has witnessed the destruction of almost the entire Nephite nation and that he believes Moroni will witness their final destruction. He hopes that Moroni will survive him and add more to the record. Then, beginning in verse three with the words, "And now, I speak somewhat concerning that which I have written," Mormon briefly outlines which records were being incorporated into his abridgement and why. This short explanation gives some of the most direct evidence available to us of how the Lord structured the Book of Mormon through his servant, Mormon.

Mormon was not the only writer to do this. Throughout the book the writers frequently tell us what they are including and why they are putting it in, and what they are leaving out and why. An examination of all their explanations (with special emphasis on those in the Words of Mormon) provides powerful evidence of some things the Lord intends that we get from the book and some ways he would have us approach the book. This paper examines that evidence.

Cheryl Brown is associate professor of Linguistics at Brigham Young University.

Reasons for Exclusion

The Overall Problem of Quantity

To appreciate how the Book of Mormon was compiled as the Lord directed the prophet-writers, we must first appreciate the fact that not everything available to the writers was included in the book. Again and again the reader is reminded of the immense amount of material the prophets had to work from and the small amount of space they had to work with. Mormon tells us that "I cannot write the hundredth part of the things of my people" (WofM 1:5). Elsewhere we read, "And now I, Nephi, cannot write all the things which were taught among my people" (2 Nephi 33:1); "And a hundredth part of the proceedings of this people, which now began to be numerous, cannot be written upon these plates" (Jacob 3:13); "And many more things did king Benjamin teach his sons, which are not written in this book" (Mosiah 1:8; see also 1 Nephi 1:16-17; 9:1-4; 10:1; Mosiah 8:1; Alma 9:34; Hel 3:14; 8:3; 3 Nephi 5:8; 26:6; Ether 15:33).

Space Limitations

The major reasons for not writing everything in the book is a physical one—there was simply too much which took place and too few plates to write everything on. Particularly in the small plates of Nephi we hear the reason of space on the plates stated frequently:

> And as these plates are small, and as these things are written for the intent of the benefit of our brethren the Lamanites, wherefore, it must needs be that I write a little. . . .And I, Jarom, do not write more, for the plates are small (Jarom 1:2, 14).

> And I, Amaleki, . . . am about to lie down in my grave; and these plates are full (Omni 1:30).

In the mid-portions of the Book of Mormon, the complaint becomes more one of the great amount which would have to be written if all the proceedings of the people were to be included:

But behold, a hundredth part of the proceedings of this people, yea, the account of the Lamanites and of the Nephites, and their wars, and contentions, and dissensions, and their preaching, and their prophecies, and their shipping and their building of ships, and their building of temples, and of synagogues and their sanctuaries, and their righteousness, and their wickedness, and their murders, and their robbings, and their plundering, and all manner of abominations and whoredoms, cannot be contained in this work (Hel 3:14).

And there had many things transpired which, in the eyes of some, would be great and marvelous; nevertheless, they cannot all be written in this book; yea, this book cannot contain even a hundredth part of what was done among so many people in the space of twenty and five years (3 Nephi 5:8).

At the end of the book, the complaint comes back again to the limitation of space on the plates: "Behold, my father hath made this record, and he hath written the intent thereof. And behold, I would write it also if I had room upon the plates, but I have not: and ore I have none, for I am alone" (Mormon 8:5).

Difficulty in Writing

Along with the problems caused by limited space, we also read that there were physical difficulties encountered in engraving on the metal plates. Both Nephi and Jacob speak of laboring "diligently" to write (2 Nephi 25:23); Jacob specifically laments, "I cannot write but a little of my words, because of the difficulty of engraving our words upon plates . . ." (Jacob 4:1). Moroni also explains, "we could write but little, because of the awkwardness of our hands" (Ether 12:24). Other times, however, the difficulty in writing was an intellectual one inherent in trying to house powerful and dynamic spiritual concepts in the fixed and structured written language. The authors of the Book of Mormon were full of the Spirit of the Lord. When they spoke to the people, they could feel that Spirit and see the effect of their words. They could perceive the thoughts and doubts of their listeners and respond to them (see 1 Nephi 15:1-4; Alma 7:17; 18:15-17; and 40:1). But once their words were written down, the authors could not respond to the effect they would have on their readers. The authors could feel, therefore, a great difference between their spoken and their written language.

Nephi, the first writer in the Book of Mormon, felt this disparity between his spoken and his written language and worried about those who would harden their hearts against the truth in written form:

> And now I, Nephi, cannot write all the things which were taught among my people; neither am I mighty in writing, like unto speaking; for when a man speaketh by the power of the Holy Ghost the power of the Holy Ghost carrieth it unto the hearts of the children of men. But behold, there are many that harden their hearts against the Holy Spirit, that it hath no place in them; wherefore, they cast many things away which are written and esteem them as things of naught (2 Nephi 33:1-2).

Moroni expressed the same worry: "Thou hast also made our words powerful and great, even that we cannot write them; wherefore, when we write we behold our weakness, and stumble because of the placing of our words; and I fear lest the Gentiles shall mock at our words" (Ether 12:25).

In Moroni's fears and the Lord's response to them comes one of the great keys to our approach to the book. The Lord offered this comfort: "Fools mock, but they shall mourn; and my grace is sufficient for the meek, that they shall take no advantage of your weakness" (Ether 12:26). Here lies one of the great keys for understanding the Book of Mormon: if we look for them, we will find weaknesses in the book, but ultimately we will mourn when our jeers turn to sorrow as we discover what we have missed because of our mocking. If we are meek, however, the Lord will speak to us from that scripture, and the concepts there will be as powerful and dynamic as if Nephi, Moroni, or any of the other prophets taught them to us personally.

Difficulty in Using a Second Language

In addition to the difficulty of engraving on metal plates, the complexities caused by writing in a second language forced at least some of the authors to limit what they wrote. Thus, the prophet Mormon writes in 3 Nephi, "there are many things which, according to our language, we are not able to write" (3 Nephi 5:18). And Moroni tells us, "And if our plates had been sufficiently large we should have written in Hebrew; but the Hebrew hath been altered by us also; and if we could have written in Hebrew, behold, ye would have had no imperfection in our record" (Mormon 9:33). But, once again, he has faith that the Lord will make up the difference: "But the Lord knoweth the things which we have written, and also that none other people knoweth our language; and because that none other people knoweth our language, therefore he hath prepared means for the interpretation thereof" (Mormon 9:34).

As we read these explanations of why the authors did not write some things and why what they did write might be weak, we are reminded that the Book of Mormon is truly the Lord's book. He knows what it is supposed to say, and the only way that we can get the full, intended meaning is through him. Through his power, what is not written by the ancient authors will not be a stumbling block for us.

Some Things to be Written Elsewhere

Another reason the Book of Mormon authors did not include certain things is that the revelations they had received were to be written in other books by other prophets. At least 17 times the Book of Mormon writers note that more was written— or would be written—in other places by other people. For example, 1 Nephi 13-15 records Nephi's vision of many of the future events of the house of Israel. But Nephi was told not to write some of the things he had seen, "for the Lord has ordained the apostle of the Lamb of God that he should write [them]" (1 Nephi 14:25). Then Nephi tells us that the name of the apostle who was to write the remainder of the vision was John. Today we know that God has given us at least some further part of this vision in the book of Revelation. He knew that we would have access to the Bible and, in his economy, did not require more to be written in the Book of Mormon.

We see the Lord's kindness in two ways here. He was kind to Nephi by not requiring the additional engraving. He was kind to us by placing a link between these two visions. Can we truly understand Nephi's vision without the part John wrote? Can we understand the Revelation of John without the part Nephi wrote? What synergism is created when these two visions "become one in thine hand" (Ezek 37:17). The Lord himself has arranged for one book of scripture to lead us to the other. This, too, is a key to understanding how the Lord intended us to use the scriptures—one volume being complementary to the other.

We do not have everything which was recorded elsewhere. Some of the Book of Mormon story was lost with the 116 pages of the original translation of the Book of Mormon. The Lord knew that this part would be lost; therefore, he had Nephi prepare the small plates and had Mormon include them with his other plates precisely because he did not want that information to be lost to us. Other writings were never intended for us, such as the accounts of the business, shipping, dealings, etc. of the Nephites and to some extent the records of the Lamanites. The authors of the Book of Mormon tell us that those records were kept, but nowhere is there evidence that the Lord was concerned that we have such records at this time. Much of the history, "the reign of the kings, and the wars and contentions" (1 Nephi 9:4) of the Nephites and Lamanites also fall into this category. Though they were written elsewhere, they have not yet come into our hands. Such issues, while interesting in establishing the fact that the principles of the book applied to real people, do not seem to be what the Lord most wanted us to get out of the Book of Mormon.

Preventing Sorrow for the Righteous and Temptation for the Wicked

Other reasons for not writing certain things show an awareness that readers of the book will also be subject to human frailties. In one very touching statement, Mormon tells why some things were not included:

> And now behold, I, Mormon, do not desire to harrow up the souls of men in casting before them such an awful scene of blood and carnage as was laid before mine eyes; but I, knowing that these things must surely be made known, and that all things which are hid must be revealed upon the house-tops—And also that a knowledge of these things must come unto the remnant of these people, and also unto the Gentiles, who the Lord hath said should scatter this people, and this people should be counted as naught among them—therefore I write a small abridgement, daring not to give a full account of the things which I have seen, because of the commandment which I have received, and also that ye might not have too great sorrow because of the wickedness of this people. And now behold, this I speak unto their seed, and also to the Gentiles who have care for the house of Israel, that realize and know from whence their blessings come (Mormon 5:8-10).

We can surely learn something from Mormon for today's depiction of blood, gore, and violence in our media.

Some other things are not included because of the temptation they might engender among weak or wicked readers. Thus, Alma instructed Helaman:

> And now, my son, I command you that ye retain all their oaths, and their covenants, and their agreements in their secret abominations; yea, and all their signs, and their wonders ye shall keep from this people that they know them not, lest peradventure they should fall into darkness also and be destroyed. Therefore ye shall keep these secret plans of their oaths and their covenants from this people, and only their wickedness and their murders and their abominations shall ye make known unto them; and ye shall teach them to abhor such wickedness and abominations and murders; and ye shall also teach them that these people were destroyed on account of their wickedness and abominations and their murders (Alma 37:27, 29).

In contrast, some things were kept back so the wicked could not destroy them. The general wickedness of people put the record in constant jeopardy. Thus Mormon was commanded that he "should not suffer the records which had been handed down by [his] fathers, which were sacred, to fall into the hands of the Lamanites, (for the Lamanites would destroy them)" (Mormon 6:6). And Joseph Smith was told in these days that "there are records which contain much of my gospel, which have been kept back because of the wickedness of the people" (D&C 6:26). The wisdom of retaining some records was demonstrated in the loss of the first 116 manuscript pages through Martin Harris. Of this matter, the Lord said to Joseph Smith, "Now, behold, I say unto you, that because you delivered up those writings which you had power given unto you to translate by the means of the Urim and Thummim, into the hands of a wicked man, you have lost them" (D&C 10:1). The Lord was well aware that not all potential readers would be happy about even the best that the book offered, and he was cautious about who should have the record at all. As he said, "My scriptures shall be given as I have appointed, and they shall be preserved in safety" (D&C 42:56).

Trying the Faith of the Readers

The Lord was also cautious about what *was* contained in the record, withholding even some very good things in order to test the faithful. We plainly see this in 3 Nephi. There, Mormon writes,

> And these things have I written, which are a lesser part of the things which he [Christ] taught the people; and I have written them to the intent that they may be brought again unto this people, from the Gentiles, according to the words which Jesus hath spoken.
>
> And when they shall have received this, which is expedient that they should have first, to try their faith, and if it shall so be that they shall believe these things then shall the greater things be made manifest unto them.
>
> And if it so be that they will not believe these things, then shall the greater things be withheld from them, unto their condemnation.
>
> Behold, I was about to write them, all which were engraven upon the plates of Nephi, but the Lord forbade it, saying: I will try the faith of my people.
>
> Therefore I, Mormon, do write the things which have been commanded me of the Lord. And now I, Mormon, make an end of my sayings, and proceed to write the things which have been commanded me (3 Nephi 26:8-12).

Moroni, too, felt the constraining hand of the Lord. However, he was allowed to write more, but he was commanded to seal up a portion of what he had written and Joseph Smith was not allowed to translate it. In Ether 4:4-7, we get the following explanation:

> Behold, I have written upon these plates the very things which the brother of Jared saw; and there never were greater things made manifest than those which were made manifest unto the brother of Jared.
>
> Wherefore the Lord hath commanded me to write them. And I have written them. And he commanded me that I should seal them up; and he also hath commanded that I should seal up the interpretation thereof; wherefore I have sealed up the interpreters, according to the commandment of the Lord.
>
> For the Lord said unto me: They shall not go forth unto the Gentiles until the day that they shall repent of their iniquity, and become clean before the Lord.
>
> And in that day that they shall exercise faith in me, saith the Lord, even as the brother of Jared did, that they may become sanctified in me, then will I manifest unto them the things which the brother of Jared saw, even to the unfolding unto them all my revelations, saith Jesus Christ, the Son of God, the Father of the heavens and of the earth, and all things that in them are.

From this statement and all the other reasons given by Book of Mormon authors for not including certain things, two points can be easily drawn about the book and what the Lord intended that we get from it. One is the fact that the Book of Mormon is the Lord's book and that a correct understanding of it comes from him alone. The other is that there is much more knowledge and truth available which we will receive only as we live in accordance with that which we already have.

Reasons for Including Certain Things

So, what *is* in the Book of Mormon and why is it there? The authors discuss their reasons for including what they included, too.

Looking Forward to Intended Readers

To begin with, it is obvious that the authors intended the writings to be of worth to particular people. Interestingly, not all of the authors specified the same groups. Nephi seems to have had a broad perspective about his potential readership—"the things which shall be written out of the book shall be of great worth unto the children of men" but he also recognizes some narrower groups for whom the book will have special meaning: "and especially unto our seed, which is a remnant of the house of Israel" (2 Nephi 28:2).

Jacob gives a feeling of a narrower perspective, viewing potential readers as being composed of Nephites and Lamanites: "Now in this thing we do rejoice; and we labor diligently to engraven these words upon plates, hoping that our beloved brethren and our children will receive them with thankful hearts, and look upon them that they may learn with joy" (Jacob 4:3). He closes his writings hoping that "many of [his] brethren may read [his] words" and saying, "Brethren, adieu" (Jacob 7:27). Enos and Jarom both seem to have views that are even narrower. Enos says, "And I had faith, and I did cry unto God that he would preserve the records; and he covenanted with me that he would bring them forth unto the Lamanites in his own due time" (Enos 1:16), and Jarom points out, "these things are written for the intent of the benefit of our brethren the Lamanites" (Jarom 1:2).

Mormon also clearly considered himself writing to the remnant of the Lamanites and the Nephites. Commenting on the hope that Moroni would survive him to write more, he said, "And it supposeth me that he will witness the entire destruction of my people. But may God grant that he may survive them, that he may write somewhat concerning them, and somewhat concerning Christ, that perhaps some day it may profit them" (WofM 1:2). But Mormon also saw more. In Mormon 5:12, he states, "Now these things are written unto the remnant of the house of Jacob."

Alma, like Nephi, also saw a broader audience. This is indicated by his comment to Helaman that the record "should be kept and handed down from one generation to another, and be kept and preserved by the hand of the Lord until they should go forth unto every nation, kindred, tongue, and people" (Alma 37:4).

The Savior himself also taught this broad view in his visit to the Nephites. He said, "Therefore give heed to my words; write the things which I have told you; and according to the time and the will of the Father they shall go forth unto the Gentiles" (3 Nephi 23:4). Earlier in his visit he had said, "These sayings which ye shall write shall be kept and shall be manifested unto the Gentiles" and then "that through the fulness of the Gentiles, the remnant of their seed, who shall be scattered forth upon the face of the earth because of their unbelief, may be brought in, or may be brought to a knowledge of me, their Redeemer" (3 Nephi 16:4). The Lord intended that everyone should have the book.

To Allow for a Fair Judgment

One reason everyone should have the book and one reason authors give for writing it involves the judgment. The Lord told Nephi, for example, that the records must be kept because "out of the books which shall be written I will judge the world, every man according to their works, according to that which is written" (2 Nephi 29:11). Then, again, during his visit to the Nephites, the Savior reminded the record keepers: "Write the works of this people, which shall be, even as hath been written, of that which hath been. For behold, out of the books which have been written, and which shall be written, shall this people be judged, for by them shall their works be known unto men. And behold, all things are written by the Father; therefore out of the books which shall be written shall the world be judged" (3 Nephi 27:24-26).

And, in the Words of Mormon, "And I know that they will be preserved; for there are great things written upon them, out of which my people and their brethren shall be judged at the great and last day, according to the word of God which is written" (WofM 1:11). The prophets wrote so that there would be a fair judgment for their people—and so that we would have the knowledge upon which our judgment will be based. This is one of the things the Lord intended for us—a "standard" work to guide our thoughts and actions.

To Express Deep Feelings of the Soul

Other items were included in the Book of Mormon because they touched the souls of the authors. Thus, Nephi declares, "And upon these I write the things of my soul" (2 Nephi 4:15) and Mormon explains his actions by saying, "And the things which are upon these plates pleas[ed] me. . . . Wherefore, I chose these things, to finish my record upon them" (WofM 1:4-5).

To Be Obedient to Others

The authors of the Book of Mormon also wrote because they had been commanded by those who had kept the records before them. Jacob tells us that he was commanded by his brother Nephi, to write on the plates (Jacob 1:1-2) and that he gave the plates to his son, Enos, with the same commandment he had received from Nephi (Jacob 7:27); Jarom wrote because he was told to by his father; Enos so that their genealogy could be preserved (Jarom 1:1); and Omni because his father, Jarom, told him the same things (Omni 1:1). Alma carefully instructed Helaman about keeping the records. Mormon himself wrote in obedience to the instructions given him by Ammaron (Mormon 1:3-4; 2:17).

To Be Obedient to God

But the main reason the prophets wrote was obedience to the Lord's command. Thus, Nephi tells us of the commandment he received to make a new set of smaller plates and what they were to contain: "And after I had made these plates by way of commandment, I, Nephi, received a commandment that the ministry and the prophecies, the more plain and precious parts of them, should be written upon these plates; and that the things which were written should be kept for the instruction of my people, who should possess the land, and also for other wise purposes, which purposes are known unto the Lord" (1 Nephi

19:3). Later he says, "And I engraved that which is pleasing unto God" (2 Nephi 5:32).

To Supply Missing Elements of Christ's Gospel

The authors also wanted to present a fuller statement of the gospel. Thus, Nephi is shown that "they have taken away from the gospel of the Lamb many parts which are plain and most precious; and also many covenants of the Lord have they taken away" (1 Nephi 13:26). Furthermore, the Lord tells Nephi:

> I will manifest myself unto thy seed, that they shall write many things which I shall minister unto them, which shall be plain and precious; and after thy seed shall be destroyed, and dwindle in unbelief, and also the seed of thy brethren, behold, these things shall be hid up, to come forth unto the Gentiles, by the gift and power of the Lamb. And in them shall be written my gospel, saith the Lamb, and my rock and my salvation (1 Nephi 13:35-36).

The Book of Mormon gives more evidence of this fact when it records Christ's ministry among the Nephites. He told his disciples: "Behold, other scriptures I would that ye should write, that ye have not" (3 Nephi 23:6). He then gave the Nephites the words of Malachi, which had been given to the Jews after Lehi departed from Jerusalem. He also made sure that they had recorded the fulfillment of one of Samuel the Lamanite's prophecies.

To Demonstrate That the Lord's Words
Do Not "Fall to the Ground"

The incident with Samuel the Lamanite's prophecies ties closely to another major reason for including certain things in the Book of Mormon; namely, to give clear evidence that the words of the Lord do not "fall to the ground" (see 1 Sam 3:19). In other words, the Lord wanted very plain evidence that all of his promises and prophecies are fulfilled. Following the passage quoted above in which Christ supplied the disciples with the teachings of Malachi, he pointed out that they had failed to record the fulfillment of Samuel's prophecy (3 Nephi 23:10-11) that many saints would arise from the dead, and should "appear unto many" (Hel 14:25). Even though the record keepers had noted the fulfillment of numerous other prophecies regarding the birth, death, and resurrection of Christ, that was not enough. The Lord wanted it made clear that *every single one* of his prophecies were fulfilled. He commanded the disciples to write the scriptures and their fulfillment, then told them to teach those things to the people.

Further evidence that the Lord wanted it clear that none of his words fail comes in Mormon's instructions to readers: "And now, whoso readeth, let him understand; he that hath the scriptures, let him search them, and see and behold if all these deaths and destructions by fire, and by smoke, and by tempests, and by whirlwinds, and by the opening of the earth to receive them, and all these things are not unto the fulfilling of the prophecies of many of the holy prophets" (3 Nephi 10:14).

Christ also had his Nephite disciples record a statement he made in Jerusalem about having other sheep, saying:

> And I command you that ye shall write these sayings after I am gone, that if it so be that my people at Jerusalem, they who have seen me and been with me in my ministry, do not ask the Father in my name, that they may receive a knowledge of you by the Holy Ghost, and also of the other tribes whom they know not of, that these sayings which ye shall write shall be kept and shall be manifested unto the Gentiles, that through the fulness of the Gentiles, the remnant of their seed, who shall be scattered forth upon the face of the earth because of their unbelief, may be brought in, or may be brought to a knowledge of me, their Redeemer (3 Nephi 16:4).

The Lord had prophesied that the gathering of Israel would take place, but, uncertain whether his disciples in the Old World would inquire about the prophecy's meaning, he reiterated it in the New World.

The Lord also made sure that there was a witness to the fulfillment of the prophecies about the Jaredites: "And the Lord spake unto Ether, and said unto him: Go forth. And he went forth, and beheld that the words of the Lord had all been fulfilled; and he finished his record" (Ether 15:33). The Book of Mormon authors wrote so that we may know what and in whom we can trust.

To Give Testimony of the Lord and His Mission

Bearing testimony that Christ is the person in whom we can trust is another major reason that the authors of the Book of Mormon give for putting certain things into their records. Very early in the Book of Mormon, Nephi is commanded: "And behold this thing shall be given unto these for a sign, that after thou hast beheld the tree which bore the fruit which thy father tasted, thou shalt also behold a man descending out of heaven, and him shall ye witness; and after ye have witnessed him ye shall bear record that it is the Son of God" (1 Nephi 11:7).

True to this purpose all the way through his record, Nephi concludes his account with his testimony of Christ:

> And now, my beloved brethren, and also Jew, and all ye ends of the earth, hearken unto these words and believe in Christ; and if ye believe not in these words believe in Christ. And if ye shall believe in Christ ye will believe in these words, for they are the words of Christ, and he hath given them unto me; and they teach all men that they should do good. And if they are not the words of Christ, judge ye—for Christ will show unto you, with power and great glory, that they are his words, at the last day; and you and I shall stand face to face before his bar; and ye shall know that I have been commanded of him to write these things, notwithstanding my weakness (2 Nephi 33:10-11).

Jacob follows Nephi's lead, telling how he labored to record sacred things on the plates, "And touch upon them as much as it were possible, for Christ's sake, and for the sake of our people" because "we knew of Christ and his kingdom, which should come. . . . Wherefore we would to God that we could persuade all men not to rebel against God, to provoke him to anger, but that all men would believe in Christ, and view his death, and suffer his cross and bear the shame of the world" (Jacob 1:4-8).

Authors throughout the Book of Mormon bear testimony of Christ, and Mormon reinforces this concept at the end of his abridgement, attempting to persuade people to believe in Christ:

> And this is the commandment which I have received; and behold, they [the records] shall come forth according to the commandment of the Lord, when he shall see fit, in his wisdom. And behold, they shall go unto the unbelieving of the Jews; and for this intent shall they go—that they may be persuaded that Jesus is the Christ, the Son of the living God; that the Father may bring about, through his most Beloved, his great and eternal purpose, in restoring the Jews, or all the house of Israel, to the land of their inheritance, which the Lord their God hath given them, unto the fulfilling of his covenant (Mormon 5:13-14).

At the beginning of this paper, I mentioned that the Words of Mormon provides some of the most direct evidence available of how the Lord structured the Book of Mormon. However, we have also seen that all parts and writers in the Book of Mormon do that. We have noted reasons and purposes for both *not* writing and writing certain things.

The Lord's Reasons and What They Mean

While all of the reasons noted thus far for the structuring of a holy book through holy men are interesting, some of them are vastly more important than others because they are reasons that the Lord himself has given. *His* reasons for *not having things written* consist of the fact that things will be written elsewhere and that the faith of the people should be tried. *His* reasons for *having things written* consist of restoring plain and precious parts of the gospel, giving evidence that all of the promises of the Lord are fulfilled, and testifying of Jesus Christ and his mission.

If we look at only these reasons, we can see a larger pattern which tells us more clearly what the Lord intends that we should get from the book. First, it is very clear that the book is "Another Testament of Jesus Christ." There is hardly a page which does not refer to him or his work or mission or love. We are to learn of Christ from the book, and to have hope in him.

Second, the Savior is very careful to make sure we know that he keeps his promises—all of his promises and prophecies are fulfilled. Both missing scripture and missing reports of fulfillment of scripture were added to the book at the Savior's specific request. We are to learn from the book to trust Christ, to have faith in him.

Third, the Lord has made it clear that he has withheld some glorious things with the promise that they will be given later. In light of the previous two points, this becomes a powerful enticement. We know the goodness of Christ. We know that his promises are all fulfilled. And now we know that, when we repent and become clean before him and exercise faith in him (Ether 4:6-7), he will unfold unto us all his revelations (Ether 4:7), even the very things which the brother of Jared saw, "and there never were greater things made manifest than those" (Ether 4:4). The book is designed to draw us upward to him, to bring us "nearer to God" than we would get "by any other book."

As we see the Lord's design in the Book of Mormon, we can also gain new appreciation for those through whom he worked. In particular, Mormon is amazing. Notice how, in just a few verses from the Words of Mormon, he is able to draw together so many reasons for writing, bringing them to focus superbly on Christ:

> And now I speak somewhat concerning that which I have written; for after I had made an abridgment from the plates of Nephi, down to the reign of this king Benjamin, of whom Amaleki spake, I searched among the records which had been delivered into my hands, and I found these plates, which contained this small account of the prophets, from Jacob down to the reign of this king Benjamin, and also many of the words of Nephi.
>
> And the things which are upon these plates *pleasing me*, because of *the prophecies of the coming of Christ*; and my fathers knowing that many of them have been fulfilled; yea, and *I also know that as many things as have been prophesied concerning us down to this day have been fulfilled, and as many as go beyond this day must surely come to pass—*
>
> Wherefore, I chose these things, to finish my record upon them, which remainder of my record I shall take from the plates of Nephi; and *I cannot write the hundredth part of the things of my people.*
>
> But behold, I shall take these plates which contain these prophesyings and revelations, and put them with the remainder of my record, for *they are choice unto me*; and I know they will be choice unto *my brethren.*

> And I do this for a wise purpose; for thus *it whispereth me, according to the workings of the Spirit of the Lord* which is in me. And now, I do not know all things; but the Lord knoweth all things which are to come; wherefore, he worketh in me to do according to his will.
>
> And my prayer to God is concerning *my brethren, that they may once again come to the knowledge of God*, yea, the redemption of Christ; that they may once again be a delightsome people (WofM 1:3-8; emphasis added).

Mormon feeds our faith in Christ. With that faith, it is now up to us to be enticed to the higher plane and greater revelation which Christ has promised.

"We Did Magnify Our Office unto the Lord"   4

Richard O. Cowan

*L*atter-day Saints generally think only of revelations in the Doctrine and Covenants as a source of information about the Church's mission and organization. Obviously these latter-day revelations contain the most detailed instructions concerning how the restored Church is to function, but the Book of Mormon also contains valuable insights into how God's church was organized in ancient America. There is much we can learn from the Nephites because the true church of the present and earlier dispensations has always had similar objectives. The sixth article of faith affirms: "We believe in the same organization that existed in the Primitive Church, namely, apostles, prophets, pastors, teachers, evangelists, and so forth."

In Joseph Smith's day, the phrase "primitive church" was understood to refer specifically to the organization among New Testament Christians. In a broad sense, however, this declaration may be applied to God's church in any dispensation. Even though organizational structure may have varied and different ecclesiastical titles were often used, there have always been those in every dispensation those who, like the Apostles, were special witnesses for the Savior (D&C 107:23), "prophets" who were God's authorized spokesmen, "pastors" or shepherds to care for the flock, "teachers" to inform the people, and "evangelists" to expound the gospel. Today, for example, stake presidents, bishops, priesthood

Richard O. Cowan is professor of Church History and Doctrine at Brigham Young University.

leaders, and others are "pastors." Similarly, today's patriarchs are "evangelists," as they reveal and apply the gospel to individuals through inspired blessings (*Teachings of the Prophet Joseph Smith* 151; hereafter *TPJS*).

Church Organization in the Old World

A review of what the scriptures teach about the Church in the Old World will provide perspective for what the Book of Mormon reveals about the Church in ancient America. From the time of Adam to Moses, the Lord's people were organized along family lines and were presided over by worthy bearers of the High Priesthood. Ideally, this position of patriarch was handed down from father to first-born son. The authority held by these leaders came to be known as the "Melchizedek Priesthood" (D&C 107:2-4).

Following the Israelites' exodus from Egypt, the Lord inaugurated a separate order of priesthood when he called Aaron and his sons to serve as "priests" (Ex 28:1). Latter-day revelations clearly set forth the relative power of these two orders of priesthood: "The Melchizedek Priesthood holds the right of presidency, and has power and authority over all the offices in the church in all ages of the world, to administer in spiritual things" (D&C 107:8). The lesser priesthood, on the other hand, has a specific responsibility for temporal affairs and administers "outward ordinances" (D&C 107:13-14).

By divine assignment the tribe of Levi assumed the duties of the lesser priesthood, and this authority came to be known as the Aaronic or Levitical Priesthood (Palmer 61-62). Aaron's direct descendants, generally known as "high priests," held the presiding keys and exercised authority comparable to today's bishops, at least so far as their Aaronic Priesthood responsibilities are concerned. The rest of the Levites, also known as "priests," functioned under their direction and had lesser assignments comparable to today's teachers and deacons (McConkie 10). In Old Testament times the term "elder" was applied to at least two different groups: (1) older and more experienced men in a community, not necessarily holding a priesthood office; and (2) those ordained to this Melchizedek Priesthood office (Ex 24:9; LDS BD 662).

When the Savior organized his church during the meridian of time, he called the Twelve Apostles and the Seventy to spread the gospel (Matt 10:1, 5-6; Luke 10:1). The New Testament mentions other priesthood officers including deacons and bishops (1 Tim 3:1, 8).

In these last days the Church's organization was not established all at once. It was restored piecemeal as conditions required and as the Saints were prepared. From Peter, James, and John, Joseph Smith and Oliver Cowdery received the authority of the Apostleship (D&C 18:9; 20:2-3). In 1830 the initial Church structure included elders, priests, teachers, and deacons. Bishops and high priests were added the following year. By 1833 there were patriarchs and a First Presidency. The first stake was established in 1834, and quorums of the Twelve and Seventy were added the following year. The process of restoration has continued, with wards, missions, auxiliaries, regions, and areas becoming part of the ecclesiastical structure. The Book of Mormon record suggests that the Church also grew in a step-by-step manner among the Nephites.

A Patriarchal Family Organization

As Lehi and Ishmael led their children from Jerusalem into the wilderness, the group may have numbered about twenty (1 Nephi 7:6). Lehi as patriarch received revelation concerning their spiritual and temporal welfare in the desert. He also took the lead in offering sacrifices for the family (1 Nephi 2:7; 5:9). Not long after the family had left Jerusalem, the Lord promised Nephi, then the youngest son, that "inasmuch as thou shalt keep my commandments, thou shalt be made a ruler and a teacher over thy brethren" (1 Nephi 2:22). Nevertheless, Nephi continued to show proper deference to his father as head of the family. For example, when Nephi broke his steel bow with which he hunted game, the group feared they might starve. Even Lehi murmured. Nephi fashioned a new bow of wood, and respectfully asked his father to inquire of the Lord for direction as to where he should hunt (1 Nephi 16:18-26).

By the time forty years had passed, the group had crossed the ocean to America and were established in their new promised land. It is likely that Lehi's and Ishmael's great grandchildren were then being born, and the colony perhaps numbered even as many as 200 souls. Following Lehi's death, a great division occurred. Nephi's older brothers resented his ruling over them and threatened to kill him. The Lord warned Nephi to take all the righteous who would follow him and flee into the wilderness. This group called themselves "the people of Nephi," or Nephites (2 Nephi 5:1-9), and these circumstances provided the setting for the first expansion beyond the simple family organization.

Ecclesiastical and Secular Officers Appointed

Nephi provided his people with both spiritual and temporal leadership, but when they wanted him to become their king, he declined but provided whatever leadership he could. This fulfilled the Lord's earlier promise that Nephi would become "their ruler and their teacher" (2 Nephi 5:18-19).

As the spiritual leader of his people, Nephi consecrated his younger brothers, Jacob and Joseph, to be "priests and teachers over the land of my people" (2 Nephi 5:26). Elder Joseph Fielding Smith explained that "the fact that plural terms *priests and teachers* were used [in recording the ordination of only two people] indicates that this was not a reference to the definite office in the [Aaronic] priesthood in either case, but it was a general assignment to teach, direct, and admonish the people. Otherwise the terms *priest and teacher* would have been given, in the singular" (Smith 1:124; emphasis in original). As will be shown hereafter, the Nephites were operating under the Melchizedek Priesthood rather than the Aaronic. Hence, Jacob and Joseph could well be described as "priests/teachers."

Following Nephi's time, religious and secular leadership responsibilities were separated. Near the end of his life, Nephi appointed his younger brother, Jacob, to record significant preaching, prophecies, and revelations on the small plates (Jacob 1:1-4). This appointment meant that Jacob also assumed the spiritual leadership of the people. Another man was appointed to be king. He and his successors were known as "Second Nephi," "Third Nephi," etc., in honor of their first great leader (Jacob 1:9-11). However, responsibility for keeping the small plates passed down through the family for several generations to Amaleki. Having no posterity and knowing king Benjamin to be "a just man before the Lord," Amaleki gave the plates to him (Omni 1:25).

This brought the ecclesiastical and civil leadership once again to one man. Benjamin exercised this dual authority near the end of his life when he designated his son Mosiah to succeed him as king and also appointed priests to teach the people (Mosiah 6:3). Mosiah was likewise acknowledged by the people not only as their king, but also as a seer, revelator, and prophet (Mosiah 8:13-18). With his ecclesiastical power, Mosiah authorized Alma to establish churches throughout the kingdom and to ordain priests and teachers (Mosiah 25:19).

Alma had served as a priest under the evil king Noah, who reigned over a colony of Nephites. Through the preaching of the prophet Abinadi, Alma and about 450 others were converted to the true faith. After fleeing for their lives, the converts were organized by Alma and called the "Church of God" or "Church of Christ." Mormon later stated that this was "the first church" among these people "after their transgression" (3 Nephi 5:12). He undoubtedly meant that this was the first church after the transgression of Noah, not the first church among the Nephites in general.

As he baptized the converts, Alma affirmed that he had authority from "Almighty God" (Mosiah 18:1-17). As Nephi had done centuries earlier, Alma also declined the people's invitation to become their king (Mosiah 23:6-7). As the founder of their church, however, he did assume the office of "high priest" (Mosiah 23:16). In this capacity as spiritual leader Alma consecrated just men as priests and teachers to "watch over their people" and to "nourish them with things pertaining to righteousness" (Mosiah 23:17-18). By the time Alma and his group reached the heartland of the Nephites in Zarahemla, a new challenge faced the Church—numbers.

Increasing Numbers Prompt Organizational Expansion

When the Nephites migrated to the land of Zarahemla, they absorbed a people even more numerous than they. Growth continued as the groups of Limhi and Alma joined the main body of Nephites. These increasing numbers posed a challenge to Alma, the high priest, as he responded to king Mosiah's commission and assumed responsibility for the Church in Zarahemla. There were too many people to hear the word of God in just one congregation, so they were divided into seven groups known as "churches." Nevertheless, they all thought of themselves as belonging to one church. In each congregation Alma appointed priests and teachers (Mosiah 25:20-23). In doing this he was following a precedent established while he and his converts were still in the wilderness. At that time he had ordained one priest for each fifty people to preach the gospel and teach them concerning God's kingdom (Mosiah 18:18). These local leaders were truly pastors or shepherds for their flocks.

Eventually the Nephites adopted a system of elected judges to replace rule by kings. Alma the Younger, who had already succeeded his father as high priest, was the first person elected chief judge (Mosiah 29:42). Hence, at least temporarily, civil and religious leadership continued to be exercised by the same person. After only eight years, however, Alma resigned as chief judge in order to devote his full time to church service (Alma 4:11-20).

At this point, "elders" are mentioned in the record for the first time (Alma 4:7) as Alma commissioned these local officers to "preside and watch over the church" (Alma 6:1). His successor as chief judge was chosen from "among the elders of the church" (Alma 4:16). Once again, ecclesiastical and secular leadership were exercised by different individuals.

Both Alma and Alma the Younger taught that local church officers should be self-supporting. From the beginning, Alma the Elder insisted that the priests he appointed should "labor with their own hands" to support themselves rather than live off the people. And yet, he explained that Church members should be willing to assist their leaders in case of need (Mosiah 18:24-28). He continued the same policy as he took charge of the Church in Zarahemla—the priests worked to support themselves except in the case of illness (Mosiah 27:5). This brought Alma the Younger into direct conflict with Nehor, who sought to introduce what they called "priestcraft." Nephi had earlier defined it as the practice of men who "preach and set themselves up for a light unto the world, that they may get gain and praise of the world; but they seek not the welfare of Zion" (2 Nephi 26:29). Alma denounced Nehor's idea that all priests should be popular and supported by the people (Alma 1:3). Under Alma's leadership the humble servants of God freely shared the gospel "without money and without price," and the priests and teachers did not esteem themselves as being any better than those whom they taught (Alma 1:20, 26).

The Growing Responsibility of Church Leaders

Alma the Younger as a high priest presided "over the church of God throughout the land" (Alma 8:23). Among other things he supervised the formation of additional local congregations. For example, "Alma established a church in the land of Sidom, and consecrated priests and teachers in [that] land, to baptize" (Alma 15:13). The sons of king Mosiah played a similar role during their fourteen-year mission; they "went forth from city to city, and from one house of worship to another, establishing churches, and consecrating priests and teachers throughout the land among the Lamanites, to preach and to teach the word of God among them; and thus they began to have great success" (Alma 23:4).

A new intermediate level of Church administration appeared when other high priests were called under Alma's supervision. Ammon, for example, was high priest over the land of Jershon, and Giddonah was high priest in the land of Gideon (Alma 30:19-23). Helaman succeeded Alma as high priest. He and his fellow high priests provided "exceedingly great care" and labored diligently to maintain order among the churches (Alma 46:6, 38). To assist in this process, Helaman and his brethren "did appoint priests and teachers throughout all the land, over all the churches" (Alma 45:22).

Accounts of judicial proceedings shed light on these various levels of church organization. For example, the teachers brought transgressors to the priests to be judged. Difficult cases were then referred to high priests for further consideration. Korihor, for example, was brought before Giddonah, the high priest in Gideon, who heard the case in conjunction with the local chief judge. They in turn referred this matter to "Alma, and the chief judge who was governor over all the land" (Alma 30:21-29).

The Nephites' Priesthood

In the Old World the Melchizedek Priesthood was withdrawn from the people as a whole, although selected individuals—the prophets—received this authority by divine ordination (*TPJS* 181). Because the Aaronic Priesthood was assigned to the tribe of Levi, and because no Levites accompanied Lehi's group (they were of the tribe of Joseph), Elder Joseph Fielding Smith concluded that "under these conditions the Nephites officiated by virtue of the Melchizedek Priesthood from the days of Lehi" (Smith 1:124). Anciently this authority was known as "*the Holy Priesthood, after the Order of the Son of God*" (D&C 107:3). Alma reminded his people that God had called priests "after his holy order, which was after the order of his Son," to teach them gospel principles. He therefore exhorted them to humble themselves as had done the people of Melchizedek, "who was also a high priest after this same order" (Alma 13:1,14).

While discussing the nature of the priesthood he bore, Alma also shed light on another important truth. He testified that those so ordained had been foreordained, being "called and prepared from the foundation of the world according to the foreknowledge of God, on account of their exceeding faith and good works" (Alma 13:3). The scriptures point out that Abraham and Jeremiah were so chosen (Abr 3:22-23; Jer 1:4-5). In fact, the Prophet Joseph Smith declared that "Every man who has a calling to minister to the inhabitants of the world was ordained to that very purpose in the Grand Council of heaven before this world was" (*TPJS* 365).

Priesthood Leaders Were to Teach

The chief role of ecclesiastical officers was to teach. Of forty Book of Mormon references to "priests," fourteen specifically state they were to teach. Another fifteen references link priests and teachers, perhaps in the combined role of "priests/teachers"; and only eleven mention priests without any reference to teaching. When the Lord outlined the duties of officers in his latter-day church, he likewise insisted that they were to "warn, expound, exhort, and teach" (D&C 20:42, 46, and 59). Alma affirmed that those bearing the High Priesthood of God were "to teach his commandments unto the children of men, that they also might enter into his rest" (Alma 13:6). On another occasion he noted with approval that the priests were out among the people preaching against a variety of evils (Alma 16:18). Because of this key teaching role of priesthood leaders, the people had been warned to "trust no one to be your teacher nor your minister, except he be a man of God, walking in his ways and keeping his commandments" (Mosiah 23:14).

General Church leaders provided the guidance needed to assure unity in this teaching. Priests and teachers in each local congregation were to preach the word "according as it was delivered to [them] by the mouth of Alma" (Mosiah 25:21). In the present dispensation, Elder Harold B. Lee similarly emphasized the key role of the Brethren teaching in general conferences: "As the Latter-day Saints go home from this conference, it would be well if they consider seriously the importance of taking with them the report of this conference and let it be the guide to their walk and talk during the next six months. These are the important matters the Lord sees fit to reveal to this people in this day" (68).

The Nephite Twelve

The next major development in Book of Mormon church organization came with the visit of the Savior after his resurrection in Jerusalem. One of the first things the Master did when he came among his "other sheep" in America was to call twelve disciples and to authorize them to build up his church there (3 Nephi 11:18-22; 12:1). Centuries earlier an angel had shown these twelve to Nephi:

> Behold the twelve *disciples* of the Lamb, who are chosen to minister unto thy seed. And he said unto me: Thou rememberest the twelve *apostles* of the Lamb? Behold they are they who shall judge the twelve tribes of Israel; wherefore, the twelve *ministers* of thy seed shall be judged of them; for ye are of the house of Israel. And these twelve *ministers* whom thou beholdest shall judge thy seed And, behold, they are righteous forever; for because of their faith in the Lamb of God their garments are made white in his blood (1 Nephi 12:8-10; emphasis added).

Some have wondered whether or not these twelve were truly apostles. Elder Joseph Fielding Smith concluded that "while in every instance the Nephite twelve are spoken of as disciples the fact remains that they had been endowed with divine authority to be special witnesses of Christ among their own people. Therefore, they were virtually apostles to the Nephite race, although their jurisdiction was, as revealed to Nephi, eventually to be subject to the authority and jurisdiction of Peter and the twelve chosen in Palestine" (Smith 1:121-22). In his "Wentworth Letter," the Prophet Joseph Smith likewise affirmed that when the Savior visited the Nephites he "planted the Gospel here in all its fulness, and richness, and power, and blessing; that they had Apostles, Prophets, Pastors, Teachers, and Evangelists; the same order, the same priesthood, the same ordinances, gifts, powers, and blessings, as were enjoyed on the eastern continent" (*History of the Church* 4:538).

Consistent with the emphasis on teaching as the dominant responsibility of church leaders, the first official act of the Nephite twelve was to instruct the people. After the Lord's visit on the first day, they divided the huge multitude into twelve groups in order to teach them (3 Nephi 19:4-6). After the Savior reascended to heaven, these disciples took the lead in establishing "a church of Christ in all the lands round about." In their ministry they performed "great and marvelous works" including healing the sick and even raising the dead (4 Nephi 1:1,5).

Moroni's Parting Instructions

As Moroni completed the Nephite record with his own book, he was prompted to include materials that might almost be regarded as an appendix to the main history that had gone before. These items included some key teachings from his father (Moroni 7 and 8) and his own exhortation to the latter-day readers of his record (chapter 10). In chapters 2 through 6 Moroni set forth basic ecclesiastical procedures that had been taught by the Savior as he ministered to the Nephites, and hence these chapters are like a short handbook of instructions.

Moroni chapter 2 records the Lord's instructions on conferring the Holy Ghost. Chapter 3 tells how elders were to ordain priests and teachers, apparently referring to specific offices in the priesthood rather than to general titles as used earlier in the record. Chapters 4 and 5 tell how elders and priests were to administer the sacramental emblems of the Lord's supper. Chapter 6 emphasized the responsibility of baptized members to bring forth good fruit. The Church was to maintain records so that the members "might be remembered and nourished by the good word of God." The Saints were to "meet together oft, to fast and to pray, and to speak one with another concerning the welfare of their souls," and these meetings were to be conducted under the direction of the Holy Ghost. Transgressors were to be brought before the elders to be removed from the Church unless they repented (Moroni 6:4-9).

The Example of Jacob and Joseph

The foregoing sections have reviewed the ecclesiastical structure of the Church among the Nephites. The Book of Mormon also provides valuable insights into how individual priesthood bearers should function. Jacob and Joseph, the youngest sons of Lehi, provide an outstanding example: "For I, Jacob, and my brother Joseph had been consecrated priests and teachers of this people, by the hand of Nephi. And we did magnify our office unto the Lord, taking upon us the responsibility, answering the sins of the people upon our own heads if we did not teach them the word of God with all diligence" (Jacob 1:18-19).

Even as Jacob and Joseph magnified their callings, latter-day priesthood bearers are admonished to do the same. To avoid being responsible for others' sins, one must faithfully perform his own duties. Elder Delbert L. Stapley explained that "to magnify

is to honor, to exalt and glorify, and cause to be held in greater
esteem or respect. It also means to increase the importance of, to
enlarge and make greater." We can bring respect to our callings
and make them appear greater by faithfully fulfilling them, and
taking advantage of all opportunities to bless the lives of those
whom we serve. Elder Stapley therefore concluded that for a man
to magnify his calling he must faithfully and worthily honor his
priesthood, accept callings willingly, abide by gospel standards,
sustain those who preside over him, "use his priesthood in
righteousness for the blessing and benefit of his fellow men," and
"banish all iniquity from his soul" (424). According to the "oath
and covenant which belongeth to the priesthood," those who
magnify their callings will inherit "all that my Father hath" (D&C
84:33-39).

Jacob especially set the example of teaching the gospel
"with all diligence." In his teachings Jacob emphasized doctrines
of greatest importance. In one great sermon, recorded in 2 Nephi
6-10, he taught the people concerning their destiny as part of the
house of Israel and emphasized the great blessings made possible
through the Savior's atonement. He also plainly taught important
practical facets of gospel living. He advocated the proper use of
wealth, denounced immorality, and encouraged setting a good
example (Jacob 2-3). Like his older brother Nephi, Jacob
"likened" (applied) the scriptures to his listeners (1 Nephi 19:23).
After quoting Zenos' allegory of the tame and wild olive trees,
Jacob made sure the people understood their responsibility in
light of these teachings:

> Wherefore, my beloved brethren, I beseech of you in words of sober-
> ness that ye would repent, and come with full purpose of heart, and
> cleave unto God as he cleaveth unto you. And while his arm of mercy
> is extended towards you in the light of the day, harden not your hearts.
> Yea, today, if ye will hear his voice, harden not your hearts; for why
> will ye die? For behold, after ye have been nourished by the good word
> of God all the day long, will ye bring forth evil fruit, that ye must be
> hewn down and cast into the fire? . . . O then, my beloved brethren,
> repent ye, and enter in at the straight gate, and continue in the way which
> is narrow, until ye shall obtain eternal life (Jacob 6:5-7, 11).

Jacob and Joseph took their stewardship to teach seriously. They realized that if they did not fulfil their commission to teach, they must bear the responsibility for the sins of those whom they had not instructed adequately. After Jacob had expounded the gospel with clarity and power, he could state that he had shaken off "your iniquities from my soul, and that I stand with brightness before [God], and am rid of your blood" (2 Nephi 9:44). This was consistent with Ezekiel's teachings that a watchman who fails to sound the alarm will be held accountable for the destruction of his people (Ezek 3:17-21; 33:1-9). In our day the Lord has warned that parents bear the same responsibility for their children (D&C 68:25).

Thus we see that the Book of Mormon not only provides interesting information concerning how the Nephites' church was organized, but it also sets forth worthy examples we should follow in order to "magnify our office unto the Lord" (Jacob 1:19).

BIBLIOGRAPHY

History of the Church. 7 vols. Salt Lake City: Deseret Book, 1980.

Lee, Harold B. *Conference Report* (April 1946) 67-72.

McConkie, Bruce R. *Mormon Doctrine.* 2nd ed. Salt Lake City: Bookcraft, 1966.

Palmer, Lee A. *Aaronic Priesthood Through the Centuries.* Salt Lake City: Deseret Book, 1964.

Smith, Joseph Fielding. *Answers to Gospel Questions.* 5 vols. Salt Lake City. Deseret Book, 1963.

Stapley, Delbert L. "Honoring the Priesthood." *Improvement Era* (May 1957) 60:423-25; also in *Conference Report* (Apr 1957) 76-77.

Teachings of the Prophet Joseph Smith. Comp. Joseph Fielding Smith. Salt Lake City: Deseret Book, 1976.

Botanical Comparisons in the Allegory of the Olive Tree   5

Wilford M. Hess

F rom a botanical point of view, Jacob 5 in the Book of Mormon is one of the most interesting chapters in all scriptures. Not only was the science of horticulture well established in biblical times, but this botanical knowledge was also used by ancient prophets to convey information about the house of Israel. However, the allegory in Jacob 5 is not completely botanically correct. Although in most ways it follows sound botanical principles, a few instances violate these principles. This paper will discuss the botanical principles in Jacob 5, identify those which are violated, and then clarify the allegory according to those principles.

Botanical Principles Behind Jacob 5

The scattering and gathering of Israel is a prominent theme in the scriptures, and is discussed again and again throughout the Book of Mormon. One of the most interesting approaches to the topic is the allegory of the olive tree in Jacob 5. In this chapter, Jacob quotes Zenos, an Old World prophet whom the Nephites knew about from the plates of brass, but whose writings were somehow not included in the Old Testament. Zenos may have used the olive tree in this allegory because of the importance of this plant to the people of his day, or he could have been inspired

Wilford M. Hess is professor of Botany and Range Science at Brigham Young University.

by the Spirit to use the olive tree, as was Lehi, who referred to a portion of the same allegory (1 Nephi 10:12; 15:7, 12, 16).

Olive trees are referred to at least 25 times in the Bible, from Deuteronomy to Revelation. The most interesting reference in the New Testament is in Romans 11, where Paul applies to the converted Gentiles of Rome the allegory of grafting olive tree branches. While many LDS readers see an immediate parallel with Jacob 5, Professor John W. Welch, of the BYU Law School, is preparing a paper which cautions that there are many significant differences between them and only a few similarities. He also notes that there is no reference to the olive tree in the Book of Mormon after Jacob's. This suggests that the olive tree was referred to only from its Old World scriptural setting and that after this time, between 550 and 480 BC, the plant was probably unfamiliar to the New World communities.

The olive tree (*olea*) has been one of the most widely grown indigenous plants of the Mediterranean basin (Zohary 56-57). It was spread throughout the Mediterranean countries by the Phoenicians, Greeks, and Romans, and for millennia has been the principal source of edible oil for the people of this area. Recent research has made us more keenly aware of the nutritional qualities of olive oil (Manousis and Moore 11). In addition to being part of a daily diet, olive oil "was used in holy ointments . . . , and for anointing the sick, for lighting . . . , and as a solvent of various spices, incenses and aromatics" (Zohary 56). Since early biblical times and the early history of mankind, the olive leaf has symbolized peace and has heralded new life and hope. A dove brought Noah a freshly plucked olive leaf (Gen 8:11) to show that the Flood had receded.

Although the scriptures frequently refer to plants, they are generally mentioned only incidentally, and sometimes even incorrectly. It has been shown that the many references to lilies should probably be to the iris, and the Isaiah 35:1 reference to the desert's blossoming as a rose is probably to a bulb (Narcissus?) rather than a rose (Klein 301-03; Balick 28). Sometimes word meanings have changed, such as in the KJV use of "corn" for what today means wheat or grain. However, it appears to be difficult to confuse the olive tree with any other plant, so the olive has likely been identified and translated correctly.

Although an ancient plant, the olive has changed little through time. The genus *olea* "contains about 35 species distributed widely from Africa to New Zealand" (Simmonds 219), but only the species *olea europaea* produces fruit eaten by man (Manousis and Moore 7). This species has many different strains. There are sixty different strains just in Italy. "Two botanical varieties [of this species] are usually recognized" (Simmonds 219); one is cultivated and the other is wild. It is believed that this wild form may have escaped from cultivation rather than being "ancestral to the cultivars" presently used. Also, the cultivated hybrid appears to have originated from another variety of wild olive plants in the eastern Mediterranean mountains, and at least one parent has probably become extinct (Simmonds 219). Apparently the cultivated and wild forms were both present in very ancient times. Olives were cultivated on the island of Crete as early as 3000 BC (Manousis and Moore 7). The antiquity of the hybrid has been demonstrated "by the great diversity of kernel types found . . . and dated to the fourth millennium BC" (Simmonds 219).

"The olive tree is more easily propagated than other fruit trees" (Manousis and Moore 8), and it is known for its longevity and capacity for regeneration by suckering from the rootstock. Cultivated trees seldom exceed 30 feet in height and are generally kept much smaller by frequent pruning. As in the days of Zenos, it is still standard procedure to graft desired varieties or cultivars onto wild olive trees that grow naturally on hillsides, or to grow seedling stocks and graft them in nurseries. In modern practice wild branches are not grafted into tame trees, and there are differences of opinion as to whether it was ever done. There is no horticultural advantage in doing this, since wild roots are normally more desirable than tame roots because they are heartier and more disease resistant. Cuttings are also widely used for olive tree propagation. These cuttings consist of branches, several inches in diameter and up to five or six feet long, planted in the ground. Stem or trunk pieces with bark can also be used for propagation. The archaeological record shows these practices go back to very ancient times. The scriptural record is generally confined to major and specific events which happened since Adam and Eve came out of the garden. Except for the creation accounts, there are only rare glimpses into very early events[1] which were important for the domestication process.

It is likely that olive trees were domesticated very early. Domesticated plant origins and plant distribution patterns have been worked out from the archaeological record and from the examination of the genetic makeup of the different forms of the plant. These procedures can also be used to help trace plant origin.

When the archaeological record is examined, it is evident that plant domestication took a very long time, and many domesticated plants rely upon man for reproduction because they are so different from their original wild forms. Domestication (tame trees) results from selection of desirable genetic characteristics, and these genetically variant plants rely upon man for maximization of production. As wild plants have been continuously tended by countless generations of people, successive selection of desirable genetic characteristics has helped to insure better production of the respective plant products. As this process has occurred, the highly selected plants have required more intensive agricultural practices to insure yield of the improved product. In many instances, highly domesticated plants fail to survive if not tended and nurtured by man. For example, maize plants produce relatively large numbers of seeds encased in husks. If an ear falls to the ground and if there is sufficient moisture for germination of the seeds, many seeds will germinate, but very few will mature

---

[1] One reference to things happening much earlier than previously thought is in Helaman 8:18, where Mormon summarized the words of Nephi, son of Helaman, and stated that "Abraham not only knew of these things, but there were many before the days of Abraham who were called by the order of God; yea, even after the order of his Son; and this that it should be shown unto the people, a great many thousand years before his coming, that even redemption should come unto them."

and produce seeds the next season because there will be a clump of plants all competing for nutrients in a small spot of soil. Thus if man does not tend these domesticated plants, they will perish and not be available for his use. On the other hand, non-domesticated (wild) plants are well-adapted genetically to survive without man's intervention. As an example, teosinte, a wild relative of maize, has a few loosely connected seeds which are not enclosed in husks. These seeds fall to the earth singly, and they easily produce plants for the next season of growth without man's intervention.

The benefits of domesticating plants, however, far outweigh the detriments. Olive trees are now being grown in areas in Israel where it was previously too dry to grow them. In fact, by use of genetic engineering procedures, olive trees can now come into production in almost half the time when root production is stimulated by a microorganism (Strobel, et al 2581). In the past, olive trees would not bear during their first fifteen years, and then often bear only every other year. Now with careful selection of root stock, irrigation, and cultivation, it is possible to get a crop when the trees are only three to four years old, and they will bear almost the same every year.

The biblical horticulturalists certainly had a knowledge of many very important biological principles like propogation and domestication. This ancient knowledge could be the subject of an extensive study. Joseph Smith probably had little knowledge of olive trees in New York, as they will not grow in the northeastern United States. When he translated the plates, he may have wondered about the plant and the botanical principles referred to in the allegory. It is also likely that Jacob in the land of Nephi did not know about olive trees and relied entirely upon the words of Zenos for this knowledge. "Olive" and "grafting" are not referred to again in the Book of Mormon after Jacob 5, as noted above. The botanical emphasis in other allegories changes to "seeds" and "sprouting" (Alma 32:28, 43).

If the olive tree had survived the journey with Lehi and his party, it probably would have been referred to by Book of

Mormon prophets who were not quoting older scripture. Possibly the Nephites and Lamanites did not commonly graft fruits, as was done with olive trees in the Old World; there is no evidence in their writings that they did. Lehi and his group either did not try to bring olive trees, or they brought cuttings which did not survive the desert wanderings and sea voyage. They probably did not bring olive seeds, as it was not the custom to use seeds for the propagation of olive trees.

It is reasonable to suppose that both Joseph Smith and Jacob received their knowledge of olive cultivation entirely from Old World sources. In the following section, I will compare Jacob's scriptural examples of botanical knowledge of olive cultivation to present-day scientific knowledge.

Examples of Botanical Knowledge in Jacob 5

A vineyard benefits from being nourished (vv 3, 4, 5, 11, 20, 22, 23, 25, 27, 28, 31, 34, 47, 58, 63, 71, 75, 76) which in some instances includes being dunged (vv 47, 64, 76) to provide plant nutrition. It is still common practice to use dung, including human dung, in most of the world, although commercial fertilizers are more commonly used in industrialized nations.

A vineyard will decay (vv 3, 4). Limbs can become infested (dead tissue) and/or infected (living tissue) with parasitic and saprophytic microorganisms and insects; thus burning infected limbs is desirable to prevent the spread of pestilence. It also keeps the ground open and uncumbered (vv 9, 44, 49, 66). Burning reduces inoculum of parasitic organisms. Although it is resistant to a number of pests, there are more than 200 insects and known fungal diseases that "attack the olive tree and its fruit. Other pests are bacteria, lichens, yeasts, nematodes, spiders, birds, and mammals," which cause estimated world losses of $500 million per year (Manousis and Moore 9).

The principle of pruning contributes to the health of the tree and improves production of fruit (vv 4, 5, 11, 27). Pruning produces a proper amount of foliage and permits sufficient light to strike the branches and maximize fruit production. Fruit production is not maximized if trees are allowed to grow without care. They become too bushy.

Proper care will cause young and tender branches to form (vv 4, 6). This principle is still used extensively today. When growing tips, plants produce biohormones which are translocated to lateral buds and branches conveying the biosignals which prevent or limit their growth. Thus, when main branch tips are cut, lateral branches grow.

Branches can be removed and grafted onto other olive trees (vv 8, 9, 10, 17, 18, 30, 34, 52, 54, 55, 56, 57, 60, 63, 64, 65, 67, 68) or can be planted to start new trees (vv 23, 24, 25, 43). As was mentioned above, the olive tree is among the easiest of trees to propagate, and it is very easily grafted. This principle is still extensively used today. Propagation by seeds results in too much genetic variation. With cuttings, however, each new vegetatively propagated tree will be genetically identical to the branch from which it came.

The amount of root needs to be balanced with the amount of foliage (vv 37, 48, 65, 66). When good branches are allowed to become too thick, the developing fruit will be of poor quality. If there is too much foliage surface area, the roots cannot supply enough nutrients and water to them for maximal rates of photosynthesis. When there is too much top growth and not enough nutrients from roots, the top dies back. When there is not enough photosynthesis in the foliage to nourish the roots, they die back. The products of photosynthesis nourish the roots and the roots provide nutrients from the soil to insure cell growth in the whole plant. Because of grafting, the foliage of a particular tree may be either from domesticated plants or wild relatives. Graft materials and recipient plants have to be closely related for grafts to take.

Fruit can be wild (bad or evil) or domesticated (good) (vv 17, 18, 20, 25, 26, 27, 30, 32, 33, 35, 36, 37, 38, 39, 40, 42, 45, 46, 52, 54, 60, 61, 65, 77). Likely, the bad fruit was small-seeded and bitter (low quality) and was from non-domesticated (wild) plants. The good fruit was large-seeded and palatable (high quality) and was from plants which had been genetically selected for a long period of time to accumulate the desirable genetic characteristics.

Land for growing trees can be poor (evil) or good (vv 21-23, 25, 43), but proper nourishment in either case can produce good fruit. Tame fruit grown on trees which have not been tended may be much smaller than normal, and wild fruit grown on trees that have been tended will be larger than normal. However, good fruit (in the sense of tame versus wild) can come only from tame tissue. Both types of fruit will be larger with proper care, but the wild will never be as large as the tame if both are tended equally under the same cultural conditions.

If the foliage of an otherwise healthy tree is removed or reduced, the roots may perish (vv 8, 18, 34, 36, 54, 60, 65, 66). When branches are grafted, the new foliage can carry on photosynthesis and supply the necessary carbohydrates to nourish the roots.

Examples of Interpretations that Seem to Violate Botanical Rules

Wild Branches Can Yield Tame Fruit

All of a tree will be genetically identical unless there is a sector of cells, called a chimera, which is of a different genetic makeup than the rest of the branch. A chimera is unusual. A graft can be considered a man-made chimera because its genetics will be different from those of the recipient plant. Therefore, if a wild olive branch is grafted onto a tame olive tree, that branch and all of its growth will retain the same genetics; it will remain wild and will produce only wild or small-seeded, bitter fruit (fruit of low quality), although the size may increase due to better nutrition. That branch will never have the genetic potential of the branches from domesticated trees. Conversely, if a tame branch is grafted onto a wild tree, that branch will produce only genetically tame large-seeded good fruit (fruit of high quality) unless the root stock is diseased or less efficient in either photosynthesis or water and mineral uptake. This principle is used extensively in horticulture today. However, with proper nourishment and care, both wild and tame branches will have fruits which are larger than fruits on unattended trees. Conversely, both wild and tame branches will have fruits which are smaller than normal when water and nutrients are limited factors. A drought will result in a restriction of fruit development.

Likely Zenos knew that wild trees would not produce the same quality of fruit that tame trees would produce with the same amount of tending. However, the quality of carefully tended wild fruit may have been better than the quality of tame fruit which was completely neglected. Most domesticated plants are genetically adapted to give maximum production with careful tending, and it is likely that the quality of the fruit is very poor without tending. When both domesticated (tame) and non-domesticated (wild) plants are properly tended, the domesticated plants will always produce superior fruit. It is common in Utah and adjoining states to see apple trees growing along roadsides or on ditch banks. These plants may be products of the sexual reproduction of domesticated plants which have become "wild" and are normally genetically inferior to plants grown in orchards. The fruits are normally small and of poor quality. Even in abandoned orchards, where the plants are genetically superior, neglected trees normally have undersized fruit of very poor quality.

Even if the wild fruit were similar in size and palatability to the tame fruit, the susceptibility or resistence to infection by parasitic fungi, bacteria, or insects could make the fruit good or bad. It would then be desirable to prune and burn the infected branches to reduce the inoculum potential of the pathogen or pathogens. If this approach is used, the allegory more nearly follows the principles of biology we are familiar with today to describe good and bad fruit, but not wild and tame fruit.

Good Plants Can Emerge from Poor Soil

A desirable rate of growth cannot be obtained from either tame or wild plants on poor soil, even with a lot of tending and digging. Soil has exchange capacity, or the ability to retain ions for plant nutrition. The amount is related to the size of the soil particle. Sand has no exchange capacity while clay has high exchange capacity. On the other hand, sand is well aerated while clay is too poorly aerated for good plant growth. Of course, a sandy loam is ideal. With an equal amount of effort, the growth in good soil will be far superior to growth in poor soil. However, by adding organic matter (dung) and by taking sufficient care, it is possible to get relatively good growth in poor soil, particulary since organic matter helps to retain moisture and also has a high exchange capacity. However, the careful tending of the plant will not cause a change in the genetic characteristics of a branch or tree.

Clarification of the Allegory

Zenos' allegory is easier to understand if the imagery and interpretation are clarified. Symbolically, the tame tree is the house of Israel (Jacob 5:3), the wild tree is the Gentiles, the roots of the tree can be interpreted as the blood of Israel among the Gentiles, and grafting refers to "com[ing] to the knowledge of the true Messiah" (1 Nephi 10:14). The vineyard is probably the world, the master of the vineyard is interpreted as Jesus Christ and the servants are prophets and missionaries. When the Gentiles accept the gospel, they become "new creatures" fully capable of producing fruit as large and delightsome as the Israelites. Conversely, when the Israelites become wild or are "overcome" by the wild roots, they have no more potential to produce large fruits of marvelous quality than do the Gentiles. Thus, the allegory violates a botanical principle to teach a spiritual truth. Regardless, this is one of the important messages of the allegory.

An outline of the major events related to the tree follows. The verses are from Jacob 5 and the house of Israel comparisons in italics are the interpretations given by Nyman (24-36).[2]

1. The olive tree "grew, and waxed old, and began to decay" (v 3).

   "The house of Israel was in Egypt, because of the famine in Canaan" (25).

2. It was tended, and young tender branches grew (vv 5-6).

   The new generation of Israelites were allowed to enter Canaan after their parents had been detained in the wilderness for forty years. Also God took the Melchizedek Priesthood from the Israelites and left "the lesser or Aaronic Priesthood" (26).

3. The main top began to perish so the tame branches were replaced with wild ones to preserve the roots (vv 6-7, 10-11).

   The Melchizedek Priesthood was taken away and the Gentiles (wild branches) were grafted in; ie, the Assyrian and Babylonian conquests (26).

4. Young and tender branches were placed in the nethermost part of the vineyard to preserve the natural branches (v 13). They were planted in different places (v 14).

   "These are the ten tribes (about 721 BC), the Jews (about 607 BC), and the Lamanites (about 600 BC)." This ends the first period from about 1800 to 400 BC (27).

5. "A long time passed away" (v 15).

   About 400 BC to about AD 30 (27).

6. On the main tree the wild branches brought forth tame fruit. Without these branches the tree would have perished (v 18).

---

[2] A recent book which presents a brief and concise discussion of the allegory is Monte S. Nyman's *An Ensign to All People*. Although obviously there are other interpretations for some of the aspects of the allegory, Nyman's interpretation is very close to my own.

This is during the ministry of Jesus (AD 30-34) when the Gentiles bore good fruit; for instance, the Samaritan woman at Jacob's well (28).

7. The first natural branch which was hidden in the nethermost part of the vineyard brought forth much good fruit (v 20). It was on the poorest spot in the vineyard (vv 21-22).

"The ten and a half tribes [were] taken into Assyria and then led further into the north" (28).

8. The second branch was planted in ground that was even poorer but brought forth much good fruit (v 23).

The Jews (29).

9. The third branch was planted in a good spot of ground and a part brought forth tame fruit and a part brought forth wild fruit (v 25).

The Nephites and Lamanites (29).

10. All of the fruit of the vineyard was nourished (v 28).

This is probably "the period between AD 34 and 36, when all were converted to the Lord (4 Nephi 1-2)" (29).

11. A long time passed away (v 29).

The Apostasy to the Restoration (29).

12. The main tree whose natural branches were replaced with wild branches had "all sorts of fruit" (v 30). It brought forth much fruit, but none of it was good (v 32). The roots of the tree were still good (vv 34-36).

The Gentiles who had been grafted into the house of Israel had many different religions (fruit), but none were true. "The blood of Israel" (roots) was, however, "scattered among the Gentiles" (30).

13. The three natural branches in the nethermost parts of the vineyard had also become corrupt (v 39). The wild fruit of the third branch "had overcome that part of the tree which brought forth good fruit" (v 40), even though it was planted in ground which was choice above all other (v 43). Thus, all of the trees of the vineyard had become corrupted although they once brought forth good fruit (v 42).

The lost tribes, the Jews, the Nephites, and the Lamanites had all become corrupt. The Lamanites overcame the Nephites even though the Nephites lived in the land choice above all other lands. "Those he had cut down so that he 'might plant this tree' (Jacob 5:44) were the Jaredites" (30).

14. The problem was the loftiness of the vineyard. The branches grew faster than the strength of the roots and the branches became corrupted (v 48).

"Apostasy crept in" (31).

15. The branches from the nethermost parts of the vineyard were grafted onto the good roots of the mother tree (v 52) and branches of the mother tree were grafted onto the good root of the branches in the nethermost parts of the vineyard (vv 54-56).

The mother tree is the fulness of the gospel in the latter days established by the house of Israel scattered among the Gentiles. Thus, the branches of this mother tree will then take the gospel to the branches from the nethermost parts of the vineyard or the lost tribes, Jews, and Lamanites. The blood of Israel (roots) is to become the mother tree (31-32).

16. Only the most bitter branches were plucked and the trees of the vineyard were nourished (vv 57-58).

Only the most wicked were removed "until the natural branches could derive nourishment from the natural roots" (32).

17. Servants were called to prepare the way to bring forth natural fruit again (v 61) for the last time (v 62).

    Missionaries are being sent out and have been seeking the natural fruit for more than 150 years (32).

18. The servants would graft in the last branches first and the first branches last (v 63).

    The last group taken away, Lehi's group, will be the first to be grafted back. The second group will be Judah and the last branch will be the lost tribes (32-33).

19. The servants would clear away the branches which bring forth bitter fruit, but not all at once, so the roots would still have strength (v 65). They would maintain equal root and top growth until the good could overcome the bad. They would cut the bad and cast it into the fire. Thus the branches of the natural tree would be grafted again into the natural tree (vv 67-68), and the bad would be cast away (v 69).

    It will be a gradual process, but eventually the Lamanites, Jews, and lost tribes will be "'like unto one body' . . . (Jacob 5:74)" (33).

20. The servants came but they were few (v 70). They were told to labor with their might because this was the last time the vineyard would be nourished for the end was nigh at hand (v 71). The natural branches began to grow and thrive exceedingly and the wild branches were cast away. The roots and top were equal in strength (v 73).

    Again, the missionaries are the instruments in bringing the natural branches back to the main tree (33).

21. They labored until all of the bad had been cast away and the trees produced natural fruit and "became like unto one body" (v 74). All the fruit was good as it had been in the beginning (v 75).

The tribes of Israel will be united under one shepherd (33).

22. The master said, "for a long time will I lay up of the fruit of my vineyard" (v 76).

The Millennium (33).

23. The master said that when the time came that evil fruit should come into his vineyard he would preserve the good and cast away the bad. "And then cometh the season and the end; and my vineyard will . . . be burned with fire" (v 77).

This is the end of the Millennium when the evil fruit appears again and the righteous are saved and the wicked are burned along with the vineyard. The mission of the house of Israel will be completed and "the temporal existence of the earth will then be completed" (33).

Conclusion

Zenos' allegory is profound for us because it reinforces in our minds the importance of our mission as members of the house of Israel among the political Gentiles. The olive tree, a very important Old World plant that to many provides life itself, was used in the allegory probably because olive horticulture so closely fit the message to be conveyed. Ephraim is the birthright tribe (Jer 31:9) and is responsible for redeeming the three branches which were planted in the nethermost part of the vineyard—the Nephites and Lamanites, the Jews, and the lost tribes (D&C 133:26-34), as well as all others who qualify themselves for adoption into the house of Israel (Gal 3:26-29; 2 Nephi 26:33; 3 Nephi 30:2). In other words, Ephraim is responsible for bearing the message of the restoration of the gospel to the entire world and for gathering scattered Israel. This responsibility includes extending the blessings of temple work to each of the branches of the house of Israel (D&C 133:26-34).

The servants in Zenos' allegory are prophets and missionaries. As an extension of the allegory, it appears that members of the house of Israel among the Gentiles could also act as servants. Although all of the tribes are represented in latter-day patriarchal blessings, a very high percentage of the members of the Church are Ephraimites. Therefore, our responsibilities are profound. The gathering has already begun. The Book of Mormon was written to enlighten all twelve tribes of Israel (Mormon 3:17-21). Even though the greater part of the gathering of Israel will not take place until after the return of Christ and the beginning of the Millennium (3 Nephi 21:23-28), the coming forth of the Book of Mormon is described as the beginning of the gathering of Israel (3 Nephi 21:1-7). When Christ returns, Judah and the ten tribes will finally accept him as their Savior (3 Nephi 21:22-23). Then they will come from the four quarters of the earth and "the remnant of the seed of Jacob, who are scattered abroad upon all the face of the earth" (3 Nephi 5:24), will be gathered and become part of the mother tree (Nyman 31-32).

BIBLIOGRAPHY

Balick, Michael. "Ecology of the Holy Land." *Horticulture* (Dec 1976) 54:28-31.

Klein, Richard M. *The Green World: An Introduction to Plants and People.* New York: Harper, 1987.

Manousis, T., and N. F. Moore. "The Olive Tree." *Biologist* (1988) 35:7-12.

Nyman, Monte S. *An Ensign to All People.* Salt Lake City: Deseret Book, 1987.

Simmonds, N. W. "Olive." *Evolution of Crop Plants.* London: Longman, 1976. 219-21.

Strobel, Gary A., Avi Nachmias, and Wilford M. Hess. "Improvements in the Growth and Yield of Olive Trees by Transformation with the Ri Plasmid of *Agrobacterium Rhizogenes*." *Canadian Journal of Botany* (Dec 1988) 66:2581-85.

Zohary, Michael. "Olive." *Plants of the Bible.* Cambridge: Cambridge Univ, 1982. 56-57.

The Religion of Moses and the Book of Mormon

6

Lauri Hlavaty

Introduction

Central to The Church of Jesus Christ of Latter-day Saints and to the great work of the Lord that has begun to roll forth is a community of believers who possess a sound knowledge of the scriptures. If we are to read the scriptures the way Brigham Young taught us—to read them as though we stood in the place of those who wrote them (*Journal of Discourses* 7:333)—it is important for us to understand the spiritual environment of these ancient men. For this reason we should be familiar with the religion of Moses, which is central to our comprehension of the Old and New Testaments, for it is infused in them. Indeed, it is infused into the restored gospel. It should surprise no one that the keystone of our religion, the Book of Mormon, is crucial to our understanding of the religion of Moses, for it contains the gospel of Jesus Christ in its most plain and therefore precious written form. "Behold, my soul delighteth in proving unto my people the truth of the coming of Christ," Nephi tells us, "for, for this end hath the law of Moses been given." Furthermore, he explains that "all things which have been given of God from the beginning of the world . . . are the typifying of him" (2 Nephi 11:4). Twenty-five centuries later Joseph Smith taught that "though there were different dispensations, yet all things which God communicated to His people were

Lauri Hlavaty is a graduate student in Ancient Studies at the University of Chicago.

calculated to draw their minds to the great object, and to teach them to rely upon God alone as the author of their salvation" (*Teachings of the Prophet Joseph Smith* 61; hereafter *TPJS*). Therefore the religion of Moses is evidence of our Heavenly Father's concern for his children because it was an implement used to teach the gospel to many of his children in the house of Israel.

Before we proceed, we must clarify our definitions. First, the term "religion of Moses" is used here to define the gospel as it was taught by Moses to his rebellious followers. This includes all doctrines, beliefs, covenants, sacrifices, and rituals associated with it. The "religion of Moses" is a constructed term and is not used in the scriptures, but it is used here because the second term, "law of Moses," is confusing. In the scriptures, "law of Moses" is often synonymous with the carnal commandments, which are only a part of the religion of Moses. But it can also refer to the Pentateuch, and it sometimes means the religion of Moses as a whole. It is difficult, with any given scriptural reference to the law of Moses, to know exactly which definition is being used. In addition, the term in our day carries to us a negative implication of something lifeless.

Our third term is "covenant of Moses," which refers to the part of the religion of Moses that was not done away with at Christ's advent. This terminology comes from 3 Nephi 15:8, where Christ states that "the covenant which I have made with my people is not all fulfilled; but the law which was given unto Moses hath an end in me." Following his example, we distinguish the covenant of Moses from the law of Moses, which together constitute the religion of Moses.

To further define the religion of Moses, a few brief statements follow. The religion of Moses:

1. is of divine origins, being given by Jehovah;
2. is administered by the Aaronic Priesthood, which means that adherents have access to Aaronic Priesthood functions and ordinances, such as baptism;
3. is the gospel without the Melchizedek Priesthood;

4. contains some additions to the gospel, usually called carnal commandments (this is what we usually think of when we think of the law of Moses);
5. is the medium or environment through which the covenant of Moses is taught, particularly to the Old Testament and Book of Mormon peoples, which is another reason why it is important for us to understand;
6. is, in its purity (that is, without the man-made additions), recognizable to us as truth.

The religion of Moses is *not*:

1. a laundry list of commandments, because the Lord does not give laundry lists; nor
2. the ritualistic stiffness accompanied by the letter-of-the-law mentality we often attribute to it—it didn't start out that way, and never was the Lord's intention.

The Religion of Moses Is Curious to Us

"The Church is the same wherever you go!" I grew up hearing this from returning vacationers and from missionaries reporting their missions. And I understood what they meant. They didn't mean that the same hymns were sung elsewhere—though they were—or that everyone used the same lesson manuals, or that everyone thought the same. They meant the gospel felt the same wherever they went. This resulted from the presence of the Holy Spirit, which is the universal way we recognize the things of God. It's the same when you learn something new or see something from a new slant, and suddenly it all makes sense. You know it's right, because it feels right and is consistent with other glimpses of truth that you've had. Therefore it is puzzling that the religion of Moses seems foreign or irrelevant to us. We are a people who have familiarity with the higher law, and one would think that the lower law, which comes from the same source, would not be a stranger who baffles or bores us. It should feel right, just as our own teachings do.

There are, I think, two reasons why the religion of Moses might seem strange to us. First of all, many distortions, omissions and additions have occurred in the law and its primary record, the Bible. The Bible in its present form is not what it once was. "I believe the Bible as it read when it came from the pen of the original writers," said Joseph Smith. "Ignorant translators, careless transcribers, or designing and corrupt priests have committed many errors" (*TPJS* 327). And referring to the first letter in the Hebrew Genesis, he once taught, "the *Baith* was not originally put there when the inspired man wrote it, but it has been since added by an old Jew" (*TPJS* 371). The Book of Mormon, with typical succinctness, tells us why such changes have occurred: "And all this have they done that they might pervert the right ways of the Lord, that they might blind the eyes and harden the hearts of the children of men"; "also many covenants of the Lord have they taken away" (1 Nephi 13:27, 26). And thus we see, as Mormon would say, that the religion of Moses as recorded in the Old Testament is now imperfect, making it necessary to defer to the Book of Mormon in order to understand it.

Not only has the Bible been changed, but the religion of Moses itself has been added to. On more than one occasion Christ himself severely criticized the Pharisees, the conservative religious leaders of the day. He called them hypocrites, blind fools, snakes, perverters of the law, and murderers of prophets. The tonguelashing recorded in Matthew 23 came not only because of their personal unrighteousness, but because they changed the law. The proliferation of fences around the original commandments had ossified and corrupted the law, leaving less room for the spiritual aspects of the religion. This tragedy is played out for us in the New Testament, where we see Christ, the Giver of the law, rejected by many who were living the religion of Moses—the schoolmaster that was to bring them to their Messiah.

In spite of this, Christ corrected the woman of Samaria while conversing with her at the well. She asserted that the religious beliefs of the Samaritans were as good as those of the Jews. He countered, saying, "Ye worship ye know not what: we know what we worship: for salvation is of the Jews" (John 4:22). The religion of Moses was the authorized religion; it was still the carrier of God-given commandments and covenants.

The second reason the religion of Moses is difficult for us to grasp is that cultural differences exist between modern Mormons and ancient Jews. Their revelations came specific to their way of life and were understood through their own cultural context, as are ours. From Doctrine and Covenants 1:24 we learn that "commandments . . . were given unto my servants in their weakness, after the manner of their language, that they might come to understanding." Nephi teaches a similar concept: "For the Lord God giveth light unto the understanding; for he speaketh unto men according to their language, unto their understanding" (2 Nephi 31:3). Thus, the Lord instructs his children in ways they can understand, not only in their own language, but in their own dialect and according to their own culture. He would not use a graduate-school vocabulary when addressing a 14-year-old boy, nor would he employ Albanian sayings to instruct a Cherokee.

The Hebrews lived long ago, but the gap of time separating us is not as great as the cultural chasm that separates the East from the West. Modern western men and women who live in urban or suburban settings and buy food from sanitized supermarkets are probably steeped in their own culture and might find it difficult to bridge the gap and learn of God from their ancient siblings.

The Covenant of Moses

The precious core of the religion of Moses is the God-given covenant around which the rest revolves. As we know, our Heavenly Father defines his relationship with his children through covenants, and the covenant of Moses is no exception, although it is quite different from the covenant that we are familiar with, which is the covenant of Christ. Under the covenant of

Moses there is no promise of individual blessings, nor is there any promise of eternal salvation. These promises belong to the higher covenant and to the ordinances that are possible through the Melchizedek Priesthood. Just as the Aaronic Priesthood is concerned with spiritual preparation and administration of temporal affairs, so is the covenant of Moses mainly concerned with this world. It is designed to bring about a moral people. With the covenant of Christ, our Heavenly Father's statement of his promise is something like this: "If you keep my commandments and know my Son, you shall be like me and you may live with me forever." It is designed to produce a spiritual being. The covenant of Moses, on the other hand, is more like this: "If you keep my commandments, I will take care of you." The covenant of Moses, like the Aaronic Priesthood, was received without an oath—that is, no eternal promises were exchanged in connection with its reception (see *TPJS* 318-19). The covenant of Moses is beautifully expressed in Leviticus: "If ye walk in my statutes, and keep my commandments . . . I will give you rain in due season, and the land shall yield her increase. . . . I will give peace in the land, and ye shall lie down, and none shall make you afraid. . . . And I will walk among you, and will be your God, and ye shall be my people" (Lev 26:3, 4, 6, 12). There are two significant insights we can glean from this passage. The first is that the covenant of Moses is a promise for temporal salvation. The second is not so obvious and is what makes the covenant of Moses different from "modern" covenants. The "you" that Jehovah is addressing here is plural. (This shows up clearly in Hebrew, but can be ambiguous in modern English.) Normally covenants are one-on-one. I covenant with my Heavenly Father to do a, b, and c, and he rewards me with x, y, and z. But the covenant attendant to the religion of Moses functions differently. This is not a one-on-one covenant, but a covenant that is made with a community. Although the worship practices of the Nephites were strikingly different from those of the Israelites, Nephi, Jacob, Abinadi, and Alma tell us they worshipped "according to the law of Moses" (2 Nephi 5:10; Jacob 4:5; Mosiah 13:27; Alma 25:15).

We can therefore assume that Book of Mormon statements of the covenant of Moses are community promises as well and not individual blessings. King Benjamin is thus explaining a promise of temporal salvation for a community when he says "all that he requires of you is to keep his commandments; and he has promised you that if ye would keep his commandments ye should prosper in the land" (Mosiah 2:22). This is a critical concept. When a Book of Mormon prophet says (and many of them do), "If you keep my commandments you will prosper in the land," he does not mean that every single person who keeps the commandments will prosper; individuals will still have challenges and difficulties, for that is part of our mortal experience. He means if the people of the community live the commandments, the community will be a prosperous one.

The Book of Mormon vividly portrays the outcome of keeping or breaking the covenant of Moses. We clearly see the roller-coaster pattern where prosperity plunges into economic chaos and war and rises again to peace and prosperity. Mormon explains that spiritual infractions cause hard times and repentance causes peace, for communities and for individuals. The Nephite nation bears silent testimony of the ramifications of keeping or breaking their covenants. The Lord takes his covenants seriously.

This covenant is the pearl of the religion of Moses. But the oyster and the shell of the religion of Moses are also worthy of our attention, and now this discussion will focus on several other aspects of the religion which are positive and good and part of the gospel of Jesus Christ.

A Rational Belief

We live in a rational world today. Because of this, it is difficult for us to appreciate the rationality of the religion of Moses. But if we consider the world in which the Israelites lived, we discover this is one of the great strengths of their religion. The Israelites were always surrounded by people they interacted with, many of whom were wealthier than they and came from lands that were politically and militarily superior. Many also had more advanced technical skills. These characteristics made foreigners admirable and worthy of imitation to many Israelites. Owing to this, foreigners who continually dealt with Israel—whether Egyptian officials, Assyrian soldiers, or Canaanite neighbors—were able to exert much influence over them, including religious influence. This was always a problem for the Israelites. Their prophets warned them not to worship the gods of others, but they did anyway. The Israelite captivities of 721 and 586 BC bear testimony of their disobedience and disregard for their covenants.

The foreign religions that influenced Israel were very different from our own. Generally speaking, the religious beliefs of the ancient Near East consisted of what we call superstitions. Their religious practices included not only sacrifice, but charms, curses, rituals, and incantations. Magic and worship were often synonymous. The realm of spirits and demons was very much a part of everyday life. For example, an Egyptian mother, fearful that a spirit might harm her child during the night, might utter the following:

> Mayest thou flow away, he who comes in the darkness and enters in furtively, with his nose behind him, and his face reversed, failing in that for which he came! . . . I have made his magical protection against thee out of *clover*—that is what *sets an obstacle*—out of onions—what injures thee—out of honey—sweet for men, (but) bitter for those who are yonder—out of the *roe* of the *abdju*-fish, out of the jawbone of the *meret*-fish, and out of the backbone of the perch (Pritchard 328; emphasis in original).

The mother could rest easier, believing her child safe from the unseen.

Chanting the proper words and acting out the proper motions were thought to net the desired results; this was true of worship activities as well. However, living the religion of Moses was to teach them the proper way they must approach Jehovah. No magic or mystical contemplation would bring them to their God; to earn his pleasure they were to do daily what he demanded, whether they were praying, eating or working. Theirs was a rational religion. They were forced, to some extent, to think about it, and through the years this gave birth to a mode of thinking, a way of viewing the world that was different from their neighbors.

The "Taste-Good" Teachings

While giving a discourse on the nature of God, Joseph Smith observed, "This is good doctrine. It tastes good. . . . I know it is good; and when I tell you of these things which were given me by inspiration of the Holy Spirit, you are bound to receive them as sweet, and rejoice more and more" (*TPJS* 355). There are many facets of the religion of Moses that taste good to us because they are part of the everlasting gospel; we could not begin to discuss them all here. One must read the Book of Mormon and the Old Testament, preferably with the help of the Spirit, to sense the goodness and the love for God which emanates from the religion of Moses. Theoretically, any part of the gospel not spe-cifically designated as a Melchizedek Priesthood privilege or ordinance is part of the religion of Moses. Therefore, most ele-ments of the gospel as we know it would be familiar to someone living the lesser law. For instance, baptism, a function of the Aaronic Priesthood, would be part of the religion of Moses, while receiving the gift of the Holy Ghost, which requires a Mel-chizedek Priesthood ordinance, is not. Adherence to most of our teachings and commandments is possible without the higher priesthood, but for our purposes we shall list only a few of the "taste-good" teachings offered by the religion of Moses.

According to Bruce R. McConkie, the religion of Moses was given for the purpose of teaching the chosen people "to bridle their passions, to overcome the lusts of the flesh, to triumph over carnal things, and to advance to the place where the Spirit of the Lord could have full flow in their hearts" (435). In other words, it teaches self-discipline to its adherents.

It also teaches concern for others. Because the covenant was a community affair, there was a collective responsibility for correct behavior. The benevolent treatment of strangers was en-couraged. Parents were to teach their children to love the Lord, to keep his commandments, and to support their neighbors in doing so. Christ reiterated this unselfish concern for others when he taught, "Therefore all things whatsoever ye would that men should do to you, do ye even so to them: for this is the law and the prophets" (Matt 7:12; 3 Nephi 14:12).

In addition, it teaches love for God. Some of the most beautiful and Christ-like exhortations and counsels are those taught to people living the religion of Moses. Consider these two examples from Deuteronomy:

> And now, Israel, what doth the Lord thy God require of thee, but to fear the Lord thy God, to walk in all his ways, and to love him, and to serve the Lord thy God with all thy heart and with all thy soul, to keep the commandments of the Lord, and his statutes, which I command thee this day for thy good? Behold, the heaven and the heaven of heavens is the Lord's thy God, the earth also, with all that therein is. Only the Lord had a delight in thy fathers to love them, and he chose their seed after them, even you above all people, as it is this day. Circumcise therefore the foreskin of your heart, and be no more stiffnecked (10:12-16).

> Hear, O Israel: The Lord our God is one Lord: And thou shalt love the Lord thy God with all thine heart, and with all thy soul, and with all thy might. And these words, which I command thee this day, shall be in thine heart: And thou shalt teach them diligently unto thy children, and shalt talk of them when thou sittest in thine house, and when thou walkest by the way, and when thou liest down, and when thou risest up (6:4-7).

These majestic verses remind us of another contribution. We can learn from the inspiration that comes from the dignity and beauty of the poetry itself. We can sense peace and calmness, and the love that we feel for our God can deepen when the spirit of these words touches our hearts. While the Book of Mormon instructs us with a plainness that we simply cannot misunderstand, the Old Testament gives a gift of words that fashion unrivaled spiritual beauty.

Teachings like these, the faith of the Jews, and the inherent rationality of the religion, have helped make Judaism a strong and viable entity to this day, surviving through the millennia as a religious tradition and as a people. The Nephites, in contrast, were often more righteous and seem to have had more access to the Melchizedek Priesthood, but they have vanished from the earth.

Living the religion of Moses has created a particular world view, in which the temporal nature of the covenant of Moses is apparent. According to Jacob Neusner:

> The Jew has been taught to engage realistically in the world's tasks, to do so with a whole heart, yet without the need, or even the power, to regard completion of those tasks as the threshold of a final and completed fulfillment of history. Because of its mode of thinking, Judaism teaches men to take seriously the wide range of worldly problems without expecting that in solving them—provisionally, let alone finally—they might save the world (11).

The Carnal Commandments

While keeping in mind all these things that were going right for the religion, we must now examine modern revelation's criticisms of it. Section 84 of the Doctrine and Covenants informs us that when the Melchizedek Priesthood was taken away, changes were made in the way Israel worshiped, changes that were independent of the loss of priesthood. These changes, the carnal commandments, were additions and variations on the commandments that remained with Israel. Joseph Smith tells us: "It is said again, in Gal. iii:19, that the law (of Moses, or the Levitical law) was 'added' because of transgression. What, we ask, was this law added to, if it was not added to the Gospel? It must be plain that it was added to the Gospel, since we learn that they had the Gospel preached to them" (*TPJS* 60). But we should not assume that the additions, or carnal commandments, were a revealed replacement, given by Moses just before he was gone. It is more likely that the changes were made gradually and the Mosaic law grew into its recognizable form, which is an exquisite elaboration rooted in God-given commandments. This hybrid creation was perennially nourished by giving the mind priority over the heart, and it was watered by not observing the covenant; therefore, it was not exactly what it could have been. Jacob writes:

> But behold, the Jews were a stiffnecked people; and they despised the words of plainness, and killed the prophets, and sought for things that they could not understand. Wherefore, because of their blindness, which blindness came by looking beyond the mark, they must needs fall; for God hath taken away his plainness from them, and delivered unto them many things which they cannot understand, because they desired it. And because they desired it God hath done it, that they may stumble (Jacob 4:14).

Abinadi tells us that the Jews couldn't grasp their religion "because of the hardness of their hearts; for they understood not that there could not any man be saved except it were through the redemption of God" (Mosiah 13:32). In the course of time the variations became more important than the theme and finally, in the minds of those not spiritually inclined, grew wild and over-powered the original commandments. It was because of the carnal commandments, so called to distinguish them from the God-given commandments, that Paul and Christ criticize the law of Moses so harshly, and why Nephi is selective in what he teaches his people about the Jews. It was the carnal commandments that angered the Lord, so that "in his wrath" he directed that they continue until the meridian of time (D&C 84:27). This is also why we distinguish between the law and the covenant of Moses, for the implications of each are quite different.

It must be stressed that the real culprit here, as Jacob and Abinadi state, was the unbelief and lack of spirituality that spawned their development rather than the carnal commandments themselves. By themselves they were not harmful, but were "to keep them in remembrance of God and their duty towards him" (Mosiah 13:30). These observances are contained in the Pentateuch.[1] For our purposes, we shall generalize them into two main categories: those codified to define social behavior and those intended to ritualize worship practices, particularly sacrifices.

The carnal commandments concerned with social behavior function as a legal code: that is, they define proper behavior and

---

[1] See Ex 20:2-17; 22:1-23; all of Lev; Deut 5:6-21; and Deut 12-16 for the Ten Commandments and primary portions of the Old Testament law code.

direct procedure in case of crime or injustice. Their purpose is to maintain stability and well-being within the community, and they tend to show how one should implement in any number of circumstances the Ten Commandments and the commandment to love one's neighbor. For instance, they illustrate how children should behave, how slaves and animals should be treated, and how killers should be dealt with. The rationality inherent in the religion of Moses often presents itself by giving a justifying motive for a commandment, thus idolatry isn't just forbidden, it is forbidden for a reason—because "I the Lord thy God am a jealous God" (Ex 20:5). Also, a benefit of the doubt emerges occasionally. For instance, if a man violates a betrothed woman outside of a town, he is to die, because death is the accepted punishment for adultery, but the woman is spared, because she might have cried for help in vain, with no one around to hear her (Deut 22:25-27).

The legal code also defines the ritualization of sacrifice, which was the principal act of worship among the Israelites. Animal sacrifice was originally established by God with Adam and Eve: "And he gave unto them commandments, that they should worship the Lord their God, and should offer the firstlings of their flocks, for an offering unto the Lord" (Moses 5:5). The original explanation for sacrifice was that it was in "similitude of the sacrifice of the Only Begotten of the Father" (Moses 5:7). By historic times sacrifice had become a widespread religious ritual, and peoples in contact with the Israelites were familiar with it. But the fundamental message—that sacrifice is a type of things to come—had been lost.

The Nephites, however, seemed to have no problem keeping the perspective of the law of sacrifice. To our knowledge they never elaborated it the way the Israelites did. No procedural explanations of sacrifice are present in the Book of Mormon, and only three instances of animal sacrifice are recorded. The first and second (1 Nephi 2:7; 5:9) were performed by Lehi in the wilderness in order to give thanks to God for his family's deliverance. The third was performed when king Benjamin gathered the people at the temple in Zarahemla and "took of the firstlings of their flocks, that they might offer sacrifice and burnt offerings according to the law of Moses" (Mosiah 2:3). Lehi and Amulek taught that sacrifice was a reminder of the great and last sacrifice of Jesus Christ (2 Nephi 2:7; Alma 34:14). Sacrifice as practiced by the Nephites seems consistent with what Adam was taught.

But sacrifice as recorded in the Old Testament seems to have diverged from the simple ordinance that had once been practiced. Perhaps owing to the Jews' spiritual blindness explained by Jacob and Abinadi, changes were introduced, and sacrifice became more elaborate. For instance, sacrifices were only to be done at the temple altar. Several kinds of sacrifice developed and were therefore described in the Pentateuch: sometimes the sacrificial victim was completely consumed by fire, and sometimes its blood was sprinkled around the altar and only a portion of the animal was burned, the rest divided between the priest and the sacrificer and then eaten. The acceptable animals were male cattle, sheep, and goats, perfectly formed and healthy. Poor people, however, could substitute birds, but only turtledoves or pigeons (see Lev 1). Wheat, corn, oil, and wine were also acceptable, sometimes as preliminary offerings and in some circumstances as a substitute for animals (see Lev 2). It was this elaboration of sacrifice that constituted an addition to the gospel, not sacrifice per se.

When we compare Israelite sacrifice with Nephite sacrifice and the earlier Adamic sacrifice, it is clear to see how the Israelite practice differed from the other two. When we recall the statements of Jacob and Abinadi citing the Israelites' hardness of heart, and the Lord's edict that the law of carnal commandments was to remain with the Jews until the meridian of time because he was angry with them (which he refers to in D&C 84:27), we should not insist that the elaboration of sacrifice was something that pleased Jehovah. It would hardly make sense for him to be angry with the Jews because of the carnal commandments if he had lovingly revealed them. The question that remains for us is this: Did the Israelites completely disregard their God and blatantly change the ordinance, or was it more a situation similar to Joseph Smith's gaining permission to give the manuscript to Martin Harris, where Deity acquiesces to man's agency? Perhaps the question is academic: allowing people to do what they want and giving them what they want essentially amount to the same thing.

The carnal commandments discussed here, those pertaining to social behavior and the law of sacrifice, are only part of the religion of Moses. The bulk of the commandments and doctrines that comprise the religion of the Israelites are God-given and timeless, practiced before the age of Moses as well as today.

The Law of Circumcision

A study of the religion of Moses would not be complete without a discussion of circumcision, for it was and is the sign of the covenant in Judaism. The ceremony in which an eight-day-old infant is circumcised is called a *b'rith*, which is the Hebrew word for covenant. Anciently the word also could mean "contract" or "treaty," and was used when a political agreement was signed by two kingdoms. Establishing such an agreement was referred to as "cutting" a treaty. Perhaps the cutting away of the foreskin became fixed in the vocabulary as a metaphor for making any kind of agreement. In any event, there was a strong correlation between circumcision and covenant. It seems strange to us that God would institute and perpetuate a covenant with circumcision, and it therefore piques our interest. What was the authority, purpose, and symbolism of circumcision?

We know that circumcision was practiced anciently by many Near Eastern people and not just the house of Israel; the nearby Philistines were an exception. Anthropologists tell us that the practice evolved as a coming-of-age ritual that was performed before marriage, not in infancy (de Vaux 1:47). The first scriptural reference to circumcision is Genesis 17:10, when it was established as the token of the covenant God made with Abraham. Thus, circumcision is not a token of the Mosaic covenant only, but a token of the covenant instituted before the Melchizedek Priesthood was taken away. Whether or not Abraham was familiar with the practice beforehand is unclear, but it is clear that he was not circumcised until the Lord commanded.

The Joseph Smith Translation of Genesis 17 tells us why circumcision was instituted:

> And God talked with [Abraham], saying, My people have gone astray from my precepts, and have not kept mine ordinances, which I gave unto their fathers; and they have not observed mine anointing, and the burial, or baptism wherewith I commanded them; but have turned from the commandment, and taken unto themselves the washing of children, and the blood of sprinkling; and have said that the blood of the righteous Abel was shed for sins; and have not known wherein they are account-able before me.... And I will establish a covenant of circumcision with thee, and it shall be my covenant between me and thee, and thy seed after thee, in their generations; that thou mayest know for ever that children are not accountable before me until they are eight years old (vv 4-7, 11).

Therefore, circumcision is a positive replacement for the erroneous doctrines that had surfaced and a sign to remind the people that children are not accountable until they are eight. Moroni corroborates this curious doctrine in the only Book of Mormon passage that mentions circumcision:

> Listen to the words of Christ, your Redeemer, your Lord and your God. Behold, I came into the world not to call the righteous but sinners to repentance; the whole need no physician, but they that are sick; wherefore, little children are whole, for they are not capable of com-mitting sin; wherefore the curse of Adam is taken from them in me, that it hath no power over them; and the law of circumcision is done away in me. And after this manner did the Holy Ghost manifest the word of God unto me; wherefore ... I know that it is solemn mockery before God, that ye should baptize little children (Moroni 8:8, 9).

It is interesting that chapter 2 of Abraham, in which the Abrahamic covenant is again discussed, does not mention cir-cumcision at all. It does, however, reiterate the fact that Abraham's posterity—the seed of his body—would be partakers of this covenant. This is perhaps why circumcision, rather than a pierced ear or tattooed arm, was the emblem of the pre-Christ covenant with Abraham.

> And I will bless them that bless thee, and curse them that curse thee; and in thee (that is, in thy Priesthood) and in thy seed (that is, thy Priesthood), for I give unto thee a promise that this right shall continue in thee, and in thy seed after thee (that is to say, the literal seed, or the seed of the body) shall all the families of the earth be blessed, even with the blessings of the Gospel, which are the blessings of salvation, even of life eternal (Abr 2:11).

Circumcision was, it seems, also a reminder of the eternal promises of the Abrahamic covenant. The responsibilities of priesthood, too, are inherent in the Abrahamic covenant, which is why its token of circumcision was by nature only applicable to males. Therefore, circumcision functioned as a sign of covenant, an indictment against erroneous doctrines, and as a reminder of eternal or Melchizedek Priesthood blessings; it was to be done away with at the coming of Christ (although the Saints in Palestine struggled with this for a time). It, like animal sacrifice, was part of the gospel before and after the Mosaic dispensation, and continued until the meridian of time.[2]

Book of Mormon Instruction

The Book of Mormon allows us to read the religion of Moses in a different light. Its teachings about "the law" are nothing like the Old Testament's; "no more like than an apple to an oyster," to quote Thomas More. Three Book of Mormon prophets (Nephi, Jacob, and Abinadi) are particularly enlightening on the religion of Moses, and we defer to them now.

The night Nephi struggled over whether or not to kill Laban, there were three factors that persuaded him to go with it. First, he recalled that the Lord had promised him that his posterity would be included in a covenant similar to that of Moses: "Inasmuch as thy seed shall keep my commandments, they shall prosper in the land of promise" (1 Nephi 4:14). Second, he

---

[2] A fourth scriptural reference to circumcision is the curious passage in Exodus 4, where the Lord is angry at Moses, apparently for not circumcising his son or being circumcised himself (Ex 4:24-26). Evidently circumcision had fallen out of use by the Hebrews at this time.

reasoned that "they could not keep the commandments of the Lord according to the law of Moses, save they should have the law" (1 Nephi 4:15). Third, the Lord had commanded him to kill Laban and had made it possible for him to do so. Nephi's commitment to God deepened considerably with this act of faith, which was partly predicated on the importance Nephi saw in obtaining Moses' law. Years later, when in their promised land, Nephi found it necessary to separate his followers from his brothers. When settled, they "observe[d] to keep . . . the commandments of the Lord in all things, according to the law of Moses" (2 Nephi 5:10), thus beginning their own tradition of living the religion of Moses. Nephi wanted his people to know that

> notwithstanding we believe in Christ, we keep the law of Moses, and look forward with steadfastness unto Christ, until the law shall be fulfilled. For, for this end was the law given; wherefore the law hath become dead unto us, and we are made alive in Christ because of our faith; yet we keep the law because of the commandments. And we talk of Christ, we rejoice in Christ, we preach of Christ, we prophesy of Christ, and we write according to our prophecies, that our children may know to what source they may look for a remission of their sins. Wherefore, we speak concerning the law that our children may know the deadness of the law; and they, by knowing the deadness of the law, may look forward unto that life which is in Christ, and know for what end the law was given. And after the law is fulfilled in Christ, that they need not harden their hearts against him when the law ought to be done away (2 Nephi 25:24-27).

Jacob continues in the footsteps of his brother. His writings too are filled with potent testimony of Christ. It is Jacob who gives us the intent and result of the religion of Moses the most plainly, exposing its beauty and its power: "[The prophets of the brass plates] believed in Christ and worshiped the Father in his name, and also we worship the Father in his name. And for this intent we keep the law of Moses, it pointing our souls to him. . . . Wherefore, we search the prophets" (Jacob 4:5, 6).

Jacob explains that the Jews' failure was caused by their spiritual blindness, and he prophesies that they will reject Christ when he comes. It seems that their disastrous results with the religion of Moses made Jacob aware that some might question why the Nephites were living it. He explains that "for this cause [ie, that the religion of Moses points people in the direction of Christ] it is sanctified unto us for righteousness, even as it was accounted unto Abraham in the wilderness to be obedient unto the commands of God in offering up his son Isaac, which is a similitude of God and his Only Begotten Son" (Jacob 4:5).

Jacob also records his debate with Sherem the anti-Christ. Sherem is well-educated and seemingly well-informed about the law; he seems curiously closer to the Old World tradition than the New. His criticism is that the religion of Moses had become too Christ-centered: "And ye have led away much of this people that they pervert the right way of God, and keep not the law of Moses which is the right way; and convert the law of Moses into the worship of a being which ye say shall come many hundred years hence. . . . [T]his is blasphemy" (Jacob 7:7). Sherem confronts Jacob, asks for a sign, is converted, confesses, and then dies. Jacob and his Christ emerge victorious. This account provides us with a dramatic word picture that illustrates and emphasizes Jacob's teachings, particularly those in Jacob 4:5, 6, and 14. It is as if Sherem were a representation of the Jews who loved the religion of Moses for its own sake, and Jacob were a repre-sentation of the Nephites who loved it because it led them to Christ. Just in case there is still any doubt in the reader's mind as to who was correct, Jacob tells us he was supported by deity in the debate: "But behold, the Lord God poured in his Spirit into my soul, insomuch that I did confound him in all his words" (Jacob 7:8).

Abinadi comes on the scene many generations later, and continues the Nephite tradition of teaching that the religion of Moses is a vehicle to bring people to Christ. He lives among a people who have separated themselves from the main body of Nephites and who are terribly uninformed about their own religion. The priests of king Noah claim they teach the religion of Moses, but when pressed they state that salvation comes from the Mosaic law. Abinadi realizes that converting these people is next to hopeless, so he begins with the basics—he quotes to them the first and second of the Ten Commandments, and accuses them of neither living nor teaching them. The priests pronounce him mad, and with an awesome dignity Abinadi delivers the message he had been sent to deliver. We are told that "his face shone with exceeding luster, even as Moses' did while in the mount of Sinai, while speaking with the Lord" (Mosiah 13:5). This is a masterful image that connects Abinadi's state of spirituality with that of Moses, especially considering the topic of discussion. Abinadi's message was that salvation does not come by the law alone— "were it not for the atonement, which God himself shall make for the sins and iniquities of his people, that they must unavoidably perish, notwithstanding the law of Moses" (Mosiah 13:28).

He explains that the children of Israel missed the point of their religion because they could not understand the concept of atonement. Atonement is a concept that requires the Spirit for understanding; the intellect doesn't do very well on its own when contemplating things of the Spirit. But the Spirit is helpless when the heart won't listen, and Abinadi reiterates Jacob, teaching that spiritual deafness was the chronic disorder that infected the Jews, "for they understood not that there could not any man be saved except it were through the redemption of God." To prove his point Abinadi continues,

> For behold, did not Moses prophesy unto them concerning the coming of the Messiah, and that God should redeem his people? . . . Even all the prophets who have prophesied ever since the world began—have they not spoken more or less concerning these things? Have they not said that God himself should come down among the children of men, and take upon him the form of man, and go forth in mighty power upon the face of the earth? (Mosiah 13:32, 33, 34).

The most striking characteristic of the Nephite view of the religion of Moses, as taught by Nephi, Jacob, and Abinadi, is its ardent Christianity. These prophets are bold in teaching that the law must have a focus and that focus is Christ and his atonement. They teach that the law is a type of things to come, that Moses knew it, and that the Jews failed to see this because they were spiritually hardened. They are so insistent in their message that misunderstanding it is difficult, if not impossible. The Book of Mormon prophets tell us they are living the religion of Moses, even though their record doesn't seem very Mosaic. But their record is, in fact, very Mosaic. While the rituals, procedures, and carnal commandments never surface, the covenant of Moses is everywhere present. The Book of Mormon stresses the covenant of Moses and underplays the law. The Old Testament, in contrast, makes a great play of the law, while only a careful reading brings out the covenant.

Conclusion

This paper was written in the pursuit of a better under-standing of the gospel of Jesus Christ. I have come away from it with added respect for the religion of Moses and its adherents on both continents. My *modus operandi* has been to examine the religion of Moses in light of what the Book of Mormon prophets have to say about it. When this is done, a new perspective emerges, a very Christ-centered one. It is not the purpose of this paper to berate anyone, and I am in no way putting black hats on the Israelites and white ones on the Nephites. This is not the judgment seat, and even if it were, traditions are not judged there, only individuals, based on what they know. Nephi, Jacob, and Abinadi said harsh things about the Jews, just as they said harsh things against their own people—and I am convinced they would say harsh things against us, given the opportunity. They were prophets whose task was calling people to repentance and preach-ing of Christ.

What relevance does the religion of Moses hold for us today? There is a treasure chest full, but there are two points that I would like to emphasize: (1) the gospel is unchanging in its purpose—no matter what the dispensation or whether the Mel-chizedek (or Aaronic) Priesthood is available, its purpose is to bring individuals to a belief in Jesus Christ; and (2) the covenant of Moses is the Lord's way of providing for his children's temporal salvation—then and now. If we keep the command-ments he will take care of us.

It is my testimony that the Book of Mormon is true. It is my prayer that we may live its precepts and become happier people. May we be more like Jacob and his people, and may we be able to say what he said:

> Wherefore, we search the prophets, and we have many revelations and the spirit of prophecy; and having all these witnesses we obtain a hope, and our faith becometh unshaken, insomuch that we truly can command in the name of Jesus and the very trees obey us, or the mountains, or the waves of the sea (Jacob 4:6).

BIBLIOGRAPHY

Journal of Discourses. 26 vols. 1854-86.

McConkie, Bruce R. *Mormon Doctrine.* 2nd ed. Salt Lake City: Bookcraft, 1966.

Neusner, Jacob. *The Glory of God Is Intelligence.* Provo, UT: Brigham Young Univ, 1978.

Pritchard, James B. *Ancient Near Eastern Texts.* 3rd ed. Princeton: Princeton Univ, 1969.

Teachings of the Prophet Joseph Smith. Comp. Joseph Fielding Smith. Salt Lake City: Deseret Book, 1976.

de Vaux, Roland. *Ancient Israel.* 2 vols. New York: McGraw-Hill, 1965.

Prophetic Decree and Ancient Histories Tell the Story of America

7

Clark V. Johnson

When Joseph Smith began receiving instructions from Moroni in 1823, he gained a new perspective on the American Indian. After his initial interview with Moroni, and before he obtained the plates, his mother observed that he described "the ancient inhabitants of this continent, their dress, mode of traveling, and the animals upon which they rode; their cities, their buildings, with every particular; their mode of warfare; and also their religious worship. This he would do with as much ease, seemingly, as if he had spent his whole life among them" (Smith 83). Yet the rest of the world had to wait until some years later for detailed information on the origin and nature of the great early American civilizations to became available. As explorers and archaeologists began to uncover the remains of these New World peoples, they also began to reevaluate previous ideas concerning them.

The records that had been kept by the Indians were purged by their Spanish conquerors either in the name of the church or for the valuable metal plates on which they were written. Many of these metal records were melted down into bullion for shipment to Spain. However, we do know of a few major pieces of Mayan literature that survived the Spanish conquest. Among these are (1) the *Popol Vuh*, (2) *Los Anales de los Cakchiquels*,

Clark V. Johnson is professor of Church History and Doctrine at Brigham Young University.

(3) *El Titulo de los Señores de Totonicapán* (hereafter *Totonicapán*), (4) *El Libro de Chilam Balam,* and (5) *La Probanza de Votan.* Of these five the *Popol Vuh* is of primary importance while the other works generally "supplement the information given in the *Popol Vuh*" (*Popol Vuh* 15). Sylvanus G. Morely said that "the *Popol Vuh* . . . is, beyond any shadow of doubt, the most distinguished example of native American literature that has survived the passing centuries" (*Popol Vuh* ix; see also Morley 255). Although these ancient books have been reviewed from several different perspectives—archaeologically, historically, linguistically, and prophetically—I will confine the parameters of this paper to prophecy and history.

Before proceeding, however, I will sketch an outline of the two works that are central to this paper, namely the Book of Mormon and the *Popol Vuh.* While I do not intend to rehearse every parallel between the Book of Mormon and the *Popol Vuh,* I will note similarities that exist in three areas: the origin of the ancient Americans, the gods they worshipped, and their belief in the Creation, the Fall, and the Flood.

Origin of the *Popol Vuh* and the Book of Mormon People

The *Popol Vuh* comes from the Quiché Indians, a tribe of Mayan people who lived in the southern highlands of Guatemala (Morley 255, 422). We do not know the name of the Quiché Indian author who wrote it, but we do know that it was written shortly after the Spanish conquest of Guatemala in 1524. The original manuscript remained in obscurity for over 150 years until early in the 18th century when the Indians in the parish of Santa Tomás Chichicastenangoa showed it to a Dominican priest named Father Francisco Ximénez. A linguist who spoke fluent Quiché, Father Ximénez first transcribed "the original Quiché text and [then] translated it into Spanish under the title *Historias del Origen de los Indios de esta Provincia de Guatemala*" (*Popol*

Vuh 4-5). His transcription has been preserved, but the original Quiché manuscript has disappeared. The Spanish translation of the *Popol Vuh* was published in Vienna in 1857 (*Popol Vuh* xi), while an English translation was not published until 1950 by Adrian Recinos.

The Book of Mormon was compiled from early records by two ancient American prophets, Mormon and Moroni, between AD 322 and 421, and was translated into English by the Prophet Joseph Smith in 1829. Shortly after the completion of his translation, Joseph Smith returned the plates to their original custodian, the prophet Moroni. The Book of Mormon was first published in Palmyra, New York, in 1830, and it remained the sole religious authority on the beliefs and cultures of ancient America from the ancient people until the publication of the *Popol Vuh* in Spanish in 1857. Although a Spanish translation of the *Popol Vuh* was available, there is no evidence that it had any impact on the North American frontier until it was translated into English 93 years later.

Both the *Popol Vuh* and the Book of Mormon are religious histories that record migrations to the New World. Both are confined to specific peoples. The *Popol Vuh* tells about the earliest settlers of Guatemala and is known as "the *Sacred Book*, or *National Book* of the Quiché" (*Popol Vuh* 5). The Book of Mormon relates the religious history of three groups who settled in the Americas and is a sacred book "written by way of commandment, and also by the spirit of prophecy and of revelation" (title page).

The *Popol Vuh* "contains the cosmogonical concepts and ancient traditions of this aboriginal American people, the history of their origin, and the chronology of their kings down to the year 1550" (*Popol Vuh* 5). The preparation of the *Popol Vuh* was done in great secrecy. Referring to his book, the author wrote: "We shall bring it to light because now the *Popol Vuh*, as it is called, cannot be seen any more, in which was clearly seen the coming from the other side of the sea and the narration of our obscurity, and our life was clearly seen. The original book, written long ago existed, but its sight is hidden to the searcher and to the thinker" (*Popol Vuh* 79-80).

The Book of Mormon clarifies much of the mystique surrounding some of the Indians who were living in America when it was discovered by Columbus. It gives insight into three separate peoples who migrated to America by boat, but does not claim to explain the origin of all those who lived on the North and South American continents anciently. Rather, it is a record containing the teachings of the Savior to a group of transplanted Israelites, and speaks of the struggle they had following their prophets and receiving God's laws through them. Other peoples may have come before, during, and after the Book of Mormon civilizations were in existence (see Gordon).

The Origin of the American Indians

The author of the *Popol Vuh* maintained that his ancestors, the ancient ones, originated on the other side of the ocean. Tradition indicates that these ancestors watched "for the coming of the star, which comes just before the sun. . . . 'We came from there, but we have separated'" (*Popol Vuh* 182).

In the 1560s, Diego de Landa, a Catholic Bishop who had lived in Yucatan since 1549, wrote that the people of Yucatan insisted they were descendants of a people "who came from the East and whom God had delivered by opening twelve paths through the sea" (Tozzer 16-17). The *Popol Vuh* says that "it is not quite clear . . . how they crossed the sea; they crossed to this side, as if there were no sea; they crossed on stones, placed in a row over the sand" (*Popol Vuh* 183). Finally, Fray Bernardino de Sahagun, a Franciscan who had lived in Mexico from 1529 until his death in 1590, states that the ancient ones came by ocean in seven caves which are seven boats or galleys (Sahagun 1:30). These people landed at the port of the Panuco River, which they called Panco, meaning "those who crossed the waters" (Sahagun 1:30). Torquemada records that these ancient ones were industrious and had no disposition for war (1:254-55).

These histories indicate that the first people came after the world had been destroyed by the Flood (*Ixtlilochitl* 1:11). According to Fernando de Alva Ixtlilxochitl, the grandson of the last king of Texcoco and an interpreter for the Viceroy in the Court of Indians, the ancient ones were giants (*Quinametzin*) who came from a very high tower when everyone's language was confused, 1964 years after the creation of the earth (*Ixtlilxochitl* 1:13). Seven friends were able to understand each other, so they brought their wives with them to the Americas. Ultimately, the Quinametzin were destroyed by punishments and calamities because of the sins they committed (*Ixtlilxochitl* 1:12, 17).

The ancient ones in the Book of Mormon also came at the time of the Tower of Babel and are known as the Jaredites. "Jared came forth with his brother and their families, with some others and their families, from the great tower, at the time the Lord confounded the language of the people" (Ether 1:33). Their prophet, the brother of Jared, asked the Lord not to confound their language (Ether 1:35). Like the Quinametzin, the Jaredites were "large and mighty men" (Ether 15:26) who were destroyed by civil war because they rejected their God (Ether 13:2, 15-17; 15).

According to the *Popol Vuh*, the second settlers, known as the Nahuales, came after the destruction of the giants. The Nahuales "came from the other part of the ocean, from where the sun rises, a place called *Pa Tulán, Pa Civán*" (*Totonicapán* 169; see also *Popol Vuh* 170-71). Quiché traditions indicate that the forefathers of the Nahuales (Tepeu, Olomán, Cohah, Quenech, and Ahau) had multiplied in the East (*Popol Vuh* 170). They were artisans and builders who built the cities of Teotihuacan, Tula, and Cholula. They suffered much for the want of food during their journey. In fact, their historian records that "they did not have sustenance; they only smelled the ends of their staffs and thus they imagined they were eating; but they did not eat when they came. . . . [T]heir hearts were troubled when they talked together, because they had nothing to eat, only a drink of water and a handful of corn they had" (*Popol Vuh* 182-83). They lamented their coming: "'Oh, we have come without joy! If only we could see the rising of the sun! What shall we do now? If we lived in harmony in our country, why did we leave it?'" (*Popol Vuh* 185).

God gave the Quiché lords a gift before they left their ancient homeland in the East and crossed the sea (*Popol Vuh* 205). This gift from God was a stone which was "the symbol of his being," the *Pizom-Gagal* (*Popol Vuh* 205 fn 3). The author of *Totonicapán* called it the *Giron-Gagal* (*Totonicapán* 170). Delia Goetz explained that, "'The great father Nacxit [1] [God] gave them a gift called the Giron-Gagal.' Giron, or quirón, is derived from *quira*, 'unfasten,' 'unroll,' 'to preserve' a thing" (*Popol Vuh* 205 fn 3).

In the Book of Mormon, the second group of people, the Nephites, left Jerusalem for the New World in 600 BC, but did not arrive until approximately 589 BC (1 Nephi 18:23; see the asterisk for that verse). They traveled "nearly a south, southeast direction until they came to the nineteenth degree of north latitude; then, nearly east to the Sea of Arabia" (Richards 272). The Prophet Joseph Smith wrote that "Lehi went down by the Red Sea to the great Southern Ocean, and crossed over to this land, and landed a little south of the Isthmus of Darien" (*Teachings of the Prophet Joseph Smith* 267).

Lehi led his family into the wilderness where, like the Nahuales, they suffered from privation and starvation (1 Nephi 16:18-19). While journeying in the wilderness Lehi also received a gift from God, which he called the Liahona (1 Nephi 16:10; Alma 37:38). The Liahona directed their travels, and writing appeared upon it which gave the colony instructions (1 Nephi 16:10, 16, 27, 29). Whether the *Giron-Gagal* and the Liahona

---

[1] The Lord Nacxit was the Quiché supreme judge of all kingdoms. Nacxit is the abbreviated name of "Topiltzin Acxitl Quetzalcoatl, the famous Toltec king" (*Popol Vuh* 207 fn 3). An earlier definition of Quetzalcoatl refers to him as the Great White God, the god of precious plumage, the god who flies through the air without sound, and the god of wind. Some feel that Quetzalcoatl is the Indian name for Jesus Christ while others maintain that there were two Quetzalcoatls. According to them the second ruled for twenty years, during which time the Indians had peace and prosperity. A conspiracy was drawn for his downfall that succeeded. He was seduced by a harlot and left Tula in shame "promising that one day he would return" (Padden 26-27).

are the same cannot be determined, but both served as a symbol of God's power among the two groups of travelers.

Indian traditions also refer to a third group of immigrants known as the Ulmecas or Xicalancas. They came by boat from the east and settled in Potochan. Later they encountered some of the giants who had escaped the calamities of their age (Ixtlil-xochitl 1:19-20), and eventually they united with the Nahuales, the second settlers (Torquemada 255). The account of the third settlers in the Indian histories is brief, probably due to their merging with the Nahuales.

The Mulekites, the third settlers in the Book of Mormon, left Jerusalem about 587 BC, during the time that Nebuchad-nezzar's forces sacked the city, slew king Zedekiah's sons, and put his eyes out (2 Kings 25:4-7; Nebuchadnezzar's forces captured Jerusalem about 587 BC [see BD 639]). King Zedekiah's youngest son, Mulek, escaped the Babylonian holocaust and migrated to the New World. After several centuries, the Mulekites were discovered by the Nephites.

Wickedness had increased so much among the second group, the Nephites, that during the days of king Mosiah I, the Lord called upon the righteous to migrate to a different part of the land. King Mosiah was "warned of the Lord that he should flee out of the land of Nephi" and take with him as many as would "hearken unto the voice of the Lord." Mosiah "did according as the Lord had commanded him. And they departed out of the land into the wilderness, . . . and they were led by many preachings and prophesyings. And they were admonished continually by the word of God; and they were led by the power of his arm, through the wilderness until they came down into the land which is called the land of Zarahemla" (Omni 1:12-13).

At Zarahemla, Mosiah and his followers found a numerous people (Omni 1:17). The people of Zarahemla were the followers of Mulek who had fled from Jerusalem during the reign of Zedekiah, the last king of Judah. They had lived in the New World for several centuries, during which time they were plagued by civil war and internal strife (Omni 1:15, 17). Even though the

Nephites arrived in the New World in 589 BC, they still did not encounter nor merge with the third group of settlers, the Mulekites, until between 279 and 130 BC. Amaleki indicates that Mosiah and the people who followed him were warmly received by the people of Zarahemla, and that they soon made Mosiah their king (Omni 1:12, 19). The merger of these two civilizations lasted between 515 and 664 years.

King Mosiah I learned about the ancient ones, or Jaredites, when the people of Zarahemla brought him "a large stone . . . with engravings on it." He interpreted the characters on the stone "by the gift and power of God" (Omni 1:20). The writings "gave an account of one Coriantumr, and the slain of his people" (Omni 1:21). They also spake a few words concerning his fathers: "And his first parents came out from the tower, at the time the Lord confounded the language of the people; and the severity of the Lord fell upon them according to his judgments, which are just; and their bones lay scattered in the land northward" (Omni 1:22).

In the Book of Mormon these three civilizations, the Jaredites, the Nephites, and the Mulekites, remained more or less apart until the Mulekites discovered the Jaredites (the giants in the *Popol Vuh* and Coriantumr in the Book of Mormon), and until the second and third migrations united.

The Gods They Worshiped

The Book of Mormon and the *Popol Vuh* also agree that once their peoples had established themselves in America they developed a culture centered around their belief in God. The Indians in the *Popol Vuh* believed in multiple gods, accepting a pantheon of deities from the other world, and looking to them for guidance. The creation of the earth was carried out by three deities, Caculhá Huracán, Chipi-Caculhá, and Raxa-Caculhá, who were known as "the Heart of Heaven" (*Popol Vuh* 82). A primitive people who migrated to Guatemala called their god Gucumatz "because their salvation was in the water" (*Popol Vuh*

81 fn 2). Bishop Núñez de la Vega said that "Gucumatz is a serpent with feathers, which moves in the water" (*Popol Vuh* 81 fn 2). Ancient records indicate that the appearance of Gucumatz, or Quetzalcoatl, changed Indian culture. Traditionally, he left peace in Yucatan and traveled to Mexico. He dwelt at Champoton and when he left the people, he promised them he would return (*Ixtlilxochitl* 1:21). Quetzalcoatl was described as a man of good disposition, grave aspect, white and bearded, and dressed in a large tunic. As a result of Quetzalcoatl's visit to Izmachi, there were no difficulties or disputes, and their kingdom was peaceful (*Popol Vuh* 212-13). Ixtlilxochitl noted that some years after the appearance of Quetzalcoatl the Indians built a temple to him (*Ixtlilxochitl* 1:21).

The god of the Book of Mormon is Jesus Christ, and he is referred to as the Only Begotten Son, the Son of God, and the Messiah, among many other titles (Jehovah, the Lamb, etc.). The Nephite record tells of the coming of the resurrected Christ to the Americas. The ancient prophet Nephi wrote that the people "cast their eyes up again towards heaven; and . . . saw a Man descending out of heaven; and he was clothed in a white robe; and he came down and stood in the midst of them; and the eyes of the whole multitude were turned upon him, and they durst not open their mouths, even one to another, and wist not what it meant, for they thought it was an angel that had appeared unto them" (3 Nephi 11:8). As the multitude at Bountiful gazed upon him, the personage identified himself, saying, "Behold, I am Jesus Christ, whom the prophets testified shall come into the world. And behold, I am the light and the life of the world; and I have drunk out of that bitter cup which the Father hath given me, and have glorified the Father in taking upon me the sins of the world, in the which I have suffered the will of the Father in all things from the beginning" (3 Nephi 11:10-11). When the people realized who the personage was, they bowed themselves to the earth, "for they remembered that it had been prophesied among them that Christ should show himself unto them after his ascension into heaven" (3 Nephi 11:12).

At his second appearance, the number of people gathered to hear him had increased many times (3 Nephi 19:3, 5). The Messiah's personal instruction changed Nephite-Lamanite society for over two centuries. The people were all converted to Jesus Christ. "There were no contentions and disputations among them, and every man did deal justly one with another. And they had all things common among them; therefore there were not rich and poor, bond and free, but they were all made free, and partakers of the heavenly gift" (4 Nephi 1:2-3; see also vv 15-17). Following these two centuries of peace, factions developed among the people and gross wickedness prevailed.

In addition to believing in the Heart of Heaven, Gucumatz or Quetzalcoatl, the Indians also believed in a god of darkness known as Vucub-Caquix, who said about himself,

> "I shall now be great above all the beings created and formed. I am the sun, the light, the moon. . . . Great is my splendor. Because of me men shall walk and conquer. . . . I am the sun, I am the moon, for all mankind. So shall it be, because I can see very far." . . . But he was not really the sun; he was only vainglorious of his feathers and his riches. And he could see only as far as the horizon, and he could not see over all the world (*Popol Vuh* 93-94).

According to Guatemalan tradition, Vucub-Caquix was eventually overthrown by two youths who were really gods (*Popol Vuh* 94).

The Nephites also believed in a god of darkness who once was an angel of light. According to Lehi, an angel of God "had fallen from heaven; wherefore, he became a devil, having sought that which was evil before God" (2 Nephi 2:17).

The Creation, the Fall, and the Flood

The first chapters of the *Popol Vuh* relate Guatemalan traditions about the Creation, the Fall, and the Flood. The Gods saw that "all was in suspense . . . nothing [was] brought together. . . . There was nothing standing; only the calm water. . . . Nothing existed" (*Popol Vuh* 81). A narrative of the creation of the earth by Gucumatz, the Heart of Heaven, follows. Under God's direction, the void was filled and man was formed. Gucumatz rejoiced in his accomplishments (*Popol Vuh* 83-84).

The Book of Mormon is silent about the details of the Creation and simply refers its reader to other records which contain detailed accounts of the Creation. Lehi said that the brass plates, which parallel some of our Old Testament, contained "an account of the creation of the world" (1 Nephi 5:11). The 24 gold plates, which were part of the Jaredite record also contained an account of the Creation, but Moroni chose not to include it in his abridgment of the story of the Jaredites (Mosiah 8:5-9; 28:11-12; Ether 1:3).

After the earth was finished and filled with plant and animal life, the Heart of Heaven held a council. Xpiyacoc and Xmucané, the old man and the old woman, were assigned to work together "'so that man . . . will nourish and sustain us, invoke and remember us.' . . . The old woman and the old man said to the Heart of Heaven, 'Your figures of wood shall come out well; they shall speak and talk on earth.' . . . And instantly the figures were made of wood. They looked like men, talked like men, and populated the surface of the earth" (*Popol Vuh* 87-89). So according to the *Popol Vuh*, it was the old woman and the old man who gave life to man, and who were charged with teaching man to remember the Heart of Heaven.

Lehi taught his children of the fall of man (2 Nephi 2). Adam, the Ancient of Days, along with his wife Eve, took an active role in transgressing a law which brought mortality to mankind (2 Nephi 2:25). Their actions allowed the spirit children of God to come to earth where they were given time to be tried and tested (2 Nephi 2:18-22). Lehi also spoke to his children of a Messiah who would come to "redeem the children of [Adam and Eve] from the fall" (2 Nephi 2:26; see also 9:21; Mosiah 3:11).

According to the *Popol Vuh*, after men were given life on the earth by the "old man and old woman" (the transgression of Adam and Eve in the Book of Mormon), they multiplied upon the face of the earth, and there were great numbers of men and women. But eventually the people of the earth forgot the Heart of Heaven.

The author of the *Popol Vuh* also related that men and women degenerated. Their faces were "without expression." They lacked strength and their "flesh was yellow. . . . They no longer thought of their Creator nor their Maker, nor of those who made them and cared for them" (*Popol Vuh* 89). Finally, the Heart of Heaven brought about a flood which destroyed man. The Quiché wrote, "The mouths and faces of all of them were mangled. And it is said that their descendants [those who survived the flood] are the monkeys which now live in the forests; these are all that remain of them because their flesh was made only of wood" (*Popol Vuh* 92). A second creation followed the destruction of the world by the Flood. The Heart of Heaven began again, and the earth was renewed and life once again abounded.

The Book of Mormon also speaks of the Flood. In the book of Alma, Amulek, a Nephite missionary, tells the Nephites that "if it were not for the prayers of the righteous, . . . ye would even now be visited with utter destruction; yet it would not be by flood, as were the people in the days of Noah" (Alma 10:22). In Moroni's abridgment of the Jaredite record, he refers to "the ark of Noah" (Ether 6:7), and speaks of when "the waters had receded from off the face of this land" (Ether 13:2).

Conclusion

As this paper has demonstrated, there are similarities in the accounts of the Creation, the Fall, and the Flood in the Book of Mormon and the *Popol Vuh*. It has also shown that the ancients believed in a former god of light, Vucab-Caquix or Lucifer, who fell from the presence of God and became evil. The narrative of the *Popol Vuh* declares that Vucab-Caquix was destroyed by two youthful gods, while the Book of Mormon testifies that Lucifer will ultimately be defeated by the Christ. The ancients of the

Popol Vuh also worshiped Gucumatz or Quetzalcoatl, while the Nephite record testifies of the Messiah or Jesus Christ. Both records teach that the god of the ancient Americans appeared to them and brought peace.

Although we have noted the similarities that exist between the *Popol Vuh* and the Book of Mormon, there are also many differences. It is sad to realize that although these early American cultures kept records, only a few are available for our study today. Even the *Popol Vuh* was not written until after the Spanish conquest of Guatemala. It is clearly the product of oral traditions passed down from generation to generation until they were finally recorded by an unknown writer between AD 1524 and 1550. The purpose of that unknown author was to preserve the historical tradition of his people for his descendants. Unfortunately, the lack of organization and the unclear language of the *Popol Vuh* hinder the reader's efforts to understand the theology and history of these ancient Americans.

Unlike the *Popol Vuh*, the Book of Mormon was written by the ancients themselves. Its writers recorded their feelings as they struggled to know and obey their God. The Book of Mormon was abridged by two prophets who recorded those parts of their history and theology that would be the most beneficial for their descendants. Their carefully prepared record was hidden away for nine centuries, until the last custodian of the record, Moroni, delivered it to Joseph Smith in 1827 to be translated into English. Although narrow in its focus, the Book of Mormon clarifies the theology concerning the fall of man and the nature of God. It also directs the reader to the life and mission of the Savior, which is the purpose for which the book was prepared. While much of the history of its peoples is missing, the Book of Mormon does give some detail concerning three migrations to America which helps to clarify our understanding of the *Popol Vuh*. In addition, the religious and cultural histories in the *Popol Vuh* and the Book of Mormon enhance our understanding of ancient America, and support Joseph Smith's early claims about the American Indians.

Finally, the Book of Mormon fulfills its divine purpose as an ancient witness to a modern world that Jesus is the Christ.

BIBLIOGRAPHY

Ferguson, Thomas Stuart. *One Fold and One Shepherd.* San Francisco: Books of California, 1958.

Gordon, Cyrus H. *Before Columbus: Links Between the Old World and Ancient America.* New York: Crown, 1971.

Hunter, Milton R. and Thomas Stuart Ferguson. *Ancient America and the Book of Mormon.* Oakland, CA: Kolob, 1950.

Morley, Sylvanus G. *The Ancient Maya.* 3rd ed. Stanford, CA: Stanford Univ, 1956.

Obras historicas de Don Fernando de Alva Ixtlilxochitl. Ed. Alfredo Chavero. Mexico, D. F.: Editora Nacional, 1965.

Padden, R. C. *The Hummingbird and the Hawk.* Columbus, OH: Ohio State Univ, 1967.

Popol Vuh: The Sacred Book of the Ancient Quiché Maya. Tran. Adrin Recinos, Delia Goetz and Sylvanus G. Morley. Norman, OK: Univ of Oklahoma, 1950.

Richards, Franklin D. and James A. Little. *A Compendium of the Doctrines of the Gospel.* Rev. ed. Salt Lake City: Deseret Book, 1925.

Sahagun, Bernardino de. *Historia general de las cosas de Nueva España.* 4 vols. Mexico: Editorial Porrua, S. A., 1969.

Sjodahl, J. M. *An Introduction to the Study of the Book of Mormon.* Salt Lake City: Deseret News Press, 1927.

Smith, Lucy Mack. *History of Joseph Smith.* Salt Lake City: Bookcraft, 1956.

Teachings of the Prophet Joseph Smith. Comp. Joseph Fielding Smith. Salt Lake City: Deseret Book, 1976.

Title of the Lords of Totonicapán. Translated from Quiché into Spanish by Dionisio José Chonay, and into English by Delia Goetz. Norman, OK: Univ of Oklahoma, 1967.

Torquemada, Juan de. *Monarquia Indiana.* 3 vols. (Bound with *The Annals of the Cakchiquels*). Mexico: Editorial Porrua, S. A., 1969.

Tozzer, Alfred M. *Landa's Relación de las cosas de Yucatan—A Translation.* Cambridge, MA: Peabody Museum of American Archaeology and Ethnology, Harvard Univ, 1941.

Warren, Bruce W. and Thomas Stuart Ferguson. *The Messiah in Ancient America.* Provo, UT: Book of Mormon Research Foundation, 1987.

Enos: His Mission and His Message

8

Dennis L. Largey

*N*ephi concluded his last recorded sermon by saying: "And now, my beloved brethren, all those who are of the house of Israel, and all ye ends of the earth, I speak unto you as *the voice of one crying from the dust*. Farewell until that great day shall come" (2 Nephi 33:13; emphasis added). Enos inherited Nephi's record-keeping responsibilities and also spoke as from the dust. What was his plea? Whom did he think his readers would be? What principles did he want them to learn? The following is a discussion of the contributions of Enos' brief but vital "cry from the dust" found in the Book of Mormon.

Enos: His Mission

Enos was a righteous son of Jacob, Nephi's younger brother. Just prior to his death, Jacob gave Enos stewardship of all the sacred records Nephi had entrusted to him. Even though they lived in a day of war and sin, Enos and others sought "to restore the Lamanites unto the true faith in God." But "our labors were vain; their hatred was fixed, and they were led by their evil nature that they became wild, and ferocious, and a blood-thirsty people, full of idolatry and filthiness . . . and they were continually seeking to destroy us" (Enos 1:20).

Dennis L. Largey is assistant professor of Ancient Scripture at Brigham Young University.

The Lamanite hatred was also directed at the Nephite records as well as their traditions. The Lamanites had sworn "in their wrath that, if it were possible, they would destroy our records" (Enos 1:14). Chief among the Nephite traditions contained in the records, was the prophecy that the Messiah would come 600 years from the time Lehi left Jerusalem (1 Nephi 10:4). The record also justified Nephite leadership in the family and chronicled the rebellion and dissension of Lamanite fathers. Enos petitioned God to preserve the record, "that it might be brought forth at some future day unto the Lamanites, that, perhaps, they might be brought unto salvation" (Enos 1:13). In this instance Enos became part of the fulfillment of one of Nephi's prophecies concerning the Lamanites and the Book of Mormon:

> After my seed [the Nephites] and the seed of my brethren [the Lamanites] shall have dwindled in unbelief, . . . and after they shall have been brought down low in the dust, even that they are not, yet *the words of the righteous shall be written, and the prayers of the faithful shall be heard*, and all those who have dwindled in unbelief [the Lamanites] shall not be forgotten (2 Nephi 26:15; emphasis added).

The Lord told Enos that his faith was like that of his fathers' whose prayers were heard in behalf of future Lamanites, and whose words would be restored for their conversion (Enos 1:18). In a revelation given to the Prophet Joseph Smith in Harmony, Pennsylvania, in July 1828, the Lord confirmed that in preserving the Book of Mormon plates he had kept his promise and that the information on the plates was intended to bring the Lamanites to a knowledge of the truth:

> And for this very purpose are these plates preserved, which contain these records—that the promises of the Lord might be fulfilled, which he made to his people; And that the Lamanites might . . . know the promises of the Lord, and that they may believe the gospel and rely upon the merits of Jesus Christ, and be glorified through faith in his name, and that through their repentance they might be saved (D&C 3:19-20).

Enos: His Message

The apostle Paul taught that "all scripture is given by inspiration of God, and is profitable for doctrine . . . [and] for instruction in righteousness" (2 Tim 3:16). As scripture, the writings of Enos contribute to both doctrine and instruction. Although Enos' words are few, his doctrine and commentary support other writers throughout the Book of Mormon and other scriptures. Gospel principles are embedded in his struggle to know God and in his determination to serve him. There are nine such supported precepts or "instructions in righteousness" that make Enos a most significant "voice from the dust."

1. To All Nations, Kindreds, Tongues, and People—
Jesus Is the Christ

Speaking to Jew or Hindu, Moslem or Buddhist, Catholic, Baptist, or Latter-day Saint, Enos witnesses that Jesus is the Messiah, the Son of God, the Redeemer of all humanity. The Lord's declaration to Enos that "thy faith [in Christ] hath made thee whole" (Enos 1:8) sums up, supports, and testifies of the New Testament record and its doctrine. The book of Enos in itself is another testament of Jesus Christ; it contains scripture consistent with the overall purpose of the Book of Mormon. Concerning his work on the small plates, Nephi wrote: "For the fulness of mine intent is that I may persuade men to come unto the God of Abraham, and the God of Isaac, and the God of Jacob, and be saved" (1 Nephi 6:4). He also commanded those who would write on the plates after him "not [to] occupy these plates with things which are not of worth unto the children of men" (v 6). True to his commission, the Book of Mormon record keepers were highly selective in what they engraved on their plates. From the revelations placed on the small plates of Nephi, those who succeeded Nephi understood that their writings would, first and most importantly, be a witness of Jesus Christ.

The Book of Mormon focuses on the Savior and his gospel. Its characters and events are always secondary to the doctrine and witness of Christ that extends from them. Consistent with this concept, the message of Jesus Christ is the central theme in the book of Enos, which is the story of how one man applied the redemptive mission of Jesus Christ to his life. The story of Enos teaches that Jesus is the answer to the hungry soul, he is the one who can say, "Thy sins are forgiven thee, and thou shalt be blessed" (Enos 1:5). In this regard the words of Enos correlate with President Ezra Taft Benson's invitation concerning reading the Book of Mormon: "Let us read the Book of Mormon and be convinced that Jesus is the Christ. Let us continually reread the Book of Mormon so that we might more fully come to Christ, be committed to Him, centered in Him, and consumed in Him" (58).

2. *Forgiveness Sometimes Requires a "Wrestle Before God"*

The story of Enos teaches us that there is a price to pay both in effort and attitude before we can receive forgiveness of our sins. Enos said: "I will tell you of the wrestle I had before God, before I received a remission of my sins" (Enos 1:2). Enos' wrestle before God was a spiritual struggle which contains lessons that can apply to all people who seek forgiveness through the Atonement. In many cases, this wrestle contains the following four elements:

(a) *A wrestle with sorrow.* Repentant persons experience deep disappointment in knowing that their sinful lives have offended God. This sorrow is intensified as they confront the great disparity between their sins and the standards which God has set.

(b) *A wrestle with guilt.* As these persons accept the fact that they have sinned and humble themselves, they will wrestle for a restoration of peace to their souls and the return of the Holy Ghost, which has withdrawn. President Spencer W. Kimball related: "There must be a consciousness of guilt. It cannot be brushed aside. It must be acknowledged and not rationalized away. . . . There must be a pricking of conscience, perhaps sleepless hours, eyes that are wet, for as Alma says: 'None but the truly penitent are saved' " (*Teachings of Spencer W. Kimball* 87).

(c) *A wrestle with time.* Often the Lord requires a period of time to elapse before lifting the burden of sin. This waiting period compels sinners to reevaluate their commitment and live the promises they have made. When this upward struggle is completed, it can then serve as an anchor to hold on to after the remission of sin is granted. During this period of struggle they school their appetites and desires so that their only focus is upon pleasing God and keeping his commandments.

Although Enos wrote that he "went to hunt beasts in the forests" (Enos 1:3), President Kimball said, "But no animal did he shoot nor capture. He was traveling a path he had never walked before. He was reaching, knocking, asking, pleading; he was being born again. He was seeing the pleasant valleys across the barren wastes. He was searching his soul. He might have lived all his life in a weed patch, but now he envisioned a watered garden" (Faith 210).

(d) *A wrestle in prayer.* If we are to receive forgiveness, we must ask for it. Enos wrote, "And all the day long did I cry unto him; yea, and when the night came I did still raise my voice high that it reached the heavens" (1:4). Of this President Kimball has taught:

> Here is no casual prayer; no worn phrases; no momentary appeal by silent lips. All the day long, with seconds turning into minutes, and minutes into hours and hours. But when the sun had set, relief had still not come, for repentance is not a single act nor forgiveness an unearned gift. So precious to him was communication with and approval of his Redeemer that his determined soul pressed on without ceasing (*Faith* 211).

Prayer is a significant key in many conversion stories recorded in the Book of Mormon. For example, king Benjamin's people all prayed "with one voice" for forgiveness of their sins (Mosiah 4:2). At the turning point in his spiritual life, Alma "cried within my heart: O Jesus, thou Son of God, have mercy on me, who am in the gall of bitterness, and am encircled about by the everlasting chains of death" (Alma 36:18). And king Lamoni's father prostrated himself upon the earth and cried mightily, saying, "O God, Aaron hath told me that there is a God; and if there is a God, and if thou art God, wilt thou make thyself known unto me, and I will give away all my sins to know thee" (Alma 22:18). Jesus said, "Behold, I stand at the door, and knock: if any man hear my voice, and open the door, I will come in to him, and will sup with him, and he with me" (Rev 3:20). The story of Enos teaches us that sometimes it takes a wrestle just to open the door. This struggling is a tutorial period which becomes a hedge against closing that door in the future, for we learn through experience that God cannot be mocked and that mercy cannot rob justice.

3. Forgiveness Comes Through Faith in Jesus Christ

At some point during Enos' lengthy prayer, he heard a voice say, "Enos, thy sins are forgiven thee, and thou shalt be blessed" (Enos 1:5). Awed by the immediate relief he felt, Enos inquired, "Lord, how is it done?" The Lord responded, "Because of thy faith in Christ, whom thou has never before heard nor seen. . . . Wherefore, go to, thy faith hath made thee whole" (Enos 1:8). Enos' faith in Jesus Christ had brought him a remission of sin and had made him spiritually whole. The scriptures abound with such stories. For example, the faith of the woman with a 12-year issue of blood made her whole, as did the faith of the man lowered through a roof in order to be healed (Luke 8:43-47; Mark 2:1-5).

There is a thread of common elements in all such renditions. Each instance shows: (1) a compelling belief that Jesus was the one who could help them; (2) a determined effort to seek Jesus and receive the desired blessing; and (3) a humble heart.

4. Removal of Sin Must Precede Removal of Guilt

Guilt is a God-given protection designed to encourage positive change. Alma taught that sin brings punishment and punishment brings remorse of conscience. The fruit of remorse of conscience is repentance, which activates the plan of mercy. The plan of mercy appeases the demands of justice, and at this point guilt is taken away. This miracle is possible because of the merits of Jesus Christ. True faith, when exercised, always leads to true repentance (Alma 42:15-23).

False prophets of the Book of Mormon sometimes tried to negate the influence of guilt on their followers and thus prevent people from repenting and living the gospel. Korihor, a noted anti-Christ, taught the Nephites to "lift up their heads in wickedness," for "whatsoever a man does [is] no crime" (Alma 30:17-18). Today's secular world reflects this belief by professing that guilt is a hinderant to "freedom." One modern professional counseling strategy concentrates on removing guilt from a client's life with little if any emphasis on modifying the behavior that produced the guilt. To sin without guilt, as this teaching implies, one must lower moral standard to correspond with behavior. This is exactly opposite from the true gospel principle that to remove guilt one must lift behavior through appropriate repentance.

The story of Enos testifies that the burden of guilt carried as a result of transgression can be swept from the heart through faith in Jesus Christ, which is indeed a miracle. Faith enables the repentant person to "[put] off the natural man and [become] a saint through the atonement of Christ" (Mosiah 3:19).

5. *Charity and Good Works Follow True Conversion*

When Enos entered the forest to pray, his first concern was for his own soul. Upon hearing the voice of the Lord announce that he had been forgiven, Enos recorded, "When I had heard these words I began to feel a desire for the welfare of my brethren, the Nephites; wherefore, I did pour out my whole soul unto God for them" (Enos 1:9). When we obtain the Spirit through sincere repentance, our hearts turn outward, having gained the capacity to forget self and love others. It seems intentional that when the

Atonement touches our lives, the Lord pours out his love in overflowing abundance. He knows his abundant love will not be wasted but will flow over and touch others. Being "born again," as Enos had experienced, introduces us to a lifetime of service. We have all of the virtues associated with the gift of charity available to us through application of the Atonement. In a letter to Moroni, Mormon wrote:

> And the first fruits of repentance is baptism; and baptism cometh by faith unto the fulfilling the commandments; and the fulfilling of the commandments bringeth remission of sins; and the remission of sins bringeth meekness, and lowliness of heart; and because of meekness and lowliness of heart cometh the visitation of the Holy Ghost, *which Comforter filleth with hope and perfect love*, which love endureth by diligence unto prayer, until the end shall come, when all the saints shall dwell with God (Moroni 8:25-26; emphasis added).

We can apply Mormon's formula to Enos' story. He began to feel for the welfare of others as he received a remission of his own sins. The Holy Ghost filled his heart with hope and perfect love. Charity, or perfect love, is a gift of the Spirit that comes as we gain and maintain our relationships with the Lord through repentance and obedience.

After gaining promised blessings for the Nephites, Enos then prayed for the Lamanites. His prayer displays a significant order in his requests: first for himself, second for his friends, and third for his enemies. Obedience to the first great commandment, "to love the Lord thy God with all thy heart, and with all thy soul and with all thy mind" brought true obedience to the second great commandment to "love thy neighbor as thyself" (see Matt 22:37-39). In essence, our first love (our relationship with God) empowers and directs our second love (our relationship with others). Unobstructed by sin, Enos now had the power to grow beyond his previous abilities. His desires progressed beyond caring mainly for his own people to include a struggle in prayer for the welfare of his enemies.

The conversion stories of Alma the Younger and the four sons of Mosiah followed this same pattern. After having their "wrestle before God" and receiving a remission of their sins, they had a consuming desire to preach the gospel. As Mormon wrote, "They were desirous that salvation should be declared to every creature, for they could not bear that any human soul should perish; yea, even the very thoughts that any soul should endure endless torment did cause them to quake and tremble" (Mosiah 28:3).

In the Church today, the most effective missionaries are those who have first reconciled themselves with God so that the Holy Ghost can assist them in their ministries. Having been born again, they can then proceed with their desires to bless others as did Enos.

This concept could have significant meaning regarding the way we interrelate with each other. For example, let Enos' prayer for his own soul represent *stage one*; his prayer for his friends represent *stage two*; and his prayer for his enemies represent *stage three*. Before attempting to resolve difficulties with others in either of stages two or three, we must spend some personal time in stage one—ie, reconciling ourselves with God, perhaps even wrestling before him in prayer, so that our emotions and desires coincide with and produce a temperament conducive to the Holy Ghost. The feeling of love generated through the warmth of the Holy Ghost enables us to *act* rather than to *react*, to *listen* rather than to *defend*, to *bless* rather than to *curse*.

The story of the martyrdom of Stephen is a dramatic example of this precept. Rather than curse those who were taking his life, Stephen "cried with a loud voice, Lord, lay not this sin to their charge. And when he had said this, he fell asleep" (Acts 7:60). The key to Stephen's ability to meet a peaceful death under violent circumstances and to forgive those who were taking his life lies in the experience he had just prior to his stoning: "But he, being full of the Holy Ghost, looked up steadfastly into heaven, and saw the glory of God, and Jesus standing on the right hand of God" (Acts 7:55).

Stephen's relationship with God led to his reception of the Holy Ghost and culminated in his glorious vision of Jesus standing at the right hand of God. This all enabled him to be obedient to the Lord's admonition: "Love your enemies, bless them that curse you, do good to them that hate you, and pray for them which despitefully use you, and persecute you" (Matt 5:44).

We in the Church are touched by the man who forgave the murderer of his missionary son, by the man who embraced and forgave the drunken driver who took the lives of his wife, daughter, and mother-in-law, and the couple who extended their love by adopting the boy who had stolen a car and accidentally ended the life of their only son. Perhaps, however, the application of this principle in our daily lives is not always seen in the dramatic episodes, but in the everyday kindness, generosity, understanding, and service we extend to our families and to our neighbors through having the "pure love of Christ."

6. Revelation

In addition to bearing testimony of the doctrine, "Ask, and it shall be given unto you" (3 Nephi 13:7), the story of Enos teaches an important principle concerning how revelation is received. Enos recorded that "while I was . . . struggling in the spirit, behold, *the voice of the Lord came into my mind* . . ." (Enos 1:10; emphasis added). This statement is consistent with what the Lord taught Oliver Cowdery when he desired to help Joseph translate: "Yea, behold, I will tell you in your mind and in your heart, by the Holy Ghost, which shall come upon you and which shall dwell in your heart. Now, behold, this is the spirit of revelation" (D&C 8:2-3).

Speaking about this mode of revelation, Elder Marion G. Romney taught that "the type of revelation most common is that which comes into our minds and feelings and induces us to do what is right" ("Peculiar" 264). In the scriptures this is often referred to as the "still small voice" (1 Nephi 17:45). In an address delivered at Brigham Young University, Elder Romney bore testimony concerning this form of revelation. He said:

> I know that God can hear prayers; He has heard mine on many occasions. I have received direct revelation from him. I have had

problems which it seemed to me that I could not solve, and I have
suffered in facing those problems until it seemed that I could not go
farther if I did not have a solution of them. Through faith, and on many
occasions fasting for a day a week over long periods of time, I have had
answers to those problems revealed to my mind in finished sentences.
I have heard the voice of God and I know his words ("Testimony"
329-30).

7. *The Lord Visits Us According to Our Diligence in Keeping the Commandments*

In answer to Enos' prayer for his brethren, the Nephites,
the Lord said: "*I will visit thy brethren according to their diligence
in keeping my commandments.* I have given unto them this land,
and it is a holy land: and I curse it not save it be for the cause of
iniquity; wherefore, I will visit thy brethren according as I have
said: and their transgressions will I bring down with sorrow upon
their own heads" (Enos 1:10; emphasis added). Nearly every
story in the Book of Mormon is a case in point verifying the truth
of these words. The repetitive promise throughout the book was
that if the Nephites kept the commandments the Lord would
prosper them and if they did not he would cut them off (2 Nephi
1:20). The Book of Mormon itself is a record of the literal
fulfillment of this promise by the Lord; its people were blessed
or cursed as they obeyed or disobeyed. In this sense, the
righteousness and wickedness of the Nephites make up two
histories in the Book of Mormon. We learn from both histories
the consistency and the reality of the consequences of making
right and wrong choices. Righteousness brought the Nephites
safety from their enemies, deliverance from their captors, refuge
from destruction, and a knowledge of the mysteries of God
through the power of the Holy Ghost. Conversely, disobedience
brought sorrow and eventual destruction upon the heads of the
people. The Book of Mormon readers learn these principles
through stories about broken bows, disabled Liahonas, burned
cities, and so forth. The plea of the prophets was for the readers
of the Book of Mormon to understand that it was written so that
we might learn to be wiser than they had been (Mormon 9:31).

Accordingly, all who read will be blessed if they can learn vicariously from the Book of Mormon experiences.

8. *The Lord Keeps His Covenants*

Enos' prayer for the Lamanites was that the Nephite record would be preserved for the welfare of their posterity. Enos said: "And I had faith, and I did cry unto God that he would preserve the records; and he covenanted with me that he would bring them forth unto the Lamanites in his own due time. And I, Enos, knew it would be according to the covenant which he had made; wherefore my should did rest" (Enos 1:16-17).

His faith enabled his soul to rest because he *knew* that God was perfectly honest in keeping all his promises. In section 1, the preface to the revelations recorded in the Doctrine and Covenants, the Lord said: "What I the Lord have spoken, I have spoken, and I excuse not myself; and though the heavens and the earth pass away, my word shall not pass away, but shall all be fulfilled" (D&C 1:38). There should be great significance in knowing that God by his very nature is "bound" to keep his word to us, if we keep our promises to him (D&C 82:10). In our lives we do not need to worry about God's being true to us. This knowledge frees us to work on our being totally true to him. Furthermore, knowing that God is obedient to his own words and promises enables us to develop the faith and trust necessary to become "as a child, . . . willing to submit to all things which the Lord seeth fit to inflict upon him, even as a child doth submit to his father" (Mosiah 3:19). This submission is a necessary requirement for entrance into the celestial kingdom. Christ said that except we become as little children we cannot enter into the kingdom of heaven (Matt 18:3).

Enos' knowledge that the Lord *would* keep his promises did not include knowing *when* he would keep them. The peace which Enos enjoyed in knowing that his prayer would be answered was not dependent upon God meeting his timetable.

Knowing that it would be accomplished was enough for him, and his soul was able to rest with that assurance.

9. *Parents in Zion Need to Teach the Gospel to Their Children*

Perhaps if Enos could speak with parents today, he would plead with them to talk often in their homes about the gospel. In the book of Proverbs we read: "Train up a child in the way he should go: and when he is old, he will not depart from it" (Prov 22:6).

The story of Enos is a powerful example of the truth of this principle. Enos wrote: *"The words which I had often heard my father speak concerning eternal life, and the joy of the saints, sunk deep into my heart.* And my should hungered; and I kneeled down before my maker, and I cried unto him in mighty prayer and supplication for mine own soul" (Enos 1:3-4; emphasis added).

It was the "words" his father had "often" taught him that motivated him to offer up his mighty prayer, which brought him forgiveness of his sins. Gospel training in the home creates a storehouse of remembrances which can be retrieved to uplift, encourage, and, in some cases, save during critical times.

A key word in this scripture is that Jacob spoke *often* of the gospel in his home. Enos truly obtained the faith of his fathers. This faith is not given genetically, but is bestowed by parents through consistent nourishment in God's word. Jacob taught his family that the rewards of eternal life and the joy of the saints are the blessings of faith in Christ and obedience to his commandments. When Enos went into the forest, his soul yearned for that joy of which his father had spoken. Often the sermons we hear have no immediate impact, but when we remember them at a later time and under different circumstances, the words "sink deep" into our hearts.

Other Book of Mormon stories support this concept. In relating his conversion story to his son Helaman, Alma said:

> And now, for three days and for three nights was I racked, even with the pains of a damned soul. And it came to pass that as I was thus racked with torment, while I was harrowed up by the memory of my many sins, behold, *I remembered also to have heard my father prophecy unto the people concerning the coming of one Jesus Christ, a Son of God, to atone for the sins of the world.* Now, as my mind caught hold upon this thought, I cried within my heart: O Jesus, thou Son of God, have mercy on me, who am in the gall of bitterness, and am encircled about by the everlasting chains of death (Alma 36:16-18; emphasis added).

Again it was the *remembrance* of the words spoken by his father about Jesus Christ and the Atonement that came to Alma as the solution in his time of spiritual crisis.

In the story of the stripling warriors, Helaman questioned his band of 2000 young men as to whether they should assist Antipus in the war against the Lamanites. They responded: "Behold our God is with us, and he will not suffer that we should fall" (Alma 56:46). In describing their extraordinary faith, Helaman said they had rehearsed to him the words of their mothers that "if they did not doubt, God would deliver them" (Alma 56:47, 48). Remembering the words of righteous mothers helped the stripling warriors develop the faith to fight and provided a catalyst for the miracle of their surviving the onslaught of the mature Lamanite army.

The stories of Enos, Alma the Younger, and the stripling warriors all teach us that children do indeed listen and learn from the spiritual training given by their parents. Parents who want their children to gain testimonies of their own and to translate faith into an active principle in their lives would do well to provide spiritual learning experiences that their children can listen to and collect in their own personal storehouses. I once attended a missionary farewell for an elderly woman, and heard her appreciative son speak of her influence: "I remember the stories my mother told me about living in Mexico. One time the saints needed rain. The members fasted, and during Stake Conference it began to rain. Those types of things have always had an effect upon me. My mother was there—she witnessed it, and that testimony has always been with me."

We who are parents need to pause and ask ourselves if our children have heard our testimonies. Do they hear them often? Do they know how we feel about Jesus and the Atonement? Have they heard our missionary experiences, and have they heard the testimonies of their aunts, uncles, grandparents, and cousins?

It may not be so much the particular words that they remember, but it is the spirit that was present when the words were spoken that lasts. It is difficult, if not impossible, to forget the "taste" of the spirit coupled with family love. People go back to a particular restaurant because they remember the taste of the food served there. Individuals often return to the gospel because they remember the sweetness of the training they received as children.

Summary

The Book of Mormon is true; consequently, the book of Enos is true. Enos' mission, though not fruitful in his own time, has proved beneficial to the Nephite and Lamanite posterity of today in the form of his short but vital message in the Book of Mormon. This "cry from the dust" witnesses of the divinity of Jesus Christ to us today. The book of Enos gives us important "instructions in righteousness" which, if we follow, will bring us nearer to God. His remarkable conversion, his ministry, his life of diligent service, and his proving himself faithful in all things after being "born of the spirit," all earned Enos the confidence he expressed just prior to writing his last amen:

> And I soon go to the place of my rest, which is with my Redeemer; for I know that in him I shall rest. And I rejoice in the day when my mortal shall put on immortality, and shall stand before him; then shall I see his face *with pleasure*, and he will say unto me: Come unto me, ye blessed, there is a place prepared for you in the mansions of my Father. Amen (Enos 1:27; emphasis added).

BIBLIOGRAPHY

Benson, Ezra Taft. *A Witness and a Warning*. Salt Lake City: Deseret Book, 1988.

Kimball, Spencer W. *The Teachings of Spencer W. Kimball*. Salt Lake City: Bookcraft, 1982.

———. *Faith Precedes the Miracle*. Salt Lake City: Deseret Book, 1972.

Romney, Marion G. "How to Gain a Testimony." *Brigham Young University Speeches of the Year*. Provo, UT: Brigham Young Univ, 1952-53. 323-30.

———. ". . . Ye Are a Peculiar People." *Brigham Young University Speeches of the Year*. Provo, UT: Brigham Young Univ, 1955-56. 257-64.

The Testimony of Christ Through the Ages 9

Joseph Fielding McConkie

*I*f all that Joseph Smith had been allowed to translate from the gold plates was what we know as Jacob chapter 4—that is, if the Book of Mormon consisted only of that single chapter—that chapter alone would be sufficient to justify the mission and ministry of Joseph Smith. Jacob 4 speaks of a universal apostasy, identifies the heart of doctrinal corruption, and bears a perfect testimony of Jesus Christ. It also includes the following significant doctrinal pronouncements:

1. The announcement that the doctrine of redemption through Christ reaches back to the days of Adam, and that all true prophets knew and testified of the Savior. (This announcement defies the theological traditions of both the Christian and Jewish worlds.)

2. The announcement that not only did all the holy prophets teach and testify that Christ is the begotten Son of God, but they also worshiped the Father in his name. (Again this denies both Jewish and Christian traditions. It also plays havoc with the doctrine of the trinity.)

3. The announcement that the law of Moses was a symbolic representation and testimony of Christ, just as was Abraham's offering of Isaac. (By so teaching Jacob establishes the fact that an apostasy had taken place among the Jews.)

Joseph Fielding McConkie is professor of Ancient Scripture at Brigham Young University.

4. A warning to religious zealots and theologians to not look beyond the mark, and thereby repeat the error of the Jews.

5. The assurance of a future day when the Jews will be brought back to the sure foundation of that Christ known to their fathers.

Let us briefly consider the biblical and other scriptural support, as well as the theological implications, of each of these pronouncements.

The Testimony of Christ:
The Central Issue in All Gospel Dispensations

The central issue of all gospel dispensations has been the divine sonship of Christ. In a real sense, the very first dispensation took place in the councils of heaven when God taught the gospel to all his spirit children even before the foundations of the earth were laid. The great issue of our pre-earth estate was the choice of our eldest brother to be the Only Begotten of the Father in the flesh. As every Latter-day Saint knows, Lucifer, a son of the morning, sought that honor for himself. When the Father chose the Firstborn, Lucifer rebelled and there was war in heaven. A third part of the hosts of heaven followed the Rebellious One and were cast out. Though the place of battle has now shifted from the heavens to the earth, the war with its central issue remains the same.

"Ye heard before the word of the truth of the gospel, which is come unto you," Paul said in his epistle to the Colossians Saints (Col 1:4-6). That is to say, your faith which centers in Christ was first made known to you in heavenly places. The Joseph Smith Translation adds the phrase, "as in all generations of the world," indicating that what is true of the Colossians is true of the Saints of all gospel dispensations.

The revelation on the degrees of glory (D&C 76) is a primary source for that knowledge in our dispensation. In that revelation, Joseph Smith and Sidney Rigdon were shown "those things which were from the beginning before the world was, which were ordained of the Father, through his Only Begotten Son" (D&C 76:12-14). In another revelation the Savior reaffirmed this doctrine by asking Joseph Smith: "Will I appoint unto you . . . except it be by law, even as I and my Father ordained unto you, before the world was?" (D&C 132:11).

From the book of Moses we learn that an angel of the Lord instructed father Adam on the role of Christ as the divine son, saying: "Thou shalt do all that thou doest in the name of the Son, and thou shalt repent and call upon God in the name of the Son forevermore. And in that day the Holy Ghost fell upon Adam, which beareth record of the Father and the Son, saying: I am the Only Begotten of the Father from the beginning, henceforth and forever, that as thou hast fallen thou mayest be redeemed, and all mankind, even as many as will" (Moses 5:8-9).

The fulness of the gospel was also taught to Adam's children though many would not listen. The scriptures tell us

> they would not "hearken unto [God's] voice, nor believe on his Only Begotten Son, even him whom he declared should come in the meridian of time, who was prepared from before the foundation of the world. And thus the Gospel began to be preached, from the beginning, being declared by holy angels sent forth from the presence of God, and by his own voice, and by the gift of the Holy Ghost. And thus all things were confirmed unto Adam, by an holy ordinance, and the Gospel preached, and a decree sent forth, that it should be in the world, until the end thereof; and thus it was. Amen (Moses 5:57-59).

Enoch also understood the doctrine of divine sonship. The Lord commanded Enoch that he "should baptize in the name of the Father, and of the Son, which is full of grace and truth, and of the Holy Ghost, which beareth record of the Father and the Son" (Moses 7:11). In response to Enoch's question, "When shall the blood of the Righteous be shed, that all they that mourn may be sanctified and have eternal life?" The Lord said, "It shall be in the meridian of time, in the days of wickedness and vengeance." Enoch was permitted to see "the day of the coming of the Son of Man, even in the flesh; and his soul rejoiced, saying: The Righteous is lifted up, and the Lamb is slain from the foundation of the world; and through faith I am in the bosom of the Father, and behold, Zion is with me" (Moses 7:45-47).

Noah also went forth teaching repentance and baptism "in the name of Jesus Christ, the Son of God," even as his fathers had done (Moses 8:24). "And the Lord ordained Noah after his own order, and commanded him that he should go forth and declare his Gospel unto the children of men, even as it was given unto Enoch" (Moses 8:19).

Of Abraham we are told that the Lord appeared to him and called him "to bear his name in a strange land," a land which would be granted to him and his seed after him as an everlasting possession if they would hearken to the Lord's voice. Indeed, Abraham's seed were to bear the priesthood and carry the gospel of Christ to all other peoples (see Abr 2:6-11).

> And Abram said, Lord God, how wilt thou give me this land for an everlasting inheritance? And the Lord said, Though thou wast dead, yet am I not able to give it thee? And if thou shalt die, yet thou shalt possess it, for the day cometh, that the Son of Man shall live; but how can he live if he be not dead? He must first be quickened. And it came to pass, that Abram looked forth and saw the days of the Son of Man, and was glad, and his soul found rest, and he believed in the Lord; and the Lord counted it unto him for righteousness (JST Gen 15:9-12).

The first chapter of the book of Moses identifies the doctrine of divine sonship as the central issue in Moses' day also. It will be recalled that when the Prince of Darkness came to Moses declaring, "I am the Only Begotten, worship me," it was "in the name of the Only Begotten" that Moses commanded him to depart (Moses 1:12-23).

The doctrine of divine sonship was introduced in the meridian dispensation with Gabriel's testimony to Mary that she would bear "the Son of the Highest," and that the Lord God would give "unto him the throne of his father David" (Luke 1:32). Thus Christ declared himself to be "the Son of God" (John 10:36), and the Father himself testified saying, "This is my beloved Son, in whom I am well pleased" (Matt 3:17).

We find the following dialogue in the Joseph Smith Translation: "And [the Pharisees] said unto him, We have the law, and the prophets; but as for this man we will not receive him to be our ruler; for he maketh himself to be a judge over us. Then said Jesus unto them, The law and the prophets testify of me; yea, and all the prophets who have written, even until John, have foretold of these days" (JST Luke 16:16-17). Again in the book of John we read of Christ saying, "I am the door of the sheep. All that ever came before me are thieves and robbers: but the sheep did not hear them" (10:7-8). The Joseph Smith Translation corrects the text to read, "All that ever came before me *who testified not of me* are thieves and robbers" (JST John 10:8; emphasis added). In harmony with this teaching, Peter declared that all the holy prophets since the world began had promised that the Messiah would rule and reign during the glorious day of refreshing we call the Millennium (Acts 3:21).

Now, if we accept Peter's testimony of Christ and his statement that there is "none other name under heaven given among men . . . whereby" salvation can be obtained (Acts 4:12), we are locked into the conclusion that reliable references to someone's having the gospel can only be interpreted as their having the gospel of Jesus Christ. To suppose that there was an Old Testament gospel and a New Testament gospel, that is, a brutish low-level gospel that was supplanted by a refined high-brow gospel, is to suggest that the atonement of Christ is not infinite or eternal, or for that matter, even necessary if one prefers the old way. Joseph Smith reasoned thus:

> It will be noticed that, according to Paul, (see Gal. iii:8) the Gospel was preached to Abraham. We would like to be informed in what name the Gospel was then preached, whether it was in the name of Christ or some other name. If in any other name, was it the Gospel? And if it was the Gospel, and that preached in the name of Christ, had it any ordinances? If not, was it the Gospel? And if it had ordinances what were they? Our friends [in the sectarian world] may say, perhaps, that there were never any ordinances except those of offering sacrifices before the coming of Christ, and that it could not be possible before the Gospel to have been administered while the law of sacrifices of blood was in force. But we will recollect that Abraham offered sacrifice, and not-withstanding this, had the Gospel preached to him. That the offering of sacirfice was only to point the mind forward to Christ, we infer from these remarkable words of Jesus to the Jews: "Your Father Abraham

rejoiced to see my day: and he saw it, and was glad" (John viii:56). So, then, because the ancients offered sacrifice it did not hinder their hearing the Gospel; but served, as we said before, to open their eyes, and enable them to look forward to the time of the coming of the Savior, and rejoice in His redemption. We find also, that when the Israelites came out of Egypt they had the Gospel preached to them, according to Paul in his letter to the Hebrews, which says: "For unto us was the Gospel preached, as well as unto them: but the word preached did not profit them, not being mixed with faith in them that heard it" (see Heb. iv:2). It is said again, in Gal. iii:19, that the law (of Moses, or the Levitical law) was "added" because of transgression. What, we ask, was this law added to, if it was not added to the Gospel? It must be plain that it was added to the Gospel, since we learn that they had the Gospel preached to them. From these few facts, we conclude that whenever the Lord revealed Himself to men in ancient days, and commanded them to offer sacrifice to Him, that it was done that they might look forward in faith to the time of His coming, and rely upon the power of that atonement for a remission of their sins (*Teachings of the Prophet Joseph Smith* 60-61; hereafter *TPJS*).

On this matter the Book of Mormon prophets are quite plain and none plainer than Jacob, who said: "For this intent have we written these things, that they may know that we knew of Christ, and we had a hope of his glory many hundred years before his coming; and not only we ourselves had a hope of his glory, but also all the holy prophets which were before us. Behold, they believed in Christ and worshiped the Father in his name, and also we worship the Father in his name" (Jacob 4:4-5). Be it remembered that when Alma compared faith to a seed the seed he was referring to was the doctrine of divine sonship. "Begin to believe in the Son of God," he said, "that he will come to redeem his people, and that he shall suffer and die to atone for their sins; and that he shall rise again from the dead, which shall bring to pass the resurrection, that all men shall stand before him, to be judged at the last and judgment day, according to their works" (Alma 33:22). This was the word or seed which he challenged the Zoramites to plant in their hearts, promising them that if they would plant and properly nourish that seed, it would become a tree, springing up in them unto everlasting life (Alma 33:1, 22-23).

In like manner, Abinadi testified to the corrupt court of king Noah saying:

> For behold, did not Moses prophesy unto them concerning the coming of the Messiah, and that God should redeem his people? Yea, and even all the prophets who have prophesied ever since the world began—have they not spoken more or less concerning these things? Have they not said that God himself should come down among the children of men, and take upon him the form of man, and go forth in mighty power upon the face of the earth? Yea, and have they not said also that he should bring to pass the resurrection of the dead, and that he, himself, should be oppressed and afflicted? (Mosiah 13:33-35).

The foundation of every dispensation of the gospel is the testimony that salvation or redemption comes only in and through the Son of God. If Jesus of Nazareth is God's Son, if he in fact worked out an atoning sacrifice, if he, through that atonement, broke the bands of death and made resurrection possible, then salvation is in him. If salvation is in him, it can be in none other; and if salvation can be in none other, then all true religion and all true scripture will harmoniously testify of him. So it must be from the days of Adam:

> Yea, and Enoch also, and they who were with him; the prophets who were before him; and Noah also, and they who were before him; and Moses also, and they who were before him; And from Moses to Elijah, and from Elijah to John, who were with Christ in his resurrection, and the holy apostles, with Abraham, Isaac, and Jacob, shall be in the presence of the Lamb. And the graves of the saints shall be opened; and they shall come forth and stand on the right hand of the Lamb, when he shall stand upon Mount Zion, and upon the holy city, the New Jerusalem; and they shall sing the song of the Lamb, day and night forever and ever (D&C 133:54-56).

God Can Only Be Worshiped in the Name of His Son

It is not necessary at this point to cite scriptural texts to support the idea that the Father can only be worshiped in the name of the Son. We have already quoted the testimony of God, angels, and prophets to that effect. The system ordained by the Father, the system by which salvation comes, is one in which we worship in the name of another—a holy name, a name above all other names—that of Jesus the Christ, who is the Son of the living God.

How is it, we ought to ask, that salvation is vested in a name? We are reminded that Jesus of Nazareth repeatedly emphasized that he had no power, authority or doctrines in and of himself. In the Gospel of John we have well over a hundred statements in which Christ attests that he is sent to do the will of the Father and that he does all that he does in the name and by the authority of the Father. His purpose was to glorify the name of the Father in all that he did. Thus the Son received the name and power of his Father, and through that name and by that power extended the promise of salvation to all who would take upon themselves his name as he had taken upon himself the name of his Father. Such is the system of salvation.

The idea that blessings come through a name finds expression in one of society's oldest traditions. It has been the custom of fathers in all ages, and we suppose among virtually all peoples, to place their name upon their posterity. As the crown of womanhood is in granting life, so the crown of manhood is the conferring upon one's posterity the family name. Often ceremony and ritual are associated with a father placing his name, his most prized possession, upon the newborn. In the giving of a name the father declares the child to be his; he makes of him or her a rightful heir of all that he possesses, and effectually promises to love and protect his progeny, for the child is but the manifestation of his own flesh and blood. The children in return are taught to love and respect their parents, and to so live as to bring honor to the name that has been given them as a sacred trust. The rebellious child can be disinherited and thus be caused to forfeit all blessings associated with bearing the family name.

Such traditions appear to reach back to man's most ancient roots. Adam was first created, then Eve was given as a help meet for him, and God "blessed them, and called their name Adam" (Moses 6:9). Thus Eve took upon herself the name of him from whom she is represented in a figurative sense as having received life, and they twain became one flesh. This perfect union that was to exist between them, represented by Eve's being created from the rib of Adam, is cited as the reason that a man was to leave his father and his mother and cleave unto his wife that they too might become one flesh or one name (see Genesis 2:23-24).

The giving of a name to something implies dominion, rule, or stewardship over that being named. Thus Adam, who had been commanded to subdue the earth and have dominion over all life forms upon it, was directed of the Lord to give all things a name (see Genesis 1:28; 2:19-20.) Again, we find that after the creation of the woman it was Adam who at God's behest gave her the name Eve (see Genesis 3:20; Moses 4:26). She would bear his name, and he would rule over her (see Genesis 3:16); that is, he would protect and provide for her, and he would be her king, while she would be his queen (*In His Holy Name* 7-8).

Such is the order and pattern of heaven. God, the Eternal Father, placed his name upon Jesus of Nazareth, his Only Begotten in the flesh, and by so doing testified that the Galilean was his own Son, and that the love and protection of heaven would be with him. Christ, a rightful heir to the dominion, power, and glory of his Father, was entrusted to act in the divine name. In turn, the Savior invited all his earthly brothers and sisters to return to that heavenly family of which they were once a part, to take again the family name, and become heirs to the blessings associated with it.

Thus, we are saved by taking upon us the name of Christ as he was saved by taking upon himself the name of his Father. The idea of taking upon ourselves the name of another is a perfect teaching device. It dramatizes the absolute necessity of our becoming one with that person or assuming in all things his nature and character. This is the nature of true worship. We can worship by doing those things that the Son did, that is by doing those things that make us one with him and that made him one with the Father. To worship in that way is to think as Christ thought, to believe as he believed, to act as he acted, and to experience as he experienced. True worship requires the heart, the might, the mind, and the soul. It is the system by which we become like the Father and the Son. It is both meditative and active, it combines both belief and works, and it cannot be deviod of either.

An Apostasy Among the Jews

From the Pearl of Great Price we know that the covenant God made with Abraham centered in the obligation of his seed to be special witnesses of Christ among all the peoples of the earth as he had been a special witness of Christ in Paddan-aram,

Palestine, and among the Egyptians (see Abr 3:15). The seed of Abraham were to bear *"the Holy Priesthood, after the Order of the Son of God"* (D&C 107:3), which Abraham had received at the hands of Melchizedek (see D&C 84:14), and by that authority they were to declare the gospel of salvation among all who were willing to hear it. The fourth chapter of Jacob affirms that the Abrahamic sacrifice was "a similitude of God and his Only Begotten Son" (Jacob 4:5). We would have a hard time supposing that Abraham did not understand this after he had been instructed by the angel of the Lord who stayed his hand from slaying his "only son" and who renewed with him the terms of that covenant which required his seed to be ministers of Christ among all men (see Gen 22:16-18). Indeed, there were many even "before the days of Abraham who were called by the order of God; yea, even after the order of his Son" (Hel 8:18), for so the priesthood had been known from the beginning (JST Gen 14:28; D&C 107:1-4).

Jacob tells us that the Nephites, a transplanted branch of the house of Israel, worshiped the Father in the name of the Son and that it was for this reason that they kept the law of Moses which pointed their "whole souls" (see Omni 1:26; Mosiah 2:21) to Christ. Further, because they kept the law for that purpose, he said, "It is sanctified unto us for righteousness" (Jacob 4:5). Now, what better evidence could we have of an apostasy among the Jews than their profession of a covenant they did not keep or their strained observance of a law they no longer understood? Their system of worship was like a grave, an ornate sepulchre without the hope of resurrection.

Theirs was no longer a personal God. The idea that they were created in the image and likeness of God was dispelled as symbolic or allegorical, or anything else as long as it was not literally so. This, of course, had a domino effect. Such doctrinal concepts as God as King, Judge, Husband, Father, and Master were each in their turn neatly labled as methaphors. The Septuagint reflects textual alterations directed at purging Holy Writ of the idea that God and man are of the same race. Rather than stating that the Lord met Moses as recorded in Exodus 4:24, he meets a divine messenger; rather than allowing the seventy elders of Israel to see God in Exodus 24:10-11, they see the place where God had been; rather than putting forth His "hand" in Joshua 4:24, he manifests his "power"; wherein the Psalmist said he would see the face of the Lord, referring to the resurrection, and then "[will] awake, with thy likeness," it was made to read, "I shall be satisfied when thy glory appears" (Ps 17:15), and so forth (Farrar 120; see also fn 2). "Later Hellenists go further by allegorizing the OT, finding abstract content in anthropomorphisms, and substituting philosophical concepts. . . . The rabbis avoid allegorizing but explain anthropomorphism as divine accommodation to human frailty" (Bromiley 329).

Thus both the Greeks and the Jews eliminated the idea that man was in the image and likeness of God as well as the idea that God could beget a child in the flesh. From the Book of Mormon, however, it is obvious that there has been a wholesale discarding of scriptural texts. We are not talking here about the altering of individual texts, nor the art of theological seduction more generally known as allegorizing, we are talking about the disappearance of some of the greatest scriptural works ever written —books written by the likes of Adam, Enoch, and Joseph of Egypt (2 Nephi 4:2); and the writings of Zenos and Zenock, both of whom were quoted by Alma to sustain the doctrine of God's Son as the source of our redemption (Alma 33:13-15).

Looking Beyond the Mark

The grand question is how such plain and precious truths as the personal nature of God and the sonship of Christ get perverted and lost. It is the prophet Jacob in the Book of Mormon who answers this question:

> The Jews were a stiffnecked people [he wrote]; and they despised the words of plainness, and killed the prophets, and sought for things that they could not understand. Wherefore, because of their blindness, which blindness came by looking beyond the mark, they must needs

fall; for God hath taken away his plainness from them, and delivered unto them many things which they cannot understand, because they desired it. And because they desired it God hath done it, that they may stumble (Jacob 4:14).

There are two equally effective ways to pervert the word of truth—add to it or take from it:

This is my doctrine [the Savior told the Nephites], and it is the doctrine which the Father hath given unto me; and I bear record of the Father, and the Father beareth record of me, and the Holy Ghost beareth record of the Father and me; and I bear record that the Father commandeth all men, everywhere, to repent and believe in me. . . . And whoso shall declare more or less than this, and establish it for my doctrine, the same cometh of evil, and is not built upon my rock; but he buildeth upon a sandy foundation, and the gates of hell stand open to receive such when the floods come and the winds beat upon them (3 Nephi 11:32, 40).

The Jews both added to and took from the law that had been given them. "My people do not know the ordinances of the Lord," said Lehi's contemporary, Jeremiah. "How can you say, 'We are wise, we have the law of the Lord,' when scribes with their lying pens have falsified it?" (New English Bible, Jer 8:8). The words of Christ sustain Jeremiah's allegation: "Woe unto you, lawyers! for ye have taken away the key of knowledge, the fulness of the scriptures; ye enter not in yourselves into the kingdom; and those who were entering in, ye hindered" (JST Luke 11:53). When he inquired about the reliability of the Apocrypha, Joseph Smith was told that "there are many things contained therein that are not true, which are interpolations by the hands of men" (D&C 91:2). The 1828 *Webster's Dictionary* defines *interpolation* as, "The act of foisting a word or passage into a manuscript or book," or, "a spurious word or passage inserted in the genuine writings of an author."

What we have here is the perfect pattern of apostasy—both taking from and adding to the law of the Lord. The emphasis of Jacob's text is that of looking beyond the mark, of going too far, of being "truer than true," of adding tradition upon tradition, rabbinical ruling upon ruling, and all of this obstensibly to protect the law. The Jewish scholars decked it and bedecked it; they jeweled and bejeweled it; they garnished and trimmed and shaped and reshaped; they preened, bordered, and embroidered; they adorned and ornamented until the law was unrecognizable, and then they worshiped the creation of their own making and forgot the God of their fathers who was the giver of the law. Fanaticism is addictive, and when we become fanatic in one area it is a short step to fanaticism in another. President David O. McKay suggested there were three kinds of sin—sins of commission, sins of omission, and virtues that were overdone. Any virtue overdone, he said, becomes a vice. In their excessive zeal the Jews made of the law a master rather than a servant. It was this obsession with the Holy Day that caused Christ to say, "The sabbath was made for man, and not man for the sabbath" (Mark 2:27).

We come back to the fact that the gospel is everlastingly the same and that the first great dispensation of the gospel took place long before the foundations of this earth were laid. The principles by which we are saved were taught to us and known by us long before we commenced our journey in this mortal probation, and they are not to be added to nor taken from. "Will I accept of an offering, saith the Lord, that is not made in my name? Or will I receive at your hands that which I have not appointed? And will I appoint unto you, saith the Lord, except it be by law, even as I and my Father ordained unto you, before the world was?" (D&C 132:9-11).

Jacob's warning about going beyond the mark strikes at the issue of theological and scriptural scholarship. It is an appropriate warning for what we vainly call "higher education." The glory of the Book of Mormon is in its simplicity. It is important that we not convey the idea that real understanding of the book rests only with scholars. The best of the world's scholarship, as it has been directed toward the Bible, has not resulted in an increase of faith in that holy book. In fact, one of the primary reasons the Lord gave us the Book of Mormon was to restore faith in the Bible, which has been under scholarly seige for many years (see D&C 20:8-11). It is not without significance that in the revelation given as a preface to the Doctrine and

Covenants the Lord warns us against trusting "in the arm of flesh" (1:19).

How then do we distinguish between genuine gospel scholarship, which is seriously needed in the Church today, and the pedantic intellectual games played by those who have gone far beyond the mark or fallen quite short of it? Perhaps we simply need to ask, "Where does this lead us?" "What is its purpose?" For instance, do the compilations of quotations from selected brethren, which are used to build fortresses to protect otherwise vulnerable theories, represent an honest search for truth? Are our files of quotations used to hide mental atrophy? Does the fact that so and so said it stop all thinking or searching? And what of our preoccupation with internal and external evidences? Is it possible to develop an expertise in scriptural geography and yet be unable to find the straight and narrow path? Are there those of us who know the stories of the Book of Mormon, but not its doctrines?

The Jews Will Return to Their Ancient Faith in Christ

In Jacob's preface to Zenos' allegory of the tame and wild olive trees, Jacob prophesies of a future day when the Jews will return to Christ and recognize him as the only "sure foundation" upon which they can build (Jacob 4:15-17). The doctrine of the gathering is not well understood among Latter-day Saints, even though the Book of Mormon repeatedly teaches it with plainness. It is supposed by many that the establishment of the modern state of Israel in 1948, together with the return of tens of thousands of Jews to their ancient covenant land, fulfills the prophecies relative to their gathering. It does not.

If we are to properly understand the doctrine of the restoration, we must have some idea of what once was, and why it is desirable that the ancient order be reinstated. Similarly, to understand the doctrine of the gathering, we must have some idea of what caused the scattering. As we have seen, the story begins with father Abraham who was sent as an apostle, or special witness of Christ, into the land of Palestine. He was promised that if he was true to his office and calling that that ancient land would be given to him and his posterity as an everlasting possession. The Lord also covenanted with Abraham that his seed would be called to hold the Holy Priesthood after the Order of the Son of God, and go into strange lands as special witnesses of his name. Thus the children of Israel became a covenant people. The fact that they were to be a covenant people, and that such covenants are made on a personal rather than a national basis, required a place of covenant. That place of covenant is, of course, the temple, or house of the Lord. Thus Israel was gathered that they might build and maintain a house for the Lord, one in which he might endow them with the knowledge and power necessary to represent him. Through all generations of time the Lord's people have been both a covenant people and a temple building people, and they have gathered together for that purpose. As long as they were true to the covenants they had made, the protecting hand of the Lord was over them. When they chose to break their covenants, to rebel, to live unworthy of his presence, then they were as over ripe fruit falling from the tree of life. If they did not repent, their land of promise—which was merely a physical symbol of their covenant, a reminder of the everlasting inheritance that would yet be theirs—would be taken from them and they would be scattered (see 2 Nephi 25:10-18).

Gathering is the child of righteousness, and scattering the heir of wickedness. The gathering described in the Book of Mormon is of two parts: first, a spiritual gathering, or a return to Christ and a covenant relationship with him; and second, a return to the promised lands which symbolize the covenant that the Jews had made. Thus we find Jacob saying that God had covenanted with "all the house of Israel—that he has spoken unto the Jews, by the mouth of his holy prophets, even from the beginning down, from generation to generation, until the time comes that they shall be restored to the true church and fold of God; when they shall be gathered home to the lands of their inheritance, and shall be established in all their lands of promise" (2 Nephi 9:1-2). Again we read:

> And as surely as the Lord liveth, will he gather in from the four quarters of the earth all the remnant of the seed of Jacob, who are scattered abroad upon all the face of the earth. And as he hath covenanted with all the house of Jacob, even so shall the covenant wherewith he hath covenanted with the house of Jacob be fulfilled in his own due time, unto the restoring all the house of Jacob unto the knowledge of the covenant that he hath covenanted with them. And then shall they know their Redeemer, who is Jesus Christ, the Son of God; and then shall they be gathered in from the four quarters of the earth unto their own lands, from whence they have been dispersed; yea, as the Lord liveth so shall it be. Amen (3 Nephi 5:24-26).

Conclusions

1. The central doctrine of the Book of Mormon is the testimony of Christ. That testimony centers in the verity that he is literally the Son of God.

2. Given that the Book of Mormon is the book ordained in the councils of heaven to gather Israel, and given that the gathering is first spiritual and only then temporal, the single greatest doctrine of the apostasy, the very doctrine that the Book of Mormon comes in response to, is that of Christ's divine sonship, for it is the doctrine upon which all other true doctrine rests. Joseph Smith declared the Atonement to be the most fundamental doctrine of our faith. All other doctrines, he maintained, were but appendages to it (*TPJS* 121). Yet, it is the doctrine of divine sonship that gives birth to the doctrine of atonement. If Christ had not been the son of a mortal woman from whom he inherited blood or mortality, and could thus lay down his life, and the son of an immortal Father from whom he inherited immortality, that he could take it up again, he could not have laid down his life and taken it up again (see John 10:17-18). It is the doctrine of divine sonship that gives birth to the doctrine of resurrection as the inseparable union of body and spirit. In like manner, it is the doctrine of divine sonship that assures us that God is a

personal being, that he is literally the father of our spirits. In turn, the knowledge that God is a personal being also gives us the hope that we can become as he is. We have no doctrines that do not trace themselves to the Book of Mormon and its testimony of Christ as the Son of God.

3. The doctrine of the divine sonship, coupled with the commandment that we are to worship the Father in the name of the Son, constitutes the sure foundation upon which salvation rests. That salvation only comes in the name of Christ is and was central to the testimony of all the holy prophets since the world began. It is the foundation of all gospel dispensations and was the central issue in the war in heaven.

4. The doctrines of the divine sonship and the personal nature of God are the chief illustrations that plain and precious things have been taken from the Old and New Testament records, and that the so-called Bible-believing world is in darkness as to the plan of salvation, and will remain so until it has received and believed the testimony of the Book of Mormon.

BIBLIOGRAPHY

Bromiley, Geoffrey W. *Theological Dictionary of the New Testament.* One volume edition. n.p.: Eerdman's, 1985.

Farrar, Frederic W. *History of Interpretation.* Grand Rapids, MI: Baker, 1961.

Millet, Robert L. and Joseph Fielding McConkie. *In His Holy Name.* Salt Lake City: Bookcraft, 1988.

Teachings of the Prophet Joseph Smith. Comp. Joseph Fielding Smith. Salt Lake City: Deseret Book, 1976.

Webster's 1828 American Dictionary. Facsimile. San Francisco: Foundation for American Christian Education, 1967.

Sherem the Anti-Christ **10**

Robert L. Millet

P resident Ezra Taft Benson has instructed that "the Book of Mormon brings men to Christ through two basic means":

> First, it tells in a plain manner of Christ and His gospel. It testifies of His divinity and of the necessity for a Redeemer and the need of our putting trust in Him. It bears witness of the Fall and the Atonement and the first principles of the gospel, including our need of a broken heart and a contrite spirit and a spiritual rebirth. It proclaims we must endure to the end in righteousness and live the moral life of a Saint.
>
> Second, *the Book of Mormon exposes the enemies of Christ.* It confounds false doctrines and lays down contention. (See 2 Nephi 3:12.) It fortifies the humble followers of Christ against the evil designs, strategies, and doctrines of the devil in our day. *The type of apostates in the Book of Mormon is similar to the type we have today.* God, with his infinite foreknowledge, so molded the Book of Mormon that we might see the error and know how to combat false educational, political, religious, and philosophical concepts of our time (3; emphasis added).

Jacob ends a lengthy recitation of and a brief commentary on the allegory of Zenos by pleading with his readers to receive and pay heed to the words of the prophets and traverse carefully that gospel path which is strait and narrow. "Finally," he concludes, "I bid you farewell, until I shall meet you before the pleasing bar of God, which bar striketh the wicked with awful dread and fear" (Jacob 6:13). This would appear to be a farewell statement, an indication to the reader that Jacob had initially planned to close his record at that point. Subsequently, however,

Robert L. Millet is associate professor and department chairman of Ancient Scripture at Brigham Young University.

he had an experience worthy of inclusion in a record which would come forth to a cynical and highly secular world—his encounter with Sherem the anti-Christ.

Portrait of an Anti-Christ

There are certain characteristics of an anti-Christ, certain patterns of belief and practice which we might expect to find among those, like Sherem, who are bent upon overthrowing the doctrine of Christ. Some of these are as follows:

They Deny the Need for Jesus Christ

The first and perhaps the most obvious characterization of an anti-Christ is that he or she denies the reality of or necessity for Jesus Christ. The anti-Christ has partaken of that spirit of rebellion which resulted in the expulsion of a third part of all the children of the Eternal Father in the premortal world. Prior to the meridian of time, the anti-Christ contended that there would be no Christ and that no man had the ability to speak authoritatively concerning future things.

Of Sherem, the Nephite record states that "he began to preach among the people, and to declare unto them that there should be no Christ. . . . that he might overthrow the doctrine of Christ" (Jacob 7:2). The doctrine of Christ is the gospel, the glad tidings that deliverance from death and hell and endless torment is available through the atoning work of Jesus Christ the Lord (see Jacob 7:6; 2 Nephi 31; 3 Nephi 27:13-22; D&C 76:40-42). Frequently, as we shall see, the message of the anti-Christ is a denial of man's fallen condition and thus of his need for anyone or anything to liberate him from the mire of mortality.

They Use Flattery to Win Disciples

"And [Sherem] preached many things which were flattering unto the people" (Jacob 7:2). To flatter is to soothe or satisfy, to make people feel comfortable. It is to whisper in their ears that all is well. To flatter is also to raise false hopes of an anticipated reward or acquisition (*Webster's*). Nehor, a different type of anti-Christ, thus taught that "all mankind should be saved at the last day . . . for the Lord had created all men, and had also redeemed all men; and, in the end, all men should have eternal life" (Alma 1:4).

Characteristically, anti-Christs are worldly-wise; they are properly trained for their persuasive ministry. Sherem was "learned, that he had a perfect knowledge of the language of the people; wherefore, he could use much flattery, and much power of speech, according to the power of the devil" (Jacob 7:4). Anti-Christs are usually glib of tongue and nimble of speech. They are sinister students of human behavior, knowing how to persuade and to dissuade; how to attract attention and create a following; and how to make their listeners feel secure and at ease in their carnality. An anti-Christ is ostensibly refined, schooled in rhetoric, and polished in homiletics. He is a peerless preacher of perversion. In Faustian fashion the anti-Christ has sold his soul to the devil: his power is not his own; he is but the pawn of him who in the end does not support his own (see Alma 30:60).

They Accuse the Brethren of Teaching False Doctrine

The devil and his disciples are neither shy nor hesitant about accomplishing their purposes. Some among the legions of Beelzebub are subtle and cunning; others are direct, assertive, and aggressive. Sherem goes directly to the prophet of the Lord—to Jacob—to gain a hearing in an effort to gain a convert. Satan would always rather capture a spiritual general than one of lesser rank. And be it remembered that the Lord himself was not immune from personal confrontation with the evil one (see Matt 4), and that Christ in turn said to Peter, the chief apostle, "Simon, Simon, behold, Satan hath desired to have you, that he may sift you as wheat" (Luke 22:31). And thus it is that Sherem "sought much opportunity" (Jacob 7:6) to engage Jacob the prophet.

Sherem accused Jacob of perverting the gospel and of uttering false prophecies concerning the coming of Jesus Christ (Jacob 7:7). Surely some Nephites who were in tune with the Spirit must have discerned in Sherem the spirit of one who "accused" the brethren (Rev 12:10), who was guilty of evil speaking of the Lord's anointed. "That man who rises up to condemn others," Joseph Smith taught, "finding fault with the Church, saying that they are out of the way, while he himself is righteous, then know assuredly, that that man is in the high road to apostasy; and if he does not repent, will apostatize, as God lives" (*Teachings of the Prophet Joseph Smith* 156-57; see also 193; hereafter *TPJS*). Sherem was on a course which would take him cross-lots to hell—by the most direct route.

They Have a Limited View of Reality

When a person refuses to exercise faith—to have a hope in that which is unseen but true (Alma 32:21)—he thereby denies himself access to the spiritual world, another realm of reality. His vision of things is at best deficient and at worst perverse; he does not see things "as they really are" (see Jacob 4:13; D&C 93:24). He is a scientist with insufficient data; his methodology is limited by his approach and his conclusions must surely be suspect.

Sherem's naturalistic view of reality precluded his appreciation of the unseen and his desire to apprehend the unknown. Those who rely exclusively upon human sensory experience and human reason to come to the truth cannot find a place in their tightly-enclosed epistemological system for such matters as spirit and revelation and prophecy. In responding to Jacob's testimony that Christ shall come as the fulfillment of the law, Sherem said: "This is blasphemy; for *no man knoweth* of such things; for *he cannot tell of things to come*." Further, "If there should be a Christ, I would not deny him; but *I know that there is no Christ*, neither has been, nor ever will be" (Jacob 7:7, 9; emphasis added). If we were to paraphrase Sherem's argument, it might be stated as follows: "If there should be a Christ—here and now, one that I could see and feel and hear, one which requires no faith or hope—then I would not deny him; I would believe." This, of course, is not true. The unbelievers and the faithless have hardened their hearts to the point that most of the time they deny or rationalize even tangible evidence (see 1 Nephi 16:38; Hel 16:21). It is usually the case that proof is the last thing that those demanding it really want. The louder the shouts for evidence, the less the inclination to accept it.

The doubter—the one whose faith centers in that which may be seen and heard and felt through natural means only—errs grossly through generalizing beyond his own experiences. What he has not experienced, he assumes no one else can. Because he does not know, no one knows (compare Alma 30:48); because he is past feeling, surely no one else has felt; because he lacks internal evidence concerning the coming of a Messiah, unquestionably the evidence amassed by every believing soul is either insufficient or naively misinterpreted. Those who dare not believe dare not allow others to believe.

They Have a Disposition to Misread and Thereby Misrepresent the Scriptures

Those whose motives are less than pure are not entitled to that which the scriptures call "pure knowledge" (D&C 121:42), knowledge from a pure source. They are unable to comprehend the scriptures in their true light, to perceive and then incorporate the purity of their messages into their own impure lives. Such persons are frequently guilty of *wresting* the scriptures, of distorting their true meanings and thus doing violence to that which was intended by the inspired writers. "Behold, the scriptures are before you," Alma said to the spiritually unstable people of Ammonihah; "if ye will wrest them it shall be to your own destruction" (Alma 13:20; compare 2 Peter 3:16). Those who wrest the scriptures do not understand them (see D&C 10:63); they have little sacred structure for their lives and wander far astray from that gospel path which must be traversed with care and caution (see Alma 41:1).

Sherem professes to know and to believe in the scriptures, but, lacking that elevated perspective and learning which comes not only by study but also by faith, he is unable to discern the undergirding message of the scriptures (Jacob 7:10-11)—that all things bear witness of the Holy One of Israel, that all things which have been "given of God from the beginning of the world, unto man, are the typifying of him" (2 Nephi 11:4; see also Moses 6:63). Devoid of that divine influence which constitutes the spirit of prophecy and revelation, Sherem cannot possess the testimony of Jesus (see Rev 19:10).

Those who have become more than distant acquaintances with the words of scripture begin to see things as God sees them: they gain "the mind of Christ" (1 Cor 2:16) and are thereby able to have "great views of that which is to come" (Mosiah 5:3). They are able to see a providential pattern in all things, to sift through the sands of the fleeting and the ephemeral, and to treasure that which is eternal. Sherem, on the other hand, seems to have been afflicted with a means-to-an-end sickness, an obsession with the here and now but a refusal to look beyond the present to greater and grander ends. In accusing Jacob of preaching false doctrine, Sherem tells him that "ye have led away much of this people that they pervert the right way of God, and keep not the law of Moses which is the right way; and convert the law of Moses into the worship of a being which ye say shall come many hundred years hence" (Jacob 7:7). Sherem, like the priests of Noah, believed that the law was all-sufficient (see Mosiah 12:31-32), that salvation would come through observance of the law without any reference whatsoever to Christ the Lawgiver. It is strange indeed that Sherem would argue for the sufficiency of the law of Moses when, in fact, the law was given by God to point the people toward the coming of Christ. Sherem's dispute was not, then, with Jacob alone on this issue, for Nephi had taught similar doctrine many years earlier (see 2 Nephi 11:4; 25:24-25). The irony and inconsistency of Sherem's argument is seen in his use of revelation—the law of Moses—to deny the principle of further revelation —the revelation of the Father in the person of Jesus Christ. Like many of his modern counterparts, Sherem was a master of scriptural manipulation: his was not a search for truth; he read with a jaundiced eye for self-justification, not sanctification.

They Are Sign Seekers

Like most anti-Christs, Sherem insisted that Jacob prove by demonstrable evidence that his was a true position—he demanded a sign (Jacob 7:13; compare Alma 30:43). Miracles or wonders or gifts of the Spirit always follow true believers; indeed, they are one of the signs of the true Church and evidence that the power of God is operating among his people. And yet Jesus taught that it is an "evil and adulterous generation [that] seeketh after a sign" (Matt 12:39). Joseph Smith added that this principle "is eternal, undeviating, and firm as the pillars of heaven; for whenever you see a man seeking after a sign, you may set it down that he is an adulterous man" (*TPJS* 157; compare 278).

Why is this so? How does a disposition to seek after signs relate to seeking after carnal pleasures? Simply stated, those who have given themselves up to their lusts, who desire that which will satiate the flesh, who have exhausted their passions in their search for the sensual—also seek for physical manifestations of spiritual sensations. They demand proof! Unable to recognize and acknowledge eternal certainties, they insist that the truths associated with the area with which they are least familiar—the spiritual—be manifest and translated into that realm they have come to know more surely than any other—the fanciful and the physical. The adulterous are those who worship at the altar of appetite, whose thresholds for gratification are ever rising, and who thereby demand something extraordinary to establish the truthfulness of a claim. Ironically, this claim may only be verified by the quiet and unobtrusive whisperings of the Spirit. Spiritual blindness and the spirit of adultery are thus common companions.

Of this fascinating but pathetic phenomenon, Elder Neal A. Maxwell has written:

> First of all, the people of the world cannot presume to command God to provide them with signs. A person can neither be a disciple and command the Master nor can he require "perpetual renewal of absolute proof." Some behave, however, as if they would set forth the conditions under which they will believe—complete with specifications; they then invite God to "bid" on their specifications! . . . Sign seekers, like adulterers, often do have a clear preference for *repeated* sensation. Those who do not understand why adultery is intrinsically wrong will also fail to understand why faith is a justified requirement laid upon us by God. We are to walk by faith and to overcome by faith (see D&C 76:53). . . . By contrast, the faithful, who are intellectually honest but are confronted with new and present challenges, sing of the Lord, "We've proved Him in days that are past." . . . Those who are adulterous have also a strong preference for "now" rather than for eternity. Impatience and incontinence, quite naturally, team up.
>
> Such erring individuals or generations also have a strong preference for meeting the needs of "me" over attending to others, a lifestyle which speeds selfishness on its endless, empty journey.
>
> By making demands of God, the proud would attach conditions to their discipleship. But discipleship requires of us unconditional surrender to the Lord. Hence the proud neither understand nor really love God. Therefore they violate the first commandment by seeing God as a sign provider upon request; as a function, not a tutoring Father (58-59).

Sign seekers have one thing going for them when it comes to convincing an audience—the servants of the Lord will not stoop to cheap theatrics to win the hearts of observers. In fact, "faith cometh not by signs, but signs follow those that believe. Yea, signs come by faith, not by the will of men, nor as they please, but by the will of God" (D&C 63:9-10). That is to say, signs and miracles fan the flame already burning in the hearts of believers. Seldom will God perform a notable miracle through his legal administrators to titillate sign seekers. And sign seekers know enough about the Lord and the prophetic past to know this. Simply stated, the anti-Christ demands a sign because he knows that the Lord does not give them in that manner. Unfortunately for Sherem (as we shall see), once in a great while the Lord does choose to make bare his mighty arm in response to taunting imps of uncleanness, but in such cases it is in wrath and proves the condemnation of the thrill seekers.

The Power of Jacob's Testimony

There are few greater prophets than Jacob, the son of Lehi. He was one of the mighty apostles of the Book of Mormon: as a special witness of Christ, he bore a perfect testimony and was true to his calling. It was to a very young Jacob that father Lehi said:

> Jacob, my firstborn in the wilderness, *thou knowest the greatness of God*; and he shall consecrate thine afflictions for thy gain. Wherefore, thy soul shall be blessed, and thou shalt dwell safely with thy brother, Nephi; and thy days shall be spent in the service of thy God. Wherefore, *I know that thou art redeemed*, because of the righteousness of thy Redeemer; for thou hast beheld that in the fulness of time he cometh to bring salvation unto men. And *thou hast beheld in thy youth his glory*; wherefore, thou art blessed even as they unto whom he shall minister in the flesh; for the Spirit is the same, yesterday, today, and forever. And the way is prepared from the fall of man, and salvation is free (2 Nephi 2:2-4; emphasis added).

In speaking of Jacob's witness of the coming Messiah, Nephi declared: "I, Nephi, write more of the words of Isaiah, for my soul delighteth in his words, . . . for he verily saw my Redeemer, even as I have seen him. And *my brother, Jacob, also has seen him as I have seen him*; wherefore, I will send their words forth unto my children to prove unto them that my words are true" (2 Nephi 11:2-3; emphasis added).

Having described Sherem's power of persuasion, Jacob noted: "And he had hope to shake me from the faith, notwithstanding the many revelations and the many things which I had seen concerning these things; for *I truly had seen angels, and they had ministered unto me. And also, I had heard the voice of the Lord speaking unto me in very word, from time to time; wherefore, I could not be shaken*" (Jacob 7:5; emphasis added). Jacob here provides a marvelous pattern for steadfastness in the face of spiritual persecution and intellectual challenge. Only when we have drunk deeply of the waters of life—when we have been grounded in revealed theology, rooted in genuine spiritual experience, and established in the things of God—can we hope to withstand the burning rays of doubt and the scorching thirst of skepticism. To be able to meet the snide remarks of the cynical head on, to be able to bear witness of the truth in the face of ridicule, and to give no heed to the enticing and otherwise convincing voices of the worldly-wise are, according to Joseph F. Smith, to have entered into the "rest of the Lord," to have partaken of the "spiritual rest and peace which are born from a settled conviction of the truth" (126). To enter the rest of the Lord "means entering into the knowledge and love of God, having faith in his purpose and in his plan, to such an extent that we know we are right, and that we are not hunting for something else, we are not disturbed by every wind of doctrine, or by the cunning and craftiness of men who lie in wait to deceive." To enter into the rest of the Lord is to enjoy "rest from doubt, from fear, from apprehension of danger, rest from the religious turmoil of the world" (Smith 58). After Enos, the son of Jacob, had prayed without ceasing; after he had wrestled in mighty supplication to the God of his fathers; after he had searched and pondered and inquired with a fervor known only to the spiritually hungry; then the voice of the Lord came to him, announced that his sins were forgiven, and regenerated his soul. "And after I, Enos, had heard these words, *my faith began to be unshaken in the Lord*" (Enos 1:11; emphasis added). Again we note that it is through being introduced into the realm of the sacred that one is able to proceed confidently and unimpeded when confronted by the profane.

The Lord explained to Joseph Smith and Sidney Rigdon in our day—at a time when the Church was under attack by those bent on its overthrow—that "there is no weapon that is formed against you shall prosper; and if any man lift his voice against you he shall be confounded in mine own due time" (D&C 71:9-10). We see this promise literally fulfilled in the ministry of Jacob, particularly in his encounter with Sherem. "But behold, the Lord God poured in his Spirit into my soul," Jacob wrote, "insomuch that I did confound him in all his words" (Jacob 7:8).

To say that Jacob *confounded* Sherem is to say that he threw him into disorder; perplexed him; terrified, dismayed, astonished, or stupefied him (*Webster's*). The power of God resting upon his servant Jacob both disarmed and disabled Sherem.

It was at the climax of his encounter with this anti-Christ that Jacob testified powerfully of the reality and necessity of Jesus Christ and again affirmed the depth of his own knowledge of the things of the Spirit (compare Alma 30:37-44):

> Believest thou the scriptures? [he asked Sherem.] And [Sherem] said, Yea. And [Jacob] said unto him: Then ye do not understand them; for they truly testify of Christ. Behold, I say unto you that none of the prophets have written, nor prophesied, save they have spoken concerning this Christ. And this is not all—*it has been made manifest unto me* [note that Jacob first appeals to the testimonies of earlier prophets and then bears his own witness—compare Alma in Alma 5:43-48], for *I have heard and seen*; and *it also has been made manifest unto me by the power of the Holy Ghost*; wherefore, I know if there should be no atonement made all mankind must be lost (Jacob 7:10-12; emphasis added).

The Woeful End of Sign Seekers

In a modern revelation the Lord explained that "signs come by faith, unto mighty works, for without faith no man pleaseth God; and with whom God is angry he is not well pleased; wherefore, unto such he showeth no signs, only in wrath unto their condemnation" (D&C 63:11). Indeed, when God does choose to manifest his power by means of the miraculous—and it is seldom—the curious sign seeker is often surprised and stunned by what is brought to pass: the sign is usually a divine judgment upon the sign seeker. After Korihor had been struck dumb by the power of God through Alma, the chief judge asked Korihor: "Art thou convinced of the power of God? In whom did ye desire that Alma should show forth his sign? Would ye that he should afflict others, to show unto thee a sign? Behold, *he has showed unto you a sign*; and now will ye dispute more?" (Alma 30:51; emphasis added). Elder George A. Smith recounted one incident from Church history in which Joseph Smith dealt with a sign seeker:

> When the Church of Jesus Christ of Latter-day Saints was first founded, you could see persons rise up and ask, "What sign will you show us that we may be made to believe?" I recollect a Campbellite preacher who came to Joseph Smith . . . and said that he had come a considerable distance to be convinced of the truth. "Why," said he, "Mr. Smith, I want to know the truth, and when I am convinced, I will spend all my talents and time defending and spreading the doctrines of your religion, and I will give you to understand that to convince me is equivalent to convincing all my society, amounting to several hundreds." Well, Joseph commenced laying before him the coming forth of the work, and the first principles of the Gospel, when [the minister] exclaimed, "O this is not the evidence I want, the evidence that I wish to have is a notable miracle; I want to see some powerful manifestation of the power of God, I want to see a notable miracle performed; and if you perform such a one, then I will believe with all my heart and soul, and will exert all my power and all my extensive influence to convince others; and if you will not perform a miracle of this kind, then I am your worst and bitterest enemy." "Well," said Joseph, "what will you have done? Will you be struck blind, or dumb? Will you be paralyzed, or will you have one hand withered? Take your choice, choose which you please, and in the name of the Lord Jesus Christ it shall be done." "That is not the kind of miracle I want," said the preacher. "Then, sir," replied Joseph, "I can perform none, I am not going to bring any trouble upon any body else, sir, to convince you" (*Journal of Discourses* 2:326).

After Jacob had borne his powerful apostolic witness, Sherem replied: "Show me a sign by this power of the Holy Ghost, in the which ye know so much. And [Jacob] said unto him: What am I that I should tempt God to show unto thee a sign *in the thing which thou knowest to be true*? Yet thou wilt deny it, because thou art of the devil." Then Jacob said: "Nevertheless, not my will be done; but if God shall smite thee, let that be a sign unto thee that he has power, both in heaven and in earth; and also, that Christ shall come" (Jacob 7:13-14; emphasis added). It is interesting to note that Jacob, like his Master and other humble servants endowed with the Spirit, discerned the true intents of Sherem's heart (see Matt 9:4; 12:25; Luke 9:47; Alma 18:16, 18); further, Jacob perceived, as is often the case (see Alma 11:24; 30:42), that the antagonist already knew that what the servant of the Lord was preaching was true and that he, the anti-Christ, was fighting the truth and thus sinning against the light.

Jacob then writes: "And it came to pass that when I, Jacob, had spoken these words, the power of the Lord came upon him, insomuch that he fell to the earth. And it came to pass that he was nourished for the space of many days" (Jacob 7:15). Sherem was struck down dramatically, even as Korihor was (Alma 30), and as Ananias and Sapphira were in the New Testament (Acts 5); his heresies were stopped, his perverse teachings silenced, and his flattering ways revealed for what they truly were. From the account it appears that from then until the time of his death Sherem was unable to care for himself; Jacob 7:15 states that he "was nourished for the space of many days." Surely he was nourished in the sense that his physical needs were met—he was fed and clothed and sheltered. Further, to *nourish* is to encourage, to educate, and to instruct (*Webster's*). It may be that Sherem was taught the gospel, was reproved and corrected in his doctrine, and was "nourished by the good word of God" (see Jacob 6:7; compare Alma 39:10). This act alone demonstrates Christianity at its highest and discipleship at its deepest—a group of Saints who had been the object of a very unchristian intellectual attack, now providing succor for him who had formerly wielded the sword of Satan, and had specialized in subtlety. This passage demonstrates one of the marvels of Christianity: the ability to truly love an enemy and to return good for evil. No true Christian takes delight in any person's demise, even if that person happens to be an anti-Christ, an avowed enemy to the cause of truth. The Saints of all ages pray for the defeat of evil and the overthrow of bitterness and opposition (see D&C 109:24-33), but they seek also to forgive and forget and welcome home the wandering prodigal. They leave judgment in the hands of the keeper of the gate, the Holy One of Israel (2 Nephi 9:41).

Life's starkest reality is death. And death is the great moment of truth. In the words of Elder Bruce R. McConkie, death is "a subject which strikes dread—even terror—into the hearts of most men. It is something we fear, of which we are sorely afraid, and from which most of us would flee if we could" (106). Even the most hardened atheists and the most elusive agnostics face what they believe to be the end with fear and trembling. Sherem, in the knowledge that he was about to face his God, sought to purge his soul of duplicity. He spoke plainly unto the people "and denied the things which he had taught them, and confessed the Christ, and the power of the Holy Ghost, and the ministering of angels. And he spake plainly unto them, that he had been deceived by the power of the devil [compare Alma 30:53]. And he spake of hell, and of eternity, and of eternal punishment" (Jacob 7:17-18). These are doctrines which would normally be scoffed at by the learned and ignored by the sophisticated. Sherem now spoke of these things because they weighed upon his mind: hell and eternal punishment were, to him, no longer religious rhetoric, but reality.

Sherem's final words are both poignant and pathetic: "I fear lest I have committed the unpardonable sin, for I have lied unto God; for I denied the Christ, and said that I believed the scriptures; and they truly testify of him. And because I have thus lied unto God I greatly fear lest my case shall be awful; but I confess unto God" (Jacob 7:19). Although the ultimate fate of Sherem is not known to us, this we do observe: deathbed repentance does not have within it the seeds of everlasting life. "It is the will of God," Joseph Smith observed, "that man should repent & serve him in health & in the strength & power of his mind in order to secure his blessings & not wait untill [sic] he is called to die" (*Words of Joseph Smith* 107). It would appear that Sherem's sin was not unpardonable—that he will not be numbered among the sons of perdition—for he still possessed a soul capable of repentance, which disposition is wholly alien to a son of perdition (*TPJS* 358). Confession at any time is to be commended, even just prior to death. But true repentance consists not only in confessing sins, but also in forsaking forbidden behavior and attitudes and in keeping the commandments thereafter (see D&C 1:32). It is well that Sherem acknowledged his lies and professed a belief in the scriptures and the coming of Christ before his demise; his situation would, however, have been far more positive had he not been compelled to believe.

A Warning to Our Day

The Book of Mormon "was written for our day," President Benson has taught us. "The Nephites never had the book; neither did the Lamanites of ancient times. It was meant for us. Mormon wrote near the end of the Nephite civilization. Under the inspiration of God, who sees all things from the beginning, he abridged centuries of records, choosing the stories, speeches, and events that would be most helpful to us" (19). Mormon's son, Moroni, having witnessed the coming forth of the Book of Mormon in a day of pride and envy and wars and pollutions, said: "Behold, I speak unto you as if ye were present, and yet ye are not. But behold, Jesus Christ hath shown you unto me, and I know your doing" (Mormon 8:35).

With this in mind—with the voice of the Nephite prophets crying out to us and stressing the eternal relevance of their messages, with the clear witness burning in our souls that the Book of Mormon is an ancient book which exposes modern falsehoods and modern anti-Christs—President Ezra Taft Benson has challenged the Saints as follows:

> Now, we have not been using the Book of Mormon as we should. Our homes are not as strong unless we are using it to bring our children to Christ. Our families may be corrupted by worldly trends and teachings unless we know how to use the book to expose and combat the falsehoods in socialism, organic evolution, rationalism, humanism, and so forth. . . . Social, ethical, cultural, or educational converts will not survive under the heat of the day unless their taproots go down to the fulness of the gospel which the Book of Mormon contains (6).

The Book of Mormon thus attests that anti-Christs are to be found in every age; that doubt and skepticism are ever with us, at least as long as Satan reigns on this planet and as long as people of the earth value the accolades of their cynical constituency more than the quiet acceptance of the Lord and his people; but that certitude and peace and power are the fruits of personal spiritual experience and the keys to remaining steadfast in the face of opposition and challenge.

One of the most effective ways to teach faith in Christ is through reading the scriptural accounts of persons who have evidenced great faith, then patterning our lives after them. Similarly, an indispensible guide in discovering the path of repentance and the miracle of forgiveness is the way of spiritual regeneration and holiness set forth in the labors and ministries of the Saints of earlier dispensations. In our own day there exists no more credible and critical source for discerning and exposing the spirit of anti-Christ than the scriptures, especially the Book of Mormon; nor is there any better formula for remaining untroubled and unhindered in our course than that put forward in the example of Jacob, who had received many revelations, had been ministered to by angels, knew well the voice and dictation of the Spirit, was a student of holy writ, and had spent many quiet hours in spiritual struggle and mighty prayer (see Jacob 7:5, 8, 11, 22). When the moment of significant confrontation came to him—just as it has or will come to individual Latter-day Saints—he stood steadfast and immovable, firm in the faith of his beloved Redeemer. Only when we are built upon the rock of Christ, are anchored and settled in true doctrine and personal spiritual experience, will we have the strength and capacity to perceive the perverse or engage the diabolical. In the words of Nephi, the son of Helaman, "when the devil shall send forth his mighty winds, yea, his shafts in the whirlwind, yea, when all his hail and his mighty storm shall beat upon you, it shall have no power over you to drag you down to the gulf of misery and endless wo, because of the rock upon which ye are built, which is a sure foundation, a foundation whereon if men build they cannot fall" (Hel 5:12).

BIBLIOGRAPHY

Benson, Ezra Taft. *A Witness and a Warning*. Salt Lake City: Deseret Book, 1988.

Journal of Discourses. 26 vols. 1854-86.

McConkie, Bruce R. "The Dead Who Die in the Lord." *Ensign* (Nov 76) 6:106-08; also in *Conference Report* (Oct 1976) 157-60.

Maxwell, Neal A. *Sermons Not Spoken*. Salt Lake City: Bookcraft, 1985.

Smith, Joseph F. *Gospel Doctrine*. 5th ed. Salt Lake City: Deseret Book, 1939.

Teachings of the Prophet Joseph Smith. Comp. Joseph Fielding Smith. Salt Lake City: Deseret Book, 1976.

Webster's 1828 American Dictionary. Facsimile. San Francisco: Foundation for American Christian Education, 1967.

The Words of Joseph Smith. Eds. Andrew F. Ehat and Lyndon W. Cook. Salt Lake City: Bookcraft, 1980.

To Learn with Joy: Sacred Preaching, Great Revelation, Prophesying

11

Monte S. Nyman

F ifty-five years after Lehi and his party left Jerusalem under the commandment and direction of the Lord (about 544 BC), Nephi, the son of Lehi and keeper of the small plates of Nephi, turned the responsibility of keeping this sacred record over to his younger brother Jacob (Jacob 1:1). He also instructed Jacob on what he was to include in his account. As Nephi was the prophet, ruler, and teacher of this people by prophecy and appointment of the Lord (1 Nephi 2:22), it is safe to assume that Jacob considered his instructions as commandments from the Lord. These commandments are important aids to us today in understanding the role of the Book of Mormon in our lives and in determining what emphasis we should place upon our study of it.

Nephi commanded that Jacob "write upon these plates a few of the things which [he] considered to be most precious; that [he] should not touch, save it were lightly, concerning the history of this people which are called the people of Nephi" (Jacob 1:2). This light touch of history is not to be interpreted as a declaration that history is unimportant. The history of Nephi's people was to be kept by other writers upon another set of plates, while Jacob and his posterity were commanded to keep the more precious

Monte S. Nyman is professor of Ancient Scripture and associate dean of Religious Education at Brigham Young University.

happenings, or what may be termed the spiritual history of the people, upon the small plates (Jacob 1:3; compare 3:13).

Jacob's people had many revelations, and the spirit of much prophecy from which to select the contents of the Book of Mormon. Because of "faith and great anxiety, it truly had been made manifest" to Jacob and others those things that were to happen to their people (Jacob 1:5). They "knew of Christ and his kingdom, which should come" (Jacob 1:6) and could select those revelations and prophecies which would be most applicable in the day that the Book of Mormon would come forth. Jacob wrote that although it was difficult to engrave upon the plates, he knew his writings would be permanent and he was concerned for future generations (Jacob 4:1-2).

For example, Jacob was concerned that we not fall because of pride, as he knew his brethren would (see Jacob's sermon on pride in Jacob 2:12-22). In 1831, when the Lord commanded the Church to move to Ohio, he warned them to "beware of pride, lest [they] become as the Nephites of old" (D&C 38:39). The Prophet Joseph Smith cautioned the Twelve in his day to beware of pride and gave them this perplexing question: "Why will not man learn wisdom by precept at this late age of the world, when we have such a cloud of witnesses and examples before us, and not be obliged to learn by sad experience everything we know" (*Teachings of the Prophet Joseph Smith* 155; hereafter *TPJS*). As believers in the Book of Mormon, we should learn with joy from Jacob's admonitions and not from the sorrow of our own experiences.

Jacob was concerned that the posterity of his people recognize the hand of the Lord in bringing Lehi and Ishmael and their families, along with Zoram, out of the Land of Jerusalem. He wanted those in the last days to "receive [the record of their fathers] with thankful hearts, and look upon them that they may learn with joy and not with sorrow, neither with contempt, concerning their first parents" (Jacob 4:1-3). While some may interpret the phrase, "their first parents," as a reference to Adam and Eve, the context strongly suggests that Jacob was referring to Lehi and Ishmael and their families who migrated to America.

Jacob was also concerned that the descendants of Lehi and Ishmael not be weighed down with sorrow over being a nation of fallen people, but would rather that they recognize the great blessings extended to them in the latter days. He also seemed concerned that they not react with contempt as descendants of the rebellious Laman and Lemuel and the sons of Ishmael. This concern may have been fostered by his knowledge that all of the remnants of Lehi and his party would be designated as Lamanites today, and that while even in his day those who sought to destroy the people of Nephi were called Lamanites (Jacob 1:13-14), he did not want the designation to carry a negative connotation in the last days. He obviously knew, as did Alma, that all those who remained after the downfall of the Nephite nation would be numbered among the Lamanites (Alma 45:13-14). As the Lord has confirmed by revelation, there are descendants of all the original families of Lehi's party among those called Lamanites today (D&C 3:16-18). This revelation confirms the teaching that a major purpose for preserving the plates was to make known to all these people the fact that the promises of the Lord would be fulfilled (v 19).

Thus, from Nephi's commandment to touch only lightly upon the history of the people, we learn that the Book of Mormon is not a history book. Neither is it a geography text or an archaeological guide book. It is a compilation of "preaching which was sacred, or revelation which was great, or prophesying" as Nephi had commanded Jacob to engrave upon the plates (Jacob 1:4). Furthermore, it is "the heads," or the most significant, of these three categories.

This compilation was "for Christ's sake, and for the sake of [Jacob's] people" (Jacob 1:4). The work of Christ is "to bring to pass the immortality and eternal life of man" (Moses 1:39). Hearkening to the messages of the Book of Mormon will enable mankind to partake of that immortality and eternal life.

Jacob and his associates "labored diligently among [their] people, [to] persuade them to come unto Christ, and partake of the goodness of God, that they might enter into his rest" (Jacob 1:7). Through his writings, Jacob desired to "persuade all men not to rebel against God, to provoke him to anger, but that all men would believe in Christ, and view his death, and suffer his cross and bear the shame of the world" (Jacob 1:8). An analysis of the Book of Mormon text illustrates how effectively Nephi, Jacob, Enos, Jarom, and the engravers of the book of Omni fulfilled the Lord's commandment to include sacred preaching, great revelations, and prophesyings (Jacob 1:4).

The Writings of Nephi

Jacob explained that the people "loved Nephi exceedingly . . . having labored in all his days for their welfare," and being desirous "to retain in remembrance his name," they called those who reigned in his stead "second Nephi, third Nephi, and so forth" (Jacob 1:10-11). It can be safely assumed that a man of such character would not ask someone to do something that he had not already done himself. To better understand Jacob and the other writers in this section of the Book of Mormon, it is important to see that Nephi also followed this pattern of emphasizing sacred preaching, great revelations, and prophesying.

1 Nephi

The book of 1 Nephi is slightly more than 52 pages long and contains 22 chapters broken into 618 verses. Over 40 of the 52 pages and 400 of the 618 verses fit into the category of sacred preaching, great revelations, and prophesying. The sacred preaching includes Nephi's explanation to his brethren concerning the plates of brass, and his counsel that they not return to live in Jerusalem. It includes Lehi's vision, Nephi's prophetic testimony of his ability to build a ship, and his explanation of Isaiah's writings. It also includes Lehi's teachings on the Messiah, the prophet who would baptize the Messiah (John the Baptist), and an explanation of the symbolism equating Israel with the house of Israel.

Five of Lehi's visions and dreams are either recorded or referred to in 1 Nephi. In these dreams and visions, Lehi saw God and Christ and the various categories of people and their reactions to the word of God. He also received commandments to leave Jerusalem and, later, to send his sons back for the plates of brass. Nephi also saw four visions. These include the same one his father had seen of the four categories of people, as well as visions of Jerusalem and other cities, his seed's future, and the nations and kingdoms of the Gentiles. This last vision was not completely recorded because parts of it were reserved for the record of John the Revelator. Nephi also received revelation to slay Laban and to build a ship. The entire group was given revelation through the Liahona to guide them in the wilderness. These are certainly great revelations, and consistent with other great revelations recorded in scripture.

Five prophecies were also recorded in 1 Nephi. First the Lord prophesied to Nephi that Laman and Lemuel would rebel and that Nephi would become their ruler and teacher (1 Nephi 2:19-24). An angel later reminded Laman and Lemuel of this prophecy and further prophesied that they would go to Jerusalem and that the Lord would deliver Laban into their hands (1 Nephi 3:29). In chapter 5, Lehi prophesied that the plates of brass would not "be dimmed anymore by time," and that they would go to every nation, kindred, tongue, and people (1 Nephi 5:18-19). In 1 Nephi chapter 10, verses 17 through 22, Nephi seems to have been prophesying concerning the power of the Holy Ghost, though this could also be classified as great preaching. And in chapter 19, Nephi intersperses the Messianic prophecy of an angel with similar prophesies from many prophets (1 Nephi 19:10-17).

1 Nephi Preaching Which Is Sacred

3:15-20; 4:1-3	Nephi to his brethren regarding the plates
5:4-5, 8	Lehi to Sariah
7:8-15	Nephi to his brethren regarding returning to Jerusalem
10:2-14	Lehi concerning the Messiah, the prophet who should baptize him, and the olive tree
15:10-16:3	Nephi to Laman and Lemuel on their father's vision
17:23-51	Nephi to Laman and Lemuel concerning his ability to build a ship
19:19-21:26	Nephi cites Isaiah to all the house of Israel
22:2-31	Nephi explains Isaiah and cites other prophets to his brethren

1 Nephi Revelation Which Is Great

1:6-14	Lehi sees God, etc.
2:1-2	Lehi commanded to leave Jerusalem
3:2-4	Lehi commanded to send his sons for the plates of brass
4:10-17	The Spirit directs Nephi to slay Laban
8:2-33	Lehi's vision of the tree of life
11	Nephi's vision of Jerusalem and other cities
12	Nephi's vision of the land of promise
13-14	Nephi's vision of the nations and kingdoms of the Gentiles
16:10, 16, 25-30; 18:12, 21-22	The directions through the round ball
17:7-10, 12-14	The Lord to Nephi on building a ship

1 Nephi Prophesying

2:19-24	The Lord concerning Laman and Lemuel
3:29	An angel to Laman and Lemuel
5:18-19	Lehi regarding the plates of brass
10:17-22	Nephi concerning the power of the Holy Ghost
19:10-17	An angel and the prophets on the Messiah

2 Nephi

The book of 2 Nephi is even more spiritually oriented than is 1 Nephi. Only one of its 64 pages and 29 of its 749 verses are historical. There are five incidents of preaching, eight great revelations, and five sections of prophesying. The sacred preaching includes Lehi to his sons in chapter 1 (vv 1-5, 12-27); Nephi to the latter-day reader as he bears his soul upon the plates in chapter 4 (vv 15-25); Jacob's sermon, or sermons, to the people of Nephi in chapters 6 through 10; the written introduction to the writings of Isaiah in chapter 11; and finally, Nephi's words on the doctrine of Christ in chapters 31-33. The eight revelations are the blessings that Lehi gave to Laman and Lemuel (2 Nephi 1:28-29), Zoram (2 Nephi 1:30-32), Jacob (2 Nephi 2), Joseph (2 Nephi 3), the sons and daughters of Laman (2 Nephi 4:3-7), the sons and daughters of Lemuel (2 Nephi 4:8-9), the sons of Ishmael (2 Nephi 4:10), and Sam (2 Nephi 4:11). The five prophecies include Lehi concerning the land of promise (2 Nephi 1:6-12), Joseph of Egypt concerning his posterity (2 Nephi 3:5-21), Lehi to his son Joseph (2 Nephi 3:22-25), Nephi concerning the Lamanites (2 Nephi 5:21-25), and Nephi interpreting Isaiah and prophesying of the last days (2 Nephi 25-30).

2 Nephi Preaching Which Is Sacred

1:1-5, 12b-27	Lehi to his sons
4:15-25	Nephi bares his soul
6-10	Jacob to the people
11	Nephi introduces Isaiah
31-33	Nephi speaks concerning the doctrine of Christ

2 Nephi Revelation Which Is Great

1:28-4:11	The patriarch Lehi's blessings to his posterity and Zoram:
1:28-29	To Laman and Lemuel
1:30-32	To Zoram
2	To Jacob
3	To Joseph
4:3-7	To the sons and daughters of Laman
4:8-9	To the sons and daughters of Lemuel
4:10	To the sons of Ishmael
4:11	To Sam
12-24	Nephi quotes Isaiah (includes many prophecies)

2 Nephi Prophesying

1:6-12a	Lehi concerning the land of promise
3:5-21	Joseph of Egypt concerning his seed
3:23-25	Lehi to his son Joseph
5:21-25	Nephi concerning the Lamanites
25-30	Nephi interprets Isaiah and prophesies of the last days (includes more of Isaiah)

The Writings of Jacob

Jacob and Enos together covered 124 years of Nephite history, from the 56th year through the 179th year after Lehi left Jerusalem (544-420 BC). Exactly how long each of the two prophets was responsible for keeping the records is not stated. Estimating that Jacob was the record keeper for 50 to 75 years, we only find two specific historical incidents in his account. The first incident took place during the reign of the second king (Jacob 1:15), which was probably Nephi's successor (see Jacob 2:1). The second incident, concerning Sherem the anti-Christ, happened after some years had passed away (Jacob 7:1). The rest of Jacob's writings are general observations and are addressed to the future reader.

Using present-day chapters and verses, the breakdown of the text is as follows. The first eight verses of the book of Jacob are Nephi's instructions concerning the keeping of the plates (Jacob 1:1-8). These verses would come under the heading of preaching that is sacred. The next four verses record the appointment of Nephi's successor as king, the great love and respect the people had for Nephi, and Nephi's death (Jacob 1:9-12). Jacob then records the segregation of the people into Nephites and Lamanites and explains their differentiating characteristics (Jacob 1:13-14). Of the first 14 verses, eight could be considered historical, but they are really just the changing of the political and ecclesiastical guard.

The next section is part of Jacob's great sermon, given at the temple, on pride, riches, and immorality (Jacob 1:17). This section includes 54 verses (1:15-3:14), 46 of which constitute the recorded portion of the sermon (3:12 is a summation of the unrecorded portion of the sermon). The other seven verses tell us that Jacob was commissioned by the Lord to give the sermon and that he and his brother Joseph had been given the priesthood (1:15-19). They also give a couple of comments about the plates (3:13-14). This sermon is one of the great examples of "preaching which is sacred."

Chapters 4 through 6 are addressed to Jacob's brethren in the last days. The fourth chapter explains why they have written —to persuade their latter-day brethren to believe in Christ and follow his teachings. Jacob then records from the plates of brass the longest chapter in the Book of Mormon (Jacob 5). This excerpt is Zenos' allegory of the tame and wild olive trees, an outline of the prophetic destiny of the house of Israel. According to chapter 4, Jacob quoted this allegory to show that the stone rejected by the builders (Christ) would yet become "the head of the corner" (vv 15-18). Chapter 6 is Jacob's testimony of the allegory and his plea to his brethren to accept it and all the other testimonies concerning Christ. Except for the first three verses of chapter 4, all of chapters 4 through 6 could be classified as prophesying, either Jacob to his latter-day brethren (Jacob 4, 6) or Zenos to the whole world. Zenos' allegory of the tame and wild olive trees could be considered as great revelation. No history of the Nephites or Lamanites appears in this section of the book of Jacob.

The second historical incident recorded by Jacob takes place in chapter seven. It is the account of Sherem the anti-Christ among the people of Nephi. The first part (vv 1-5) introduces and describes Sherem. The last part relates the outcome of Sherem's visit (vv 20-23) together with a couple of verses giving a general description of the times that followed (vv 24-25). The verses in between are an account of the conversations between Jacob and Sherem and would be considered prophecy. This is certainly only a light touch of history.

The last two verses written by Jacob are long and melancholy. They are a lamentation, and technically not historical, except for the fact that Jacob has become old and turns the record over to his son Enos. Of the nearly 19 pages of the present text of the book of Jacob, only about ten percent are historical, one and one-half of those pages, or about 23 of the 203 verses. Jacob's record, a great doctrinal contribution, has ended. He recorded preaching that was sacred, a great revelation, and prophesying.

The Writings of Enos

The history in the estimated 50 to 75 years covered by Enos is certainly only lightly touched upon (Jacob 1:2). The book covers only one specific incident in his life, his conversion. This event is related in the first 18 of Enos' 27 verses. The other nine verses give a general description of the people at this time (vv 19-24), and a concluding testimony of Enos' life as a servant of Christ (vv 25-27). While the six verses describing the people are historical, they are certainly brief, covering the space of a lifetime in about three-quarters of a page. Enos' conversion would qualify as a great revelation, with the voice of the Lord coming to his mind to tell him that his sins were forgiven. He also appears to have received a revelation that his calling and election had been made sure (v 27). In his concluding verses, Enos bears witness of his preaching and prophesying but does not enumerate. Although his book is short, he followed Nephi's commandments concerning what to include on the small plates.

The Writings of Jarom

Jarom's record covers 59 years. He divides his comments on these years into two periods: one from the 180th year, when he began to keep the record, through the 200th year (vv 1-4); and the other from the 201st year until he turned the record over to his son Omni 38 years later (vv 5-15). Concerning the first time period, a span of 21 years, Jarom gives a very general description of the contrast between the wicked and the righteous among his people (vv 3-4). He also gives a couple of introductory verses explaining why he is writing so little on the plates, stating that the plan of salvation has already been given. Jarom bears witness that he has prophesied and that he, and many others, received revelation and communed with the Holy Spirit (vv 2, 4).

Jarom only gives a very general description of the second time period (398-361 BC). Though he does include more about the people's lives and accomplishments (vv 5, 8), he does not include any specific incidents in the history. He relates that the Nephites were fairly righteous, due to the work of the prophets, and were therefore prospered in many ways, particularly against the Lamanites who often came against them. Jarom bears witness of the prophets, persuading the people to believe in Christ. His book is brief but bears testimony of the principles commanded by Nephi; preaching, revelation, and prophesying.

The Book of Omni

Five different authors wrote on the plates of Omni, covering about two hundred years.[1] Of these five writers, only Amaleki relates any historical detail. Omni kept the record for 44 years, recording only that they had seasons of war and seasons of peace. Amaron kept the record for at least 38 years, witnessing that the more wicked Nephites were destroyed while the righteous were spared, showing that the people prospered when they kept the commandments. In the one verse Chemish recorded he did not state how long he kept the record, but since he was a brother of Amaron rather than a descendant, it was probably less time than the others. Abinadom wrote only two verses, stating that there had been wars with the Lamanites and an absence of revelation and prophecy. Perhaps this is the reason these four recorded so little. There were no sacred preachings, no great revelations, and no prophesyings to write upon the plates, and Nephi had commanded that nothing else be written.

Amaleki wrote of the departure of the righteous Nephites from the land of Nephi under the leadership of Mosiah. During their travels, Mosiah and his party discovered the people of Zarahemla who had been led out of Jerusalem at the time it was destroyed by Babylon (about 589 BC). The departure of the

---

[1] Two hundred thirty-seven years are covered from the end of the book of Jarom (v 13) to the appointment of Mosiah, the son of Benjamin, who replaced his father as king (Mosiah 6:4). The first two writers, Omni and Amaron, covered 82 years, leaving 155 years for Chemish, Abinadom, Amaleki, and Mormon's abridgment of king Benjamin's life. Their individual time periods and the time period of the first six chapters of Mosiah are not recorded. The estimate of 200 years is based on this limited knowledge.

righteous Nephites from the land of Nephi, and that of Lehi from Jerusalem, are two examples of the principle taught by Nephi, that the Lord leads the righteous out of wicked nations and into promised lands (1 Nephi 17:38). The exodus of the people of Mosiah also fulfilled a prophecy made earlier by Jacob, that unless the Nephites would repent, the Lord would lead the righteous out from among them (Jacob 3:4).

In addition to these events, Amaleki also records that the people of Zarahemla had discovered Coriantumr, a survivor of the Jaredites. Thus the Nephite record links together the three migrations from the eastern hemisphere to the promised land of America. He wrote of king Benjamin's succession as ruler of the people of Zarahemla after the death of his father Mosiah, and of a certain number of people who sought to return to the land of Nephi. Many in this group were killed en route due to internal contention, their survivors returning to Zarahemla. A considerable number of people left later on a similar mission and had not been heard from before Amaleki completed his record. It seems that Amaleki quit recording only because he ran out of space. His contribution was short but significant.

In summary, Amaron preaches to us concerning the fulfilment of the Lord's promises (Omni 1:6-7); Amaleki exhorts us to come unto Christ and partake of his salvation (Omni 1:25-26) and speaks of the revelation received by king Mosiah which instructed him to lead his people to Zarahemla. The book of Omni fits the pattern set by Nephi.

The Words of Mormon

A careful reading of verses five through ten of the Words of Mormon discloses that Mormon wrote this brief insert upon the small plates of Nephi. Although Amaleki said that the plates were full (Omni 1:30), he apparently left enough space for Mormon to record a few words. Perhaps Amaleki had been instructed to do so. Mormon wrote many hundreds of years after the coming of Christ (WofM 1:2).

The first nine verses of the Words of Mormon explain how Mormon came to include the small plates in his abridgement of the Nephite record. He records that he was pleased with their many "prophecies of the coming of Christ" and that the Spirit whispered to him that he should include them "for a wise purpose" unto the Lord (WofM 1:4, 7). The last nine verses explain that after receiving the plates from Amaleki, king Benjamin defeated the Lamanites and, with the help of the prophets, established peace by putting down false Christs, false prophets, false preachers, and false teachers. Although these verses are largely historical, the book is divided about equally among history, revelation, and preaching. Mormon, in this brief space, testifies that he received a revelation to include the plates, and bears witness of the preaching of king Benjamin and the other prophets that helped establish peace.

Preaching Which Is Sacred

Jacob	1:2-8	Nephi's instructions to Jacob concerning the plates
	2:1-3:12	Jacob's sermon in the temple
Enos	1:26	Enos' life
Jarom	1:2-11	Jarom teaches us of his people
Omni	1:6-7	Omni teaches us of his people
	1:25-26	Amaleki teaches us of Christ
WofM	1:17-18	King Benjamin and the prophets establish peace

Revelation Which Is Great

Enos	1:1-18	The conversion of Enos
Omni	1:12-22	Mosiah leads his people to Zarahemla
WofM	1:3-8	Mormon includes the small plates of Nephi

Prophesying

Jacob	4:4-6:13	Jacob prophesies of Christ and quotes Zenos' prophetic allegory
Jacob	7:3-19	Jacob debates Sherem
Enos	1:26-27	Enos' life

Conclusion

In fewer than 28 pages, the record from the book of Jacob to the book of Mosiah covers about 421 of the total 1021 years covered by the entire Nephite record. This is about 41 percent of the entire time period written on less than six percent of the pages. Seventy-five percent of these pages contain "preaching which was sacred, or revelation which was great, or prophesying" (Jacob 1:4). It is definitely a light touch of history (Jacob 1:2). The books that precede and follow this section of the Book of Mormon follow a similar pattern.

Since this was the pattern set for writing on the Nephite record, should it not also be our pattern for studying, teaching, and applying its precepts to our lives, and to the lives of those whom we teach? Should we not learn and teach what the Book of Mormon itself teaches concerning the sacred preaching, the great revelations, and the prophecies rather than what others have said about its contents, literary styles, or external evidences? When I first began teaching the Book of Mormon about 30 years ago, I taught much about the external evidences and what others had said about it. Although I still appreciate and look at these things today, I now concentrate on the internal message of the book, and yearn for more time to analyze and synthesize these messages for myself and my students. This is what I believe Nephi, Jacob, Mormon, Moroni, and the Lord intended for us to do. The Lord has blessed us by restoring this record in these latter days. Two and one-half years after the Book of Mormon had been published, the Lord said he was displeased with the Saints because they were not using it properly (D&C 84:54-58). Today he has raised up another prophet to emphasize the importance of the Book of Mormon in bringing us out of spiritual bondage (Benson 78). Where much is given, much is required (Luke 12:48). May we follow the pattern set by Nephi, and followed by other writers and abridgers of the Book of Mormon, and learn with joy now instead of with sorrow at a later day.

As readers and teachers of the Book of Mormon, we should analyze each account to try to determine what the Lord is telling us through his inspired prophets. We can do this best by understanding the historical setting that produced the sacred preaching, the great revelation, or the prophecy. Then we should isolate the doctrinal message or precept and evaluate our own lives in accordance with it. We will then be following Nephi's admonition to "liken all scriptures unto us, that it might be for our profit and learning" (1 Nephi 19:23). A testimony of the importance of the preachings, revelations, and prophesyings found in the Book of Mormon is available to all those who will follow the pattern set by Nephi and continued by the other abridgers. Finally, in the words of king Benjamin, "if [we] believe all these things [we must] see that [we] do them" (Mosiah 4:10).

BIBLIOGRAPHY

Benson, Ezra Taft. "A Sacred Responsibility." *Ensign* (May 1986) 16:77-78.

Teachings of the Prophet Joseph Smith. Comp. Joseph Fielding Smith. Salt Lake City: Deseret Book, 1974.

The Small Plates of Nephi and the Words of Mormon   12

Eldin Ricks

A lthough the title of this paper is, "The Small Plates of Nephi and the Words of Mormon," it could just as properly be called, "The Large Plates of Nephi, the Plates of Mormon, the Small Plates of Nephi, and the Words of Mormon." The reason for this more extended title is that we need to know something of the several records that Mormon was working with before we can make much sense of his "Words of Mormon" appendage to the small plates of Nephi.

The Large Plates of Nephi

Let us turn the clock back to the fourth century AD in ancient America. It was an era of conflict between the Nephites and Lamanites, two rival factions that had lived in the Western world for nearly a thousand years. During this tumultuous period, a Nephite prophet named Mormon became custodian of a great record, engraved on sheets of metal, that had been handed down by his ancestors from their beginnings as a nation (Mormon 1:1-4; 2:17-18; 6:6). We refer to this record as the large plates of Nephi. Mormon explains the circumstances surrounding his appointment to add the history of his generation to the large plates of Nephi as follows:

Eldin Ricks is emeritus professor of Ancient Scripture at Brigham Young University.

> And about the time that Ammaron hid up the records unto the Lord, he came unto me, (I being about ten years of age, and I began to be learned somewhat after the manner of the learning of my people) and Ammaron said unto me: I perceive that thou art a sober child, and art quick to observe; Therefore, when ye are about twenty and four years old I would that ye should remember the things that ye have observed concerning this people; and when ye are of that age go to the land Antum, unto a hill which shall be called Shim; and there have I deposited unto the Lord all the sacred engravings concerning this people. And behold, ye shall take the plates of Nephi unto yourself, and the remainder shall ye leave in the place where they are; and ye shall engrave on the plates of Nephi all the things that ye have observed concerning this people (Mormon 1:2-4).

In due time Mormon did as he was instructed. He obtained the large plates of Nephi from their repository in the hill Shim and engraved on them the history of his times. That history turned out to be the tragic tale of the fall of his nation. Imbedded in his story is the brief but important revelation from God that the survival of his nation—and, by extension, the survival of the human family in our day of nuclear weapons—depended on more than military preparation. The following lesson comes out of the decade preceding AD 360: "And it came to pass that the Lamanites did not come to battle again until ten years more had passed away. And behold, I had employed my people, the Nephites, in preparing their lands and their arms against the time of battle. And it came to pass that the Lord did say unto me: Cry unto this people—Repent ye, and come unto me, and be ye baptized, and build up again my church, and ye shall be spared" (Mormon 3:1-2).

Just before the final battle, when Mormon finished his important literary mission, the large plates of Nephi included the books of Lehi, Mosiah, Alma, Helaman, 3 Nephi, 4 Nephi, and Mormon, and spanned Nephite history from about 600 BC to AD 385.

The book of Lehi section of the plates deserves special consideration here. In his preface to the 1830 edition of the Book of Mormon, Joseph Smith explains the loss of the first 116 manuscript pages of his translation and identifies the lost part as an abridgment of the book of Lehi. In addition, we learn in the Doctrine and Covenants that this missing portion extended to the reign of king Benjamin (D&C 10:41). It may then be said that the book of Lehi covered Nephite history from the time Lehi left Jerusalem (about 600 BC) to the opening of the book of Mosiah (approximately 130 BC). Since Lehi himself lived but a fraction of this vast period (Lehi's death is mentioned in 2 Nephi 4:12), the book of Lehi—like the books of Omni, Alma, Helaman, and 4 Nephi—was necessarily the product of several successive historians. The book of Lehi title evidently originated with Lehi's journal, or sacred personal record, that Nephi transcribed at the beginning of his large plates of Nephi (1 Nephi 19:1).

The large plates of Nephi underwent certain changes as they were passed down through a long line of historians. In their first stage they were an overall civil and religious record kept by the prophet-king Nephi. In their second stage, which lasted for several hundred years, they were strictly a civil record. In their third stage, which began near the opening of the book of Mosiah, they were restored to their original composite civil and religious character and remained so until Mormon's day.

To elaborate a little on the foregoing, Nephi included both civil and religious matters on the large plates until thirty years following his departure from Jerusalem. At that point the Lord, very probably in anticipation of the separation of the roles of kings and prophets that followed the death of Nephi, commanded Nephi to limit the large plates of Nephi to "an account of the reign of the kings, and the wars and contentions" (1 Nephi 9:4; see also Jacob 1:1-9, 18-19). He also commanded him to make the small plates of Nephi for a sacred history that would be kept by a line of record keepers apart from the kings. When we get to the book of Mosiah, however, prophets are again serving in the kingly office. Not surprisingly, the large plates of Nephi again contain both civil and religious matters, while the small plates of Nephi are discontinued.

The Plates of Mormon—A Digest of the Large Plates of Nephi

At or near the close of his literary efforts on the large plates of Nephi, Mormon was inspired to write a small digest of the moral and spiritual contributions of that entire record. It would be a selection of the best that nearly a thousand years of Nephite history had to offer, directed mainly to the descendants of the survivors of the Lamanite-Nephite wars. It would illustrate the principle, "Righteousness exalteth a nation: but sin is a reproach to any people" (Prov 14:34). It would also include an account of the most important event in all of Nephite history, the personal visitation of the resurrected Christ among them (3 Nephi 11-28). Writing this digest of the large plates of Nephi was a monumental task and very likely took Mormon years to complete. To accomplish it he first formed a separate metal volume. I judge that he did so in some degree of secrecy as he employed no craftsmen to make it, but constructed it, he says, "with mine own hands" (3 Nephi 5:11). On these plates, which we call the plates of Mormon, he carefully engraved, in his own words and style of writing, a summary of the entire history of his ancestors. He even summarized the history of his own generation which he had personally inscribed at the end of the large plates of Nephi (Mormon 2:18 and 5:9).[1] In the course of composing his book-by-book digest, he paused at one point to make the following explanation to the reader:

> And it hath become expedient that I, according to the will of God, that the prayers of those who have gone hence, who were the holy ones, should be fulfilled according to their faith, should make a record of these things which have been done—Yea, a small record of that which hath taken place from the time that Lehi left Jerusalem, even down until the present time. Therefore I do make my record from the accounts

---

[1] Mormon's abridgment of his own history apparently comprises Mormon chapters 1-5. Chapters 6 and 7, which contain an account of the fateful outcome of the hill Cumorah battle, were written after the large plates of Nephi were buried (Mormon 6:6) and, hence, strictly speaking, could not have been part of the abridgment. For convenience, however, in the diagram presented herein, we represent Mormon's abridgment of his own history as embracing all of chapters 1-7, which mark the conclusion of his writings.

which have been given by those who were before me, until the commencement of my day; And then I do make a record of the things which I have seen with mine own eyes. . . . I am Mormon, and a pure descendant of Lehi . . . (3 Nephi 5:14-17, 20).

In a later period Joseph Smith was to receive and translate the plates of Mormon—the abridgment of the large plates of Nephi—but not the original large plates of Nephi. This fact should be kept clearly in mind as we proceed.

The Small Plates of Nephi

One day while Mormon was working on his digest, he discovered a little volume of the prophetic writings of his early forefathers in his library of ancient records (WofM 1:3). An examination of its contents revealed that it had been started by the same prophet Nephi who began the large plates of Nephi. Because of its brevity we call it the small plates of Nephi. About one-third of our published Book of Mormon is a translation of the small plates of Nephi. It is important, therefore, that we know something about that sacred work.

Soon after the arrival of the original colony from Jerusalem, which was somewhere around 590 BC, the young prophet Nephi was commanded by the Lord to prepare a record for the history of his people. This record was the large plates of Nephi that we have been discussing. Then, about twenty years later, the Lord commanded him to prepare the small plates of Nephi as an exclusively religious record.

And thirty years had passed away from the time we left Jerusalem. And I, Nephi, had kept the records upon my plates, which I had made, of my people thus far [the large plates of Nephi]. And it came to pass that the Lord God said unto me: Make other plates; and thou shalt engraven many things upon them which are good in my sight, for the profit of thy people. Wherefore, I, Nephi, to be obedient to the commandments of the Lord, went and made these plates upon which I have engraven these things. And I engraved that which is pleasing unto God. And if my people are pleased with the things of God they will be pleased with mine engravings which are upon these plates. And if my people desire to know the more particular part of the history of my people they must search mine other plates (2 Nephi 5:28-33).

The sacred record that we know of as the small plates of Nephi is indebted to a yet earlier volume that the colony of Lehi brought from Jerusalem in 600 BC. This previous work, known as the brass plates of Laban, probably set the pattern for the Nephite practice of preserving their most precious writings on metal plates. It also appears to have influenced the language of some of these works (Mosiah 1:4; compare 1 Nephi 1:2 and Mormon 9:32-33). About one-third of the small plates of Nephi is directly or indirectly related to the brass plates of Laban. About one-fourth is quoted from that record verbatim.

The small plates of Nephi served the Lord's purpose as a repository of religious writings during an age in which the Nephite kings, who were custodians of the large plates of Nephi, were not qualified, I suspect, to cope with the writing of sacred history. By the time of king Benjamin, however, prophet-kings again occupied the throne. It was at this juncture that Amaleki concluded the small plates of Nephi and turned them over to king Benjamin for safekeeping. Thereafter, sacred and secular writings alike were entered on the large plates of Nephi as had been the case at the beginning of Nephite history.

The Book of Lehi and the Small Plates of Nephi

Mormon's purpose in culling out for us the moral and spiritual treasures of his ancestors' great history was, in the words of his son Moroni, "to the convincing of the Jew and Gentile that Jesus is the Christ, the Eternal God, manifesting himself unto all nations" (title page). In view of this lofty religious goal, it is no surprise to find that the abridgment of the large plates of Nephi that he inscribed on the plates of Mormon abounds in prophecies of Christ, missionary experiences, doctrinal discourses, and miracles. Even the fascinating stories of war and political change that he selected to condense and pass on to us carry faith-promoting lessons. It was probably not hard for Mormon to draw religious elements from the combined secular and religious part of the large plates of Nephi, meaning from the book of Mosiah to the end of that record. It must have been considerably more difficult, however, to glean such material from the book of Lehi part, for, as we have already observed, the book of Lehi was almost exclusively a political and civil record. So we can understand his joy when, just as he came to the reign of king Benjamin near the close of his digest of the book of Lehi, he discovered the small plates of Nephi in his repository of ancient records and learned that they formed a religious work covering almost all of the book of Lehi period (WofM 1:3-4). The thing that pleased him especially about the small plates, he says, was their "prophecies of the coming of Christ" (WofM 1:4). And no wonder, for that was exactly the kind of evidence for the messiahship of Jesus that he was seeking for his own record. What was he to do? Could he discard his abridgment of the book of Lehi and substitute the small plates of Nephi?

Before we consider what Mormon finally did with the volume that he found, we should note that the small plates of Nephi had been kept by a private line of record keepers and extended from the time of Nephi to the early reign of king Benjamin. In contrast, the book of Lehi had been written by an entirely different line of record keepers (see Jarom 1:4, Omni 1:11), and extended from the time of Nephi to the late reign of the same king Benjamin.[2]

Mormon Adds the Words of Mormon to the Ancient Small Plates of Nephi

To learn what Mormon did with the small plates of Nephi, we turn to an intriguing little section that he wrote late in life. The

---

[2] That the book of Lehi ended in the late reign of king Benjamin is based on the assumption that it closed at the point where the next book, the book of Mosiah, begins. The book of Mosiah begins shortly before Benjamin's retirement from the throne (Mosiah 1:9; 2:30).

year appears to have been AD 385, at which time Mormon was 74 (Mormon was born about AD 311; see Mormon 2:2). It was then that he took the already ancient small plates of Nephi, which had been discontinued as a record over five hundred years before, and added a little historical appendage to them.[3] The opening verse identifies the late period of his writing: "And now I, Mormon, being about to deliver up the record which I have been making into the hands of my son Moroni, behold I have witnessed almost all the destruction of my people, the Nephites" (v 1). Quite clearly the months or years of careful composing and engraving were at an end when he inscribed these lines.

Interestingly enough, after explaining how he found the small plates of Nephi during an early period of his abridgment work (v 3), why he treasured them (v 4), and how he felt impressed to include them with his own metal book (vv 6-7), he proceeds in a few short paragraphs to give the highlights of king Benjamin's life.

As he shifts from the explanatory portion of the Words of Mormon to the historical portion, he announces, "And now I, Mormon, proceed to finish out my record, which I take from the plates of Nephi . . ." (v 9). We understand this statement simply to mean that he returned to the large plates of Nephi, his basic source book, to obtain the information for the historical addition to the small plates of Nephi that comprise verses 9-18.

As we probe futher into the abbreviated historical notes that Mormon added to the small plates of Nephi, we see that they carry the reader from the point in the early lifetime of king Benjamin where the small plates of Nephi end to the point late in Benjamin's

---

[3] Notwithstanding the fact that Amaleki, the last writer of the small plates of Nephi, closed the volume with the words, ". . . and these plates are full. And I make an end of my speaking" (Omni 1:30), we are still obliged to conclude that Mormon, more than five centuries later, actually added the Words of Mormon to the small plates of Nephi. Whether he did so on a kind of cover sheet, which may have been employed to protect the sacred engravings from getting scratched or damaged, or whether he simply inserted an extra leaf, or found and utilized a little unused space at the end of the record, there can be little question but that he added the Words of Mormon to the original small plates of Nephi. This interpretation seems to be confirmed by his statement, "Wherefore, I chose these things [the small plates of Nephi] to finish my record upon them . . ." (WofM 1:5).

lifetime where the book of Mosiah begins. Mormon's appendage leads one smoothly and directly into his abridgment of the book of Mosiah.

The fact that Mormon extended the small plates of Nephi to the book of Mosiah is more significant than appears on the surface. The greater significance becomes apparent when we recall that the small plates of Nephi formed a religious record of early Nephites and that Mormon's abridgment of the large plates of Nephi—*from the book of Mosiah to the end*—formed a religious record of later Nephites. The few lines of history that Mormon added to the small plates of Nephi thus served to combine two great religious records into one. In Mormon's eyes, incidentally, his digest of the secular book of Lehi must now have seemed a supplement to the composite religious record.

Reflections

There is much more to the story of the Book of Mormon than we have thus far considered. Most of the continued story has to do with experiences of Mormon's son, Moroni, who succeeded his father as prophet-custodian of the sacred record. Indeed, my topic, "The Small Plates of Nephi and the Words of Mormon," is only the first part of the entire tale. We conclude this first part by shifting attention abruptly to the emergence of the Book of Mormon in the nineteenth century.

Mormon's inspiration to include the small plates of Nephi with his own plates and even to extend that record to the opening of the book of Mosiah was remarkably verified in Joseph Smith's day. This is what happened. The Prophet first translated Mormon's abridgment of the book of Lehi, which work proceeded very slowly but afforded him valuable translating experience. Then his assistant, Martin Harris, lost the 116 page translation of this section (*History of the Church* 1:56). Although at first the Prophet was filled with despair, we may suppose that his despair turned to joy when he learned that: (a) the small plates of Nephi, with the appended

Words of Mormon, covered precisely the same period of history that the book of Lehi did and (b) the small plates of Nephi formed a superior tool for "convincing the Jew and Gentile that Jesus is the Christ."

Afterward the Lord revealed to Joseph Smith that the small plates of Nephi were "more particular concerning the things" (D&C 10:40) that we should have. It is my humble opinion that from the foundation of the world it had been so.

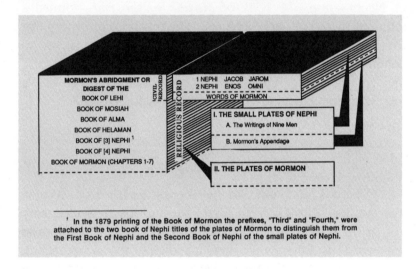

¹ In the 1879 printing of the Book of Mormon the prefixes, "Third" and "Fourth," were attached to the two book of Nephi titles of the plates of Mormon to distinguish them from the First Book of Nephi and the Second Book of Nephi of the small plates of Nephi.

BIBLIOGRAPHY

Cannon, George Q. *Young People's History of Joseph Smith*. Salt Lake City: Deseret News, 1914.

History of the Church. 7 vols. Salt Lake City: Deseret Book, 1980.

Journal of Discourses. 26 vols. 1854-86.

Pratt, Orson. "Remarkable Visions." Liverpool: Franklin D. Richards, 1851. Reprinted in *Orson Pratt: Writings of an Apostle*. Vol 2 of Mormon Collectors Series. Salt Lake City: Mormon Heritage, 1976.

Ricks, Eldin. "Story of the Formation of the Book of Mormon Plates: An Analysis of the Sources and Structure of the Sacred Record." Bound with *Book of Mormon Wide Margin Edition.* Provo, UT: Mountain West, 1987.

Pride and Riches   13

Chauncey C. Riddle

*O*ne of the most memorable and striking passages of the Book of Mormon is Jacob's instructions to his people on the subjects of pride and riches. Our purpose here is to examine the detail of this message and to apply it to our own day. We will proceed by giving a verse by verse commentary on the short passage on this subject found in Jacob 2:12-21, and will then draw some relevant conclusions for our own time.

Parentheses and superscripts are used to mark the portions of the text upon which specific commentary will be made. Commentary is then made without further reference to substantiating evidence. The supposition is that each reader will compare notes with the author's opinions and submit any differences of opinion to the Lord in prayer for resolution. That, of course, is what must be done with any evidence or opinion, footnoted or not.

The setting for Jacob's message is that his older brother Nephi, the son of Lehi, and leader and prophet unto the Nephites, has died. Jacob has been consecrated to be the spiritual leader of the Nephites, and on the occasion of the message concerning riches he is addressing those whom we might well presume are the more faithful of the Nephite peoples because his discourse takes place within the confines of the temple (Jacob 1:17). In response to Jacob's prayer, the Lord has given him instruction, specific word, to deliver to these covenant people on this occasion, and Jacob delivers that word as quoted below.

Chauncey C. Riddle is professor of Philosophy at Brigham Young University.

Jacob 2:12. And now behold, my brethren, this is the word which I declare unto you, that many of you have begun to search for gold, and for silver, and for all manner of precious ores, in the which (this land, which is a land of promise unto you and to your seed)[a], doth abound most plentifully.

a. A land of promise is a place designated by the Lord where he will go before those who are assigned to go there. The promise is that there they may find righteousness and the Lord himself, to be personally redeemed from the fall of Adam. There is no guarantee that a promised land will be fruitful or that it will abound in ores, such as Lehi's promised land did. If it is fruitful and abounds with treasures, this may actually prove to be a snare to the people if they forget the real purpose of their being in the land and if they then substitute temporal desires for the promised spiritual blessings.

13. (And the hand of providence hath smiled upon you most pleasingly, that you have obtained many riches)[a]; (and because some of you have obtained more abundantly than that of your brethren)[b] (ye are lifted up in the pride of your hearts)[c], and (wear stiff necks and high heads)[d] (because of the costliness of your apparel)[e], and (persecute your brethren because ye suppose that ye are better than they)[f].

a. The Lord is the provider, the hand of providence. He wants his children to enjoy the good things of the earth.

b. The Lord gives different gifts in differing amounts to each of his children. He deliberately does not equally bestow his temporal blessings. He wishes to give each of his children the opportunity voluntarily to share with others who have less of some temporal gift. Sometimes the temporal blessings are given to those who seem to deserve them least. The initial distribution of spiritual blessings also often seems to be unequal and unearned. But any subsequent spiritual blessings must be earned upon the principles of righteousness. In this area of further spiritual blessings, the Lord is immediate, equitable and absolutely just in bestowing his blessings, even as he will be in bestowing physical blessings in the next world.

c. We lift up our heads in pride as if we were something special among men, supposing that it has been our intelligence and industry which have provided for our desires rather than the Provider. Thus we look down on those whom we consider to be less industrious and less intelligent.

d. We have stiff necks in that we will not bow to the God of the land and acknowledge the source of our blessings. We have high heads in the haughtiness of pride.

e. The common way of showing wealth the world over is to wear expensive clothing. Expensive clothing is labor intensive, and wearing it shows that we are able to buy the time and skill of others more than most persons can.

f. Persecution comes in so many forms that it is impossible to name them all. But standard ways of persecuting are to look down on others, to speak down to them, and to segregate them because of their lack of wealth.

14. And now, my brethren, (do ye suppose that God justifieth you in this thing)ᵃ? Behold, I say unto you, Nay. But (he condemneth you)ᵇ, and (if ye persist in these things his judgments must speedily come unto you)ᶜ.

a. God justifies men by teaching them what is just or righteous, then empowering them to live up to the standard. He never calls an evil thing just, and can never make a person who persists in doing evil things into a just person. The only hope an unjust person has to become just is personal repentance through faith in Jesus Christ.

b. Jacob is the Lord's anointed; he represents Jesus Christ to them. Thus they need to take very seriously his flat statement that the Lord condemns them.

c. This is a plain warning of peril. The Lord will not always immediately bring misery and woe upon a people who are wicked if they know him not. But when a people have covenanted to become his children and obey his commandments, he warns them through his prophet and then shakes them temporally if they will not hearken to the spiritual warning. This has the goal of causing them to be humbled through physical suffering if they will not be humbled by spiritual warnings. Only as they are humble can they repent and receive the promises.

15. (O that he would show you that he can pierce you, and with one glance of his eye he can smite you to the dust)[a].

a. Jacob seems to be saying: I would that he would impress you by letting you see his great power, without having actually to smite you so that you and your children suffer.

16. O (that he would rid you from this)[a] (iniquity)[b] and (abomination)[c]. And, O (that ye would listen unto the word of his commands)[d], and (let not this pride of your hearts destroy your souls)[e]!

a. It is the Lord who makes it possible for a person to repent. He does not take the iniquity out of the world or the person, but enables the person to depart from the iniquity by turning to the corresponding righteousness. When we have departed from iniquity by making the good things the Savior would have us do part of our character, then we can also receive a permanent forgiveness for the iniquity once committed.

b. Iniquity is inequity, and it is never seen more plainly than when some are rich and some are poor and there is no attempt on the part of the rich to create equity in righteousness. Unrighteous ways to create equity in wealth are theft and governmental redistribution. Both of these attempted solutions use force to negate agency, and never do create real equity, for they are based on the faulty "wisdom" of men. The righteous way to attain equity in society is for the rich to humble themselves before God and share their wealth with the poor as he directs, until they have achieved a just equity (D&C 104: 11-18).

c. Abomination is that which departs from, is different from, the revelations of God. All righteousness comes through faith in God, which is loving obedience to his revealed instructions.

"Omin" is the equivalent of "omen," which refers to revelation. "Ab" means away from.

d. Faith comes by the hearing of the word. If only they will inquire of the Lord to know for sure that this is his word and then do what he says in full faith, they can and will be released from the curse under which they operate.

e. The curse under which they operate is their own doing. They have departed from the way of the Lord, and the destruction of their souls, spirit and body, awaits them if they will not now return to that strait and narrow way.

17. (Think of your brethren like unto yourselves)[a], and (be familiar with all)[b] and (free with your substance)[c], (that they may be rich like unto you)[c]

a. The Lord's celestial way is for us to love one another even as he loves us. If we are not quite up to that, at least we ought to think of and treat our brethren and sisters of the covenant the same way we treat ourselves.

b. The desire to make money, especially to benefit unduly, is one of the great spiritual traps of the world. Spiritually, we might well be much better off if there were no money and we were under the necessity of trading labor. That would be one step toward equity. But another, more immediate step, is simply freely to give of our possessions to those who have less than we do, being aware of their needs and circumstances and imparting to them under the direction of the Holy Spirit.

c. Richness is relative. It is not required that all men rise to a certain absolute level of physical wealth. It is only required that we of the new and everlasting covenant be equal, voluntarily equal, with each other in whatever we have. Then the Lord promises that he will give us the abundance of spiritual blessings. (D&C 70:14)

In any mortal situation, a righteous person who has the strength to do so will be voluntarily producing physical goods and services for the society in which he dwells. He will consume only what is necessary of these self-gained benefits, and will voluntarily share the surplus with others who are in need of his surplus.

One such surplus is knowledge, skills and tools which enable us to produce physical benefits. These may be righteously shared with others and are even more helpful to the recipient in most cases than are consumable goods.

18. But (before ye seek for riches, seek ye for the kingdom of God)[a].

a. There is nothing wrong in itself about seeking for riches. But we must put things in proper perspective, in proper order. The correct order is first to straiten our hearts and minds into the pattern of the Lord's love. That we do by finding his kingdom, accepting the covenant to enter that kingdom, then fully participating in the proffered salvation of our souls from the evil which is within our own breasts, which evil keeps us from becoming just and upright in all that we do.

19. And (after ye have obtained a hope in Christ)[a] (ye shall obtain riches, if ye seek them)[b]; and (ye will seek them for the intent to do good)[c]—(to clothe the naked)[d], and (to feed the hungry)[e], and (to liberate the captive)[f], and (administer relief to the sick and the afflicted)[g].

a. Hope in Christ is the pivotal concept which helps us to bridge from the beginnings of faith in Jesus Christ to the attaining of the fullness of faith, which is charity. After we receive a manifestation from the Savior which reveals his will, we have the opportunity to exercise faith by believing and obeying that instruction. Obeying the Savior gives us a right to hope for the spiritual blessings which the Savior can so richly bestow. The principal blessing which a person of faith can hope for is to receive a new heart, a pure heart which no longer desires any form of evil. This pure heart is called "charity" and is the greatest mortal attainment of any human being. Attaining it makes it possible to be able to ask for and to receive any other blessing from the Savior. Such a further blessing can be either spiritual or temporal. Additional gifts can then be given freely by the Savior to the individual who has charity because there is then no danger that the person will use any gift for an evil purpose. Thus to attain to a genuine hope in Christ is another way of saying that we have attained unto charity, which is the pure love of Christ. Then we are ready to endure to the end of our lives in righteousness, in doing pure and godly works in behalf of others. We are then ready to seek riches of any kind to be used for righteous purposes.

b. The Savior tells us that when we are pure and cleansed from all sin, we can ask for anything and will surely receive it as we obey him, because we will not ask amiss but will ask for good things to do the work of righteousness.

c. The intent to do good is the intent to do the will of God, even Jesus Christ, who is the fountain of all righteousness for the inhabitants of this earth. This good sought may be of four forms or types, each one corresponding to part of the nature of each individual human being.

We humans consist of heart, mind, strength, and might. The heart is the heart of the spirit body and is the decision center in the human being. The mind is the brain of the spirit body and is the knower, planner, executor function of the human being. The strength is the mortal human body especially including the power of procreation. The might is whatever power or influence the person has in his or her sphere of action resulting from the abilities of the heart, mind and body and also from any wealth, property, persuasive power, or ability to command the efforts of other persons which anyone might enjoy. Thus there are good things of the heart, such as pure desires; good things of the mind, such as truths; good things of the body, such as health and strength; and good things of might, such as food, clothing, shelter, fuel, money, land, political position, priesthood power, etc.

d. The naked may be those who have no clothing with whom we might share our excess clothing. Or they might be naked emotionally, such as the bereaved or hopeless to whom we can extend love. Or they might be naked intellectually, and we can share with them a knowledge of just how this world works so that they need no longer be so buffeted because of their ignorance.

e. Some hungry persons need physical food. But others are hungry in heart; they need love and kindness in a world that offers much hate and tyranny. Or they may have an insatiable curiosity which they cannot satisfy because they lack the opportunity to learn.

f. Some captives are political or military prisoners who are incarcerated through no fault of their own. To use our might to free them may be most important. Or they may be justly imprisoned, where influence might be brought to bear to help them to square a debt with society so that they may be honorably released. They might be emotional captives who are under the spell of an evil person and need an alternative to which to turn. They may be intellectual captives whose vision of the world is constrained to the point that they know not God. They may be captive to drugs or sin, from which they might be released through the assistance of the ordinances of the holy priesthood.

g. Administering relief to the sick and the afflicted may be caring for someone who has had a stroke or a debilitating disease. But it may also be nurturing someone who is suffering under a load of guilt and does not know of the mercies of the Savior. It may be to help someone who has a preoccupation with a false idea or cause, who needs to see the world another way. It may be to help a person who is possessed of evil spirits who can find no relief except in Christ.

Whatever the virtually infinite variety of need, the Savior has a solution which faithful servants may obtain and administer for every malady save one: A hard heart which will not admit the Holy Spirit. Only that person himself can change that.

20. And now, my brethren, I have spoken unto you concerning pride; and those of you which have afflicted your neighbor, and persecuted him because ye were proud in your hearts, of the things which God hath given you, (what say ye of it)[a]?

a. When the prophet speaks to those of the covenant, they of necessity must respond. If they are repentant, they will confess their sins and forsake them; thus Jacob asks his people what they will say. If they wish to continue the apostasy, they will murmur under their breath and persist in the way of evil. In either case they are judging themselves and setting the direction of their own future unto good or evil, whichever they choose; and out of their own mouths they are exonerated or condemned.

21. Do ye not suppose that such things are abominable unto him who created all flesh? And the one being is as precious in his sight as the other. And all flesh is of the dust; and (for the selfsame end hath he created them, that they should keep his commandments and glorify him forever)[a].

a. God is a god of righteousness. He desires that we should worship and glorify him because that increases the righteousness in the universe and enables him to enlarge us without end. The dust of the earth and we humans were both created, or organized, for that same purpose, but most of the time the dust is more faithful than are most humans.

Reflection on Jacob's message brings three strong conclusions to mind. The first is that there is a good reason why it is hard for people to share: the differences of values and commitments which they have. The second is that to live the gospel of Jesus Christ we must be willing to be poor. The third is that before we do anything else in our life we should seek for a hope in Christ.

Having differences of values and commitments does not make sharing impossible or unnecessary, only harder. When people have the same values and allegiances, it is easier to share. When they do not, sharing can become more difficult. To use an extreme example to emphasize the point, let us suppose two families living as neighbors. One family is very frugal and saving, and through years of living by those principles have gathered a small surplus. They are in a position to share. Suppose the other family is very needy. The first family sees that need and takes part of its hard earned savings to the other family to buy groceries.

Then suppose that the second family takes the gift, rejoices in it, but decides that the best way to spend it would be to invite all of their friends over for a big alcohol bust. In one evening they squander the hard earned savings of the frugal family and are even poorer than they were to start with. Sharing has gone awry there.

For this reason, the first thing people should share with one another is the restored gospel of Jesus Christ in the hope that there can be a common set of values, and service under a common Master. That would greatly facilitate sharing. But even if those in need will not change their values, they may yet have needs that must be addressed.

This brings us to the general rule laid down by the Savior: Sharing needs to be done under his instruction and in his way. That is why there is a gift of the Holy Ghost, for men are not wise enough to know how to do all things in righteousness. That is why there needs to be a priesthood structure in the Church to be an established channel of inspiration and sharing among the children of the Savior. Difficult though sharing maybe, it must be done, but in his own way by the guidance of his own Spirit. When done in the Savior it is always worthwhile to impoverish ourselves in the service of our fellowmen.

Clearly we do not need to be impoverished or poor to be servants of Christ. But we must always be *willing* to be poor. If we are already poor, we are admonished to remain poor before seeking wealth until we have obtained a hope in Christ. Thus we must be willing to be poor. If we have wealth, we must be willing to share our wealth with our brethren to the point that they are equal with us in physical wealth; if we have many brethren, our wealth may help many only a little, leaving us and everyone else in relative poverty. Sometimes our mission in life may cause us to be impecunious, as are some persons who spend most of their lives on a series of missions, or who may be dedicated to an enterprise which completely drains them financially, such as sustaining a fledgling educational institution. Or they may be moved to contribute heavily to the construction of a new temple, and making that contribution leaves them impoverished.

The general principle is, of course, that all we have is at the Lord's disposal. Whenever he instructs us to give it all away to the cause of righteousness, we gladly do so, knowing that we are pleasing our Master and furthering his work. We cannot be faithful servants of Christ unless we are willing to be poor, even as he, the Father of Heaven and Earth, was willing to be poor to fulfill his earthly ministry in righteousness.

But who can look so dispassionately on material possessions as to count them nothing dear when the time comes to be stripped of them? This is not easy for most mortals. It surely is not the natural inclination of the vast majority of mankind. But it must be the attitude of all who are true followers of Jesus Christ.

The true followers of Jesus Christ know that the only riches worth counting are the riches of eternity. They know that all flesh is as grass and will be gone tomorrow. They know that God is good, and amply rewards the faithful for any sacrifice of worldly goods they might make. They trust completely in the wisdom of their Master, having tried him and having found him to be trustworthy in every particular. So their faith commends only one thing as the first priority in their lives: Seek first for a hope in Christ before doing *anything* else.

The time called "youth" is looked upon by the world as a time of freedom from responsibility, a time of learning, of indulging, of exploration before settling into the sacrifices and rigors of adulthood. That largely perverse view is a very poor preparation for adult, responsible life for most of its adherents. No wonder so many want to be supported by society throughout their lives, or to be perpetual students, or to indulge their ever increasing desire for pleasure, or to avoid the responsibility of family and a productive life.

The ideal pattern for Latter-day Saint youth would seem to be that of the life of Jacob himself, who in his youth sought for a hope in Christ and found it. As a youth he beheld the glory of the Savior(2 Nephi 2:4). Then Jacob could ask for anything and know that he would receive it because of the promise of his God. If we become pure and spotless, we may ask whatsoever we will and we will receive it, for we will not ask amiss (D&C 46:30). We will ask to be able to succor the weak, the helpless, the poor, the abused, the ignorant, the hopeless. The riches of both time and eternity are standing ready to be given to the faithful to minister to the needs of the poor of all nations, kindreds, tongues and peoples if only the covenant servants of Jesus Christ will seek first for the kingdom of heaven and for a hope in their Beloved Master before they seek for anything else.

The real problem is not with riches, of course. The real problem is with hearts. When our hearts are not pure, we cannot love with a pure love. We cannot love the Savior as we should, nor can we love our neighbors as we should. The Savior came to save us from this deficit of love by extending the arms of mercy, through our own faith and repentance, to each of us.

Why do some of us resist? Is it not because we somehow see ourselves as being sufficient as we are? Do we not believe in our hearts that we are already good enough, that the Savior may indeed have to forgive us of a few things, but his love and generosity will easily take care of those things and we will then be ushered ceremoniously into the blessings of the great beyond? (2 Nephi 28:7-9). Such a belief is what the scriptures call pride. It is the belief that *we* are good, though perhaps our deeds are not. This is the belief that the old us does not need to die and become a new creature, but only our garments need to be cleansed. In pride we see ourselves as eternal creatures who may need to be forgiven and lifted up by Jesus Christ, but who do not need to be essentially changed by him. We do not need that new and pure heart which only he can give to us.

My understanding of the gospel of Jesus Christ is that no mortals are just and righteous enough of themselves to go to the same kingdom as Jesus Christ unless they are remade in the image of Christ, heart and mind, body and soul. For without that pure heart, that charity, we are nothing (Moroni 7:44), and can, of ourselves, do no good thing (John 15:1-5). We must cease to exist as the old selfish persons we were and take upon ourselves new hearts and new minds.

Then in the humility of being salvaged from damnation by the Savior's love, we will never again consider that we are better than anyone else. Then we will know that we stand only in the grace of Christ, and will never be found looking down on anyone, including the worst sinner and Satan and his angels. We will then know our true place and being in the universe, and will say of the sinner, "There, but for the grace of God, go I."

Pride is the root of our evil, the source of our selfishness, the great barrier to our salvation. It is the pride of our hearts from which we need to be saved more than from anything else. Once we are saved from that, then all good things can be added to us. Then we will see as we are seen, know as we are known, and we will be familiar and free with our substance, treating all men as brothers. Then indeed we will have heaven on earth.

Enos and the Words Concerning Eternal Life

14

David R. Seely

*T*he Book of Mormon contains many detailed accounts illustrating the power of the "word," or "words," in bringing individuals to Christ through repentance. Its inspired authors and editors were conscious of its mission: to come forth in the latter days to bring men to Christ. They were also aware that this mission was to be fulfilled through the words which they were writing. Nephi says of the Book of Mormon, "The words of the faithful should speak as if it were from the dead" (2 Nephi 27:13), and Moroni says the Lord will say to us at the judgment bar: "Did I not declare my words unto you, which were written by this man, like as one crying from the dead, yea, even as one speaking out of the dust?" (Moroni 10:27; see also 2 Nephi 33:13; Mormon 8:26).

The Book of Mormon contains the "words . . . concerning eternal life" (Enos 1:3), meaning the doctrines of salvation as delivered by the Lord and his servants. Through historical examples it demonstrates the power of such words to change lives. In addition, the collection of the words about eternal life contained in the Book of Mormon invites all men to come unto Christ by serving as a witness to the divine work accomplished by Joseph Smith in the restoration of the correct doctrines and the ordinances necessary for salvation (see D&C 20:9-12).

David R. Seely is assistant professor of Ancient Scripture at Brigham Young University.

I have been impressed with the story of Enos for two reasons: first, because my own father influenced me in much the same way Enos's did him; and second, the role that words have played in my conversion is similar to the role of words in Enos' conversion. The story of Enos after all is a story of his lifelong conversion to the gospel. It contains many elements that are familiar to all of us since they are common to all of our conversions. At several places in his account Enos mentions the role of words in his conversion: first, they act as a catalyst for his desire to gain a remission of his sins; second, they form a powerful agent in his conversation with the Lord; and finally, they are the means by which he attempts to share the experience of his conversion with others. It is the role of words in the conversion of Enos that I wish to focus on here.

Using the story of Enos as a model, I will examine the Book of Mormon concept of the "word" or "words" as it relates to the conversion process. This paper will consist of two parts. First, I will attempt to illuminate the episode of Enos' conversion by examining three pertinent questions: What was the source of the words concerning eternal life that moved Enos to action? What is the message of these words? and What were the effects of the words on Enos? In the second part I will show that the role of words in the conversions of other Book of Mormon characters is parallel to the conversion of Enos and that this concept of the role of words relates to the mission of the Book of Mormon as a whole.

Enos' Conversion

The first 18 verses of the book of Enos contain the account of Enos' conversion. He writes, "Behold, I went to hunt beasts in the forests; and the words which I had often heard my father speak concerning eternal life, and the joy of the saints, sunk deep into my heart" (v 3). The image of the words of his father "concerning eternal life, and the joy of the saints" sinking into his heart is a wonderful description of the Holy Ghost working on his soul, revealing the truth of those words as well as the need to act on them. The natural result of receiving the word through the Holy Ghost is repentance (see Mosiah 4:1-2). The words of Enos' father caused his "soul to hunger" (Enos 1:4), presumably for the "eternal life, and the joy of the saints" of which his father had spoken. Thus the "words . . . concerning eternal life, and the joy of the saints" provided the catalyst for Enos to seek the Lord through repentance.

After a day of "mighty prayer and supplication," Enos heard the voice of the Lord saying, "Enos, thy sins are forgiven thee, and thou shalt be blessed" (vv 4-5). When Enos asked how this was possible, the Lord said, "Because of thy faith in Christ" (v 8). Enos' repentance was made possible through the Atonement.

In verse nine Enos records, "Now, it came to pass that when I had heard these words I began to feel a desire for the welfare of my brethren, the Nephites; wherefore, I did pour out my whole soul unto God for them." Again the voice of the Lord responded and promised him that the Nephites would be blessed according to their faithfulness. In verse 11 Enos writes, "And after I, Enos, had heard these words [that the Nephites would be blessed on condition of their faithfulness], my faith began to be unshaken in the Lord; and I prayed unto him with many long strugglings for my brethren, the Lamanites" (his enemies!). The Lord once again responded to Enos' request according to his desires. Enos knew the Nephites would be destroyed if they were not faithful, and so he asked the Lord to preserve their record that it could be brought forth at some future day to bring salvation to the Lamanites (v 13). The Lord covenanted that this would be so: "And I, Enos, knew that it would be according to the covenant which he had made; wherefore my soul did rest" (v 17). Thus the experience of Enos demonstrates that a consequence of true conversion is the reception of the gift of charity, a gift of the Spirit, through which an individual feels concern for the welfare and the salvation of his brothers, both friends and enemies.

In the nine remaining verses of his book, Enos writes of his efforts to teach the "words . . . concerning eternal life, and the joy of the saints," to the Nephites and the Lamanites, who were in a state of serious spiritual decline. The experience of Enos demonstrates that the result of receiving the word and feeling the promptings of the Holy Ghost is the desire to share it with others. This brings to mind the injunction Christ later gave to his apostles: "When thou art converted, strengthen thy brethren" (Luke 22:32). Near the end of his life Enos said, "And I saw that I must soon go down to my grave, having been wrought upon by the power of God that I must preach and prophesy unto this people, and declare the word according to the truth which is in Christ" (v 26). Enos shared his witness valiantly throughout his life. In the words of Nephi and Jacob, he had "endured to the end" (1 Nephi 22:31; 2 Nephi 9:24; 33:4). In his closing verse Enos expressed his desire to hear the words of the Redeemer, words concerning eternal life: "Come unto me, ye blessed, there is a place prepared for you in the mansions of my Father" (v 27). This final verse provides a wonderful link between the opening and closing of the story of Enos, which begins with the words of his righteous father inspiring him to seek forgiveness of the Lord and ends with the words of the Savior inviting him to come and dwell with his Eternal Father.

The Source of the Words Concerning Eternal Life

Enos identifies the immediate source of the words concerning eternal life as his father Jacob. Enos says of his father in verse one, "I, Enos, knowing my father that he was a just man—for he taught me in his language, and also in the nurture and admonition of the Lord." Lehi, in describing Jacob, alludes to the fact that as a young boy Jacob had beheld the glory of the Lord (2 Nephi 2:1-4), and Nephi states it implicitly (2 Nephi 11:3). We can also assess Jacob's character by studying the accounts we have of his own words: five chapters in 2 Nephi 6-10 and seven chapters in the book of Jacob. Enos further explains the role his father had in teaching him the gospel, "Behold, I went to hunt beasts in the forests; and the words which I had often heard my father speak concerning eternal life, and the joy of the saints, sunk deep into my heart" (Enos 1:3). The observation that his father's words had "sunk . . . into [his] heart" is reminiscent of the comment Nephi made at the end of his record, "When a man speaketh by the power of the Holy Ghost the power of the Holy Ghost carrieth it unto the hearts of the children of men" (2 Nephi 33:1). Just men who take the time to teach their children by the Holy Spirit have a powerful influence on their lives. This principle is taught by the Book of Mormon in the stories of Enos, Lehi and his sons, Alma the Elder and Alma the Younger, and Mormon and Moroni. The words concerning eternal life have power because they come from the Lord and are confirmed to each individual by the Holy Ghost. As we look for the source of these words, we note that Jacob teaches that the Lord uses three means to teach us the words concerning eternal life: first, living mortals, including parents and other inspired men (Jacob 6:3); second, the scriptures (Jacob 6:3); and third, the Lord himself either directly (Jacob 2:11; 7:5) or through divine messengers (2 Nephi 6:8-11).

The Message of the Words Concerning Eternal Life

Enos says his father Jacob, "taught me in his language, and also in the nurture and admonition of the Lord" (Enos 1:1), and later, "The words which I had often heard my father speak concerning eternal life, and the joy of the saints, sunk deep into my heart" (Enos 1:3). Although in a general sense we can understand the phrase, "the words . . . concerning eternal life, and the joy of the saints" to mean the gospel of Jesus Christ, comprising all of those teachings and ordinances necessary for salvation and exaltation as well as the fulfillment gained by righteous living, the precise meaning Enos saw in the words of these two phrases may prove elusive. However, we can still gain some insight by examining the context in which Enos' father uses them. In fact, even from what little we have (Nephi tells us that he

recorded only a small portion of Jacob's sermons [2 Nephi 11:1])
we see some interesting correlations which suggest that Enos'
language may sometimes reflect the teachings of his father Jacob.

Taught me in his language. Judging from similar passages
in 1 Nephi 1:1 and Mosiah 1:2-3, 16;[1] the reference to his father's
language surely must refer to the level of literacy needed to read
and understand the plates as well as to continue the tradition of
writing on them. It seems clear in the cases of Nephi, Enos, and
Mosiah that their fathers took the responsibility to have them
educated in the secular as well as the spiritual matters necessary
for the keeping of the records.

Taught me in the nurture and admonition of the Lord. The
phrase "in the nurture and admonition" occurs in the Bible only
in the King James translation of Ephesians 6:4 where it also
occurs in the context of the family.[2] The English word *nurture*
does not occur elsewhere in the Old or New Testament in the KJV
and the word *admonition* is only slightly more common. Both
Greek words in Ephesians 6:4 (*paideia*, "nurture," and *nouthesia*,
"admonition") are quite common in the Septuagint translation of
numerous Hebrew verbs both in the context of the Lord and of
the family. Thus such a concept could have been known to Enos
from the brass plates, and it is at least possible that both passages
are derived from a common antecedent in the Hebrew tradition
that is no longer extant in our English translation of the scriptures.
For our purposes we are interested in seeing if there is anything
in the teachings of Jacob to which Enos may have been referring
with this phrase.

---

[1] In 1 Nephi 1:1 Nephi acknowledged that he "was taught somewhat in all the
learning" of his father. Benjamin also "caused that [his three sons Mosiah, Helorum, and
Helaman] should be taught in all the language of his fathers, that thereby they might become
men of understanding; and that they might know concerning the prophecies which had been
spoken by the mouths of their fathers" (Mosiah 1:2-3). In Mosiah 1:16 Benjamin gave charge
of the records to his son Mosiah who continued to write on the plates.

[2] Ephesians 6:1-9 is a list of instructions regarding the roles of individuals in a
household. Following the KJV, Ephesians 6:4 reads, "And, ye fathers, provoke not your
children to wrath: but bring them up in the nurture and admonition of the Lord."

As noted above, the word *nurture* does not occur elsewhere in the Book of Mormon, but it is possible that the concept Enos refers to with *nurture* may be found in its English cognate nourish (both of which derive from the Latin root *nutrire*) which occurs 25 times (in various forms) in the book of Jacob, all but one in the context of the allegory of the olive tree where the term is used in reference to the care the Lord and his servants give to the vineyard.[3] Jacob also applies it to the people in conjunction with hearing the word when he mentions their being "nourished by the good word of God all the day long" (Jacob 6:7). The same concept may also be found in the English cognate *nursing* which is found in Jacob's quotation of Isaiah referring to the "nursing fathers" and "nursing mothers" (2 Nephi 6:7). Enos' use of "nurture of the Lord," as taught him by his father Jacob, might refer to the Lord's care for his children as demonstrated by Jacob's quotations and his discussion of the allegory of the olive trees (Jacob 5-6).

The word *admonition* and its variants *admonish, admonished, admonishing*, and *admonitions*, occur only eight times in the Book of Mormon. In the small plates they occur four times, once here in Enos 1 and once in the mouth of Jacob when he speaks of "the strict commandment which I have received from God, to admonish you according to your crimes" (Jacob 2:9). It also appears in Nephi's writings when he remarks, "And it came to pass that not many days after his death, Laman and Lemuel and the sons of Ishmael were angry with me because of the admonitions of the Lord" (2 Nephi 4:13); and in Omni 1:13 we read that Mosiah's followers "were admonished continually by the word of God." In each of these cases, as well as in the other four occurrences in the Book of Mormon, "admonish" means "to exhort," usually with the connotation of repentance (see Mosiah 26:6, 39 [twice]; and Alma 1:7).

---

[3] This word occurs 45 times in the Book of Mormon, 25 of which appear in the writings of Jacob. This also argues for individual authorship apart from the influence of Joseph Smith or the KJV. Only one of the occurrences (Jacob 7:15) appears in a context other than that of the allegory of the olive trees.

The Words Concerning Eternal Life and the Joy of the Saints.
Jacob received the words he spoke from his father, from the
scriptures, from the Lord through his voice or in vision, through
messengers, and through the Holy Ghost. While the phrases
"words . . . concerning eternal life" and "joy of the saints" do not
occur in any of Jacob's sermons, all of the components of these
phrases occur enough times separately to give us a sense of what
they may have meant to Jacob and thus to Enos.

Jacob mentions "word" 27 times and "words" 39 times. Of
note are the occurrences of the phrases: "I have spoken the words
of your Maker. I know that the words of truth are hard against
all uncleanness; but the righteous fear them not" (2 Nephi 9:40)
and, "Remember the words of your God; pray unto him continually
by day, and give thanks unto his holy name by night" (2 Nephi
9:52). Both of these passages may be related to the phrase used
by Enos because Enos was concerned about repentance and was
moved by the weight of the words in his heart to seek a remission
of his sins through prayer.

Jacob refers to "life eternal" and "eternal life" three times,
always in the context of the need for repentance: "Remember, to
be carnally-minded is death, and to be spiritually-minded is life
eternal" (2 Nephi 9:39); "Therefore, cheer up your hearts, and
remember that ye are free to act for yourselves—to choose the
way of everlasting death or the way of eternal life" (2 Nephi
10:23); and, "O then, my beloved brethren, repent ye, and enter
in at the strait gate, and continue in the way which is narrow, until
ye shall obtain eternal life" (Jacob 6:11). As in these passages,
Enos' use of the phrase "eternal life" very likely refers to his
immediate concern about eternal life, repenting and gaining a
remission of his sins.

While the phrase "joy of the saints" does not occur in the
teachings of Jacob, each part of this phrase is used separately in
relevant passages, and synonymous phrases occur in 2 Nephi
9:18, 43. The occurrence that is most likely an antecedent for the
language of Enos is a combination of both "joy" and "saints" in
the same verse in 2 Nephi 9:18: "But, behold, the righteous, the

saints of the Holy One of Israel, they who have believed in the Holy One of Israel, they who have endured the crosses of the world, and despised the shame of it, they shall inherit the kingdom of God, which was prepared for them from the foundation of the world, and their joy shall be full forever." This verse gives us a good definition of a saint, one who has believed in the Holy One of Israel, endured the crosses of the world, and who is destined to receive an inheritance in the kingdom of God. It also explains that "the joy of the saints" is the happiness they will feel when they receive their reward of eternal life.[4] That "the joy of the saints" is closely related to the idea of eternal life is further supported by Lehi's statement in his vision of the tree of life when he said, "the fruit thereof . . . filled my soul with exceedingly great joy" (1 Nephi 8:12).[5]

Much of the terminology Enos uses to describe his spiritual upbringing, which he attributes to his father, can be found in his father's teachings. At the core of the teachings of Jacob is the need for repentance, a need expressed and acted upon by Enos.

Results of Hearing the Words

Referring back to the conversion of Enos, we may now summarize the results of these words in his life as follows: first, *receive the words through the Holy Ghost* (vv 1-3); second, *repent* (vv 4-8); third, have *charity* (vv 9-18); fourth, *share the word* (vv 19-26); and fifth, *endure to the end* (vv 25-27). These steps are

---

[4] The word *joy* occurs six times, twice in the words of Isaiah (2 Nephi 8:3, 11), once in the context of the hoped-for effects of receiving the words (Jacob 4:3), and three times in the allegory of the olive trees (Jacob 5:60, 71, 75). In light of Enos' concern for his brethren and his lifelong efforts to convert them to the gospel, it may be significant that joy is explicitly related to missionary work in the Lord's invitation: "If ye labor with your might with me ye shall have joy in the fruit which I shall lay up unto myself" (5:75). The word *saints* occurs three times—all in Jacob's discussion of the Fall and Atonement in 2 Nephi 9. The first occurrence, "He delivereth his saints from that awful monster the devil" (v 19), is only generally related to the language of Enos, but the remaining two are much closer (vv 18, 43).

[5] Incidentally, this definition of the "joy of the saints" is also suggested in section 51 of the Doctrine and Covenants. "And whoso is found a faithful, a just, and a wise steward shall enter into the joy of his Lord, and shall inherit eternal life," (v 19), as well as in section 52 where the Lord says he will "crown the faithful with joy and with rejoicing" (v 43).

not unique to Enos but are the true fruits of conversion common to all. An understanding of these steps can help us to measure the ongoing processes of our own conversions to Christ and our own spiritual progress.

Other Book of Mormon Examples of Conversion

The story of Enos is typical of the Book of Mormon doctrine of conversion. As other examples, let us look at the conversion of the people of king Benjamin, in Mosiah 2-6, the conversion of Alma the Younger and the sons of Mosiah, as found in Mosiah 27 and Alma 36,[6] and the Book of Mormon message as a whole.

Mosiah 2-6: The Conversion of the People of King Benjamin

Receive the word through the Holy Ghost. King Benjamin delivered "the words which had been delivered unto him by the angel of the Lord" (4:1). His sermon centered on the atonement of Christ and the need for repentance. His words, through the power of the Spirit, had a mighty impact on the people, and he saw that "they had fallen to the earth, for the fear of the Lord had come upon them" (4:1).

Repentance. The people fell to the earth as they viewed themselves in their carnal state and cried out: "O have mercy, and apply the atoning blood of Christ that we may receive forgiveness of our sins" (4:2). Through their faith in Jesus Christ they received a remission of their sins, peace of conscience, and were filled with joy (4:3).

Charity. King Benjamin continued his sermon telling them that now that they have "come to the knowledge of the glory of God . . . and have tasted of his love, and have received a remis-

---

[6] Another example that closely follows this pattern can be found in the story of the conversion of Alma the Elder (Mosiah 17-18).

sion of [their] sins" they should always remember to have charity toward their brothers (4:11-28).

Share the word. The people were all converted and accepted Benjamin's message by covenant (5:2-6). Priests were appointed to "teach the people . . . and to stir them up in remembrance of the oath which they had made" (6:3). Chapters seven through eight record that the conversion of the people was followed by missionary work in the land of Lehi-Nephi, where it is recorded that Ammon taught the people of Limhi "the last words which king Benjamin had taught them" (8:3).

Endure to the end. While we do not know how many individuals who heard the words of king Benjamin actually endured to the end, the textual evidence suggests that a large number of them did. In Mosiah 26:1, we learn that many of those who had been children at the time "could not understand the words of king Benjamin" and therefore "did not believe the tradition of their fathers." This suggests that those who had understood the words at the time king Benjamin delivered them had remained faithful their whole lives, but they had not been completely successful in transmitting this same conviction to the next generation.

Mosiah 27 and Alma 36: The Conversion of Alma and the Sons of Mosiah

Receive the word through the Holy Ghost. Alma the Younger did not listen to the words of the Lord as delivered by his father, but the Lord did hear his father's pleas on his behalf (Mosiah 27:14, 16, 20-24). Consequently, Alma the Younger was granted the "privilege" of receiving the word of the Lord directly from an angel (Mosiah 27:11; Alma 36:5). Alma is described as "a man of many words" who "did speak much flattery to the people; therefore he led many of the people to do after the manner of his iniquities" (Mosiah 27:8). As part of the sign which the Lord gave to Alma he struck him with dumbness, a symbolically fitting punishment since his mouth had before spread only flattery and dissension. However, when his tongue was finally loosened, it was full of the words concerning eternal life. The words of the angel had a dramatic impact on Alma. He said when the angel spoke to him it was "as it were the voice of thunder" (Alma 36:7), and when he heard the indicting words "seek no more to destroy the church of God", he "was struck with . . . great fear and amazement lest perhaps [he] should be destroyed" (Alma 36:11). The implication was clear that the first step was repentance.

Repentance. Alma suffered "the pains of a damned soul" (Alma 36:16), but through the atonement of Jesus Christ he received a remission of his sins and "[his] soul was filled with joy as exceeding as was [his] pain" (Alma 36:20). In his excruciating circumstances Alma sought the Lord and his forgiveness through prayer.

Charity. The charity of Alma and the sons of Mosiah is of note. Much like Enos, their concern was for the Nephites, and they ministered to them in an attempt to correct the harm they had wrought (Mosiah 27:32-37). Next the sons of Mosiah felt compassion and concern for the Lamanites, and they volunteered to "impart the word of God" to them also (Mosiah 28:1-9). In spite of the fact that the Lamanites were the "enemy," the sons of Mosiah "could not bear that any human soul should perish" (Mosiah 28:3). Alma, meanwhile, remained among the Nephites to serve as their chief judge and high priest. In fact, Alma would remain a public servant for the rest of his life, later relinquishing the office of chief judge to serve full-time in the ministry.

Share the word. Alma and the sons of Mosiah are among the greatest missionaries recorded in all of scripture. They "began from this time forward to teach the people" (Mosiah 27:32), in spite of persecution and tribulation, and "were instruments in the hands of God in bringing many to the knowledge of the truth, yea, to the knowledge of their Redeemer" (Mosiah 27:36).

Endure to the end. That Alma endured to the end is witnessed by the account of his disappearance from among the people: "Behold, this we know, that he was a righteous man; and the saying went abroad in the church that he was taken up by the Spirit . . . therefore, for this cause we know nothing concerning his death and burial" (Alma 45:19).

These two examples show that the story of Enos is not unique, rather it includes many of the basic principles common to the doctrine of conversion seen elsewhere in the Book of Mormon. All of the doctrines and examples of conversion in the Book of Mormon, taken together, teach us that while the circumstances and details often vary, the process and result of true conversion are always very much the same. The Book of Mormon thus presents us with the words concerning eternal life as an invitation to "come unto Christ" (Moroni 10:32), and then gives us specific historical examples of how we should do this.

The Mission of the Book of Mormon: To Deliver the Words Concerning Eternal Life

As stated on its title page, the mission of the Book of Mormon is to convert men to Christ. The ancient authors and editors of the Book of Mormon were concerned that their message have the impact that it should. Impassioned statements directed to the modern reader about the power of their words to convert men to Christ are found throughout their narratives. Following our five-point typology of conversion derived from the story of Enos, let us examine a few of the things the first and last of the ancient authors of the Book of Mormon said about its mission to convert men and women to Christ.

Receive the word with the Holy Ghost. Both Nephi and Moroni recognized the importance of their words and the need for the Holy Ghost to affirm the truth of them to their readers. Nephi says, "Neither am I mighty in writing, like unto speaking; for when a man speaketh by the power of the Holy Ghost the power of the Holy Ghost carrieth it unto the hearts of the children of men" (2 Nephi 33:1). Despite their self-perceived weakness in writing, they give us the key to receiving the words concerning eternal life through the Spirit—prayer. Nephi urges us to "feast upon the words of Christ" and "hearken unto the Spirit which teacheth a man to pray" (2 Nephi 32:3, 8). It may surprise us that they both thought they were better speakers than they were writers. But Moroni says, "Thou hast not made us mighty in writing; for thou hast made all this people that they could speak much, because of the Holy Ghost which thou hast given them; And thou hast made us that we could write but little, because of the awkwardness of our hands" (Ether 12:23-24). He also counsels us saying, "I would exhort you that when ye shall read these things, . . . that ye would remember how merciful the Lord hath been . . . and ponder it in your hearts. . . . [A]nd if ye shall ask with a sincere heart, with real intent, having faith in Christ, he will manifest the truth of it unto you, by the power of the Holy Ghost. And by the power of the Holy Ghost ye may know the truth of all things" (Moroni 10:3-5).

Repentance. Knowing the truth must lead to repentance and baptism. Nephi included an entire chapter (2 Nephi 31) on the importance of repentance and baptism for the remission of sins. He said, "The gate by which ye should enter is repentance and baptism by water; and then cometh a remission of your sins by fire and by the Holy Ghost" (v 17). Moroni also spoke of the importance of repentance as part of the process of attaining perfection: "And again, if ye by the grace of God are perfect in Christ, and deny not his power, then are ye sanctified in Christ by the grace of God . . . unto the remission of your sins, that ye become holy, without spot" (Moroni 10:33).

Charity. Nephi urged us to "press forward with a steadfastness in Christ, having a perfect brightness of hope, and a love of God and of all men" (2 Nephi 31:20). At the end of his section of the record he spoke of the gift of charity which he had gained from his conversion to Christ: "I have charity for my people, . . . I have charity for the Jew[,] . . . I also have charity for the Gentiles" (2 Nephi 33:7-9). Moroni expressed the same sentiment when he said, "And except ye have charity ye can in nowise be saved in the kingdom of God" (Moroni 10:21).

Share the word. Nephi and Moroni both demonstrated their dedication to teaching the gospel to their contemporaries as well as recording their teachings for those in the distant future. Their laborious work in writing on the plates is a great witness to their concern for the remnants of their people, the Lamanites, as well as for the Jews and the Gentiles.

Endure to the end. Nephi and Moroni also testified that to attain eternal life it is necessary to endure to the end. Nephi said that he knows the Lord God will hear his prayers in behalf of his people and he will make strong his words that "speaketh of Jesus, and persuadeth them to believe in him, and to endure to the end, which is life eternal" (2 Nephi 33:4). As evidence of their faithfulness to the end, they both promised that they will be present at the judgment bar of God as witnesses that the words they wrote are true (2 Nephi 33:11; Moroni 10:34). Then and there we will give an accounting of our performance to the very source of these words, for Nephi promises us: "Christ will show unto you, with power and great glory, that they are his words, at the last day; and you and I shall stand face to face before his bar" (2 Nephi 33:11).

Conclusion

The Book of Mormon teaches the word of God in two distinct but related ways, and words are an important part of each. First, it records the actual words concerning eternal life, the words of God, as transmitted to God's servants in various ways and then delivered to the people of their day as well as ours. Second, the Book of Mormon uses biography and history to illustrate the consequences of accepting or rejecting these words.

The process of conversion is succinctly illustrated in the story of Enos and further illuminated in great detail throughout the Book of Mormon. It is a message to all of us, illustrated by the examples of men who accepted the word and received it by the Holy Ghost, repented, had true charity, shared the word, and endured to the end. This is the message and living example of men like Nephi, Jacob, Enos, king Benjamin, Alma, the sons of Mosiah, Mormon, Moroni, and many others. On the other hand we have the vivid examples of those who rejected the words concerning eternal life, men like Laman and Lemuel, Sherem, king Noah, Nehor, Korihor, and countless others. The choice is well defined and placed before us in unsurpassed plainness in the Book of Mormon. There the natural results of conversion to Christ are put forth doctrinally and illustrated by real historical circumstances, serving us as standards in our own spiritual quests to come unto Christ.

As Enos of old, may we respond to the words concerning eternal life as they come to us from our parents and other mortals, from the scriptures, and directly from the Lord. May they sink deep into our hearts through the power of the Holy Ghost which bears witness of them, and may they cause us to seek the Lord for a remission of our sins, to receive the gift of charity, to share the words with others, and to endure to the end. And may we, like Enos, rejoice to think of the day when we shall go to the place of our rest, which is with our Redeemer, when our mortal shall put on immortality and we shall stand before him and he will speak the "words concerning eternal life and the joy of the saints" (Enos 1:3) to us: "Come unto me, ye blessed, there is a place prepared for you in the mansions of my Father" (Enos 1:27).

Literary Reflections on Jacob and His Descendants

15

John S. Tanner

The Small Plates as Literature

*T*his volume completes a four-volume study of the small plates. Taken together, these volumes attest to the doctrinal richness of Nephi's record. What may be less apparent is their literary diversity. The small plates range from the sublime (eg, Nephi's vision of Christ's birth) to the mundane (eg, parts of the book of Omni). They develop the Book of Mormon's most elaborate symbols (the vision of the tree of life and the allegory of the vineyard), and recount its grandest story—an epic of exodus and resettlement like that of Moses. The small plates also provide an intimate glimpse into a family in conflict, comparable to stories about the Patriarchs in Genesis. Moreover, the plates assemble all this in a truly impressive array of genres: vision, narrative, psalm, scriptural exegesis, allegory, sermon, prophecy, father's blessing, spiritual autobiography, and more. No wonder that, of the handful of Book of Mormon literary studies to date, so many are drawn from the small plates (see bibliography). To echo Dryden's comment on Chaucer: "Here is God's plenty" (497)! In this essay, I shall sample portions of this plenty.

My focus will be the record left by Jacob and his descendants, or what may be called the "Jacobite" component of the small plates.

John S. Tanner is associate professor of English at Brigham Young University.

I shall first review the general nature of the Jacobite text, and then examine in more detail Jacob himself as a writer. We do not, as a church, sufficiently appreciate the literary qualities of Jacob and his descendants—nor of scriptural authors generally. Our inattention to scripture as literature stems partly from our great attention to scripture as doctrine. Emphasizing scripture's universal, timeless doctrines—crucially important in their own right —we tend to forget how our favorite verses relate to a particular speaker in a specific historical and rhetorical situation. For example, I recently heard a religion professor refer to Nephi's teaching that "to be learned is good if they hearken unto the counsels of God" (2 Nephi 9:29). This quotation, however, is not Nephi's but Jacob's; though recorded in 2 Nephi, it derives from Jacob's magnificent two-day sermon. My colleague remembered the doctrine but forgot both the author and his rhetorical situation. Therefore, a literary reading of scripture such as mine below is largely an effort to restore authors to their authorship.

In the case of the Book of Mormon, this effort is complicated by the double obstacles that (1) the text exists only in translation, often a translation of a redaction, which leaves the reader several removes from the speaker's original words; and (2) God is twice its co-author, inspiring its ancient authors as well as its modern translator. These obstacles should induce caution, particularly about inferences drawn from stylistic evidence. Yet neither is so formidable as to rule out literary analysis altogether, especially of the small plates.

Of all Book of Mormon texts, translation is least a problem for the small plates. These plates invite stylistic analysis because they constitute the only complete source-text included intact, presumably without an editor's transcription or redaction; the only place where Joseph likely found someone's "handwriting" other than that of Mormon or Moroni.

From the first words of 1 Nephi ("I, Nephi") to the last sentence of the Book of Omni ("And I make an end of my speaking"), we are dealing with a collection of first-person documents. Naturally these writers seem more individuated than those elsewhere, even in translation. This is particularly evident from Jacob through Omni, after Nephi's dominant voice has ceased. The Jacobite record displays all the complex variety one expects of a text from many hands.

By corollary, the juncture between Omni and Words of Mormon evinces precisely the disjointedness one would expect of a bridge between an unedited primary text and a heavily condensed narrative history. Despite Mormon's best efforts to smooth the transition, readers are inevitably confused at this juncture. And well they might be. At this point every major record (the small plates, Mormon's abridgment of the large plates, the plates of brass, and the 24 plates), and every major civilization (the Nephites, Mulekites, and Jaredites), and two different time frames (Mosiah's and Mormon's) are fitted snugly together. Though this transition is usually taught perfunctorily, I regard it as a powerful textual witness that we are dealing with the genuine article. Its textual complexity is of a piece with the small plates' stylistic diversity. Both attest that the small plates are a different sort of document from Mormon's redaction; they testify that the small plates are a first-person document.

As a literary critic, I am naturally drawn to first-person documents like the small plates. I savor truths bred in the bone, supposing that nuances of style reveal the man (see Thomas 156), and I listen for echoes of a human voice in every sort of discourse, however ostensibly impersonal—even in prophetic speeches. I do not believe that God's co-authorship normally eradicates an individual's voice, since the Lord speaks through his servants "in their weakness, after the manner of their language" (D&C 1:24). Hence, we can distinguish the inspired discourse of Jeremiah from Hosea's, Matthew's from Mark's, Peter's from Paul's, and one General Authority's from another's. Early in my marriage, my wife used to read conference talks aloud while I tried to guess, from their style and themes alone, who had given them. Below, I try to do something similar with Book of Mormon writers, such as Nephi and Jacob, trying to catch glimpses of the men behind the messages. This does not discredit divine inspiration; rather, it corroborates it, verifying that the text contains the writing of many different prophets. Close attention to a prophet's words can be—and I mean it to be—an expression of love for those through whom the Lord speaks.

My surmises about Jacobite authors may be quite wrong, of course, just as my surmises about the author of a conference address were sometimes mistaken. But my analysis neither pretends nor aspires to the stature of scientific proof. I come without computer word-prints—a complete concordance is my only tool (I have relied on concordances by Reynolds and Shapiro). I come, rather, with conjectures about the timely, human contexts of timeless, divine utterances, and with confidence that more attention to the human context of the Book of Mormon can greatly enrich our appreciation of its content.

For example, consider the relation between text and context in Nephi's psalm. Nephi's lament occurs just after he records the death of his father and the renewed hatred of his brothers. Of what significance is this for the psalm that follows? Much, I suspect. Think of what Lehi's death meant to Nephi. Father Lehi had held the family together, and that only barely. He and Nephi had shared the same vision, literally and figuratively. Nephi lost a friend as well as a father and prophet in Lehi. He was Nephi's confidant, advisor, and shield against fratricide. Before Lehi's death, Nephi foresaw in revelation the tragic division between Lamanite and Nephite that would occur (1 Nephi 12:22-23). When Lehi died, Nephi must have known that the long-forestalled crisis was now inevitable—and in the New World there were no larger institutions nor higher authorities to protect Nephi and his family from his brothers' barbarism. With no father to turn to but the Father, Nephi cries to him for strength, so lonely is his new burden of leadership, so dangerous his newly empowered enemies, and so strong the old temptation to be "angry because of [his] enemy" (2 Nephi 4:27)—meaning, certainly, his brothers. I approach his psalm, then, by reading it in the immediate human situation the text provides: "And it came to pass that he [Lehi] died, and was buried. And . . . Laman and Lemuel and the sons of Ishmael were angry with me . . ." (2 Nephi 4:12-13).[1]

The Nature of the Jacobite Record

Now let us turn to the Jacobite portion of the small plates. Let us first review the nature of the Jacobite text as a whole—what literary critics would call its "genre"—in order to better interpret it doctrinally, historically, and in every other way. The record changed in three ways because it passed into Jacob's hands. First, by this act the small plates moved permanently from the line of Nephi to the house of Jacob, eventually to dwindle into little more than a chronicle of Jacob's genealogy. Recognizing the text as family chronicle is critical. Many of its distinctive features can be explained by the fact that its authors wrote because they were related to Jacob, not because they were otherwise the most qualified to write. Eventually, Jacobite authors came to see their function as primarily recorders of genealogies.

Second, with Jacob the plates passed out of the royal line (Jacob 1:9).[2] Jacobite authors were not kings; nor, from all we can tell, were they even political or military leaders. This, too, has major consequences for the nature of the record they left. After Nephi, never again did the authors of the small plates also occupy the central position in the government. Always deliberately non-secular anyway (see 1 Nephi 19:1-6; Jacob 1:2), the small plates were inscribed increasingly from the margins of the community's political life (eg, Enos 1:24).

---

[1] My emphasis upon the timely, emotional context of the psalm differs somewhat from Steven Sondrup's on the timeless, formal content of the lyric.

[2] According to Daniel H. Ludlow some unnamed "Book of Mormon scholars have surmised that Nephi's [political] successor was probably Jacob" (156). I see no evidence for this conjecture and much for the opposite conclusion—especially Jacob 1:9 and 15, in which Jacob refers to Nephi's royal successor in the third person. If Jacob were not king, then his temple sermon assumes political implications: it was likely directed specifically against the political-social elite, who would be most likely to take concubines like David and Solomon, and not simply to the people at large.

Last, Jacobite authors eventually passed out of the prophetic line as well. Only Jacob himself appears to have exercised dominant priestly authority, equivalent to that of presiding high priest (Jacob 1:17-19). His son Enos and grandson Jarom each characterizes his position as, at most, but one among many prophets (Enos 1:19, 22; Jarom 1:4). Jarom may not have engaged in a public ministry at all. For, though he refers to "my prophesying" and "my revelations," Jarom speaks pointedly in the third person of "the prophets, and the priests, and the teachers [who] labor diligently, exhorting . . . the people to diligence; teaching the law of Moses" (1:11). Similarly, he writes "our kings and our leaders were mighty men in the faith of the Lord; and *they* taught the people the ways of the Lord" (1:7; emphasis added). This phrasing sounds like that of a sympathetic bystander, one outside the loop of government power and cultic responsibility as well.

By contrast, Jarom refers to Nephite warfare and trade in the first person: "Wherefore, *we* withstood the Lamanites. . . . And *we* . . . became exceeding rich in gold, . . . in buildings, and in machinery, and also in iron and copper, and brass and steel, making all manner of tools of every kind to till the ground, and weapons of war" (1:7-8; emphasis added). This shift from prophecy to weapons of war foreshadows things to come for the descendants of Jacob. Jarom's son Omni fights for the Nephites, but there is no evidence that he does so as a major military leader, nor that he has any prophetic calling. Far from it: he confesses that he is a "wicked man" (1:2). So is it with the other authors of Omni: Abinadom explicitly acknowledges he "knows of no revelation save that which has been written"; Amaleki says that the people "were led by many preachings and prophesyings"— the impersonal, passive construction again implying that he did not himself act as one of the prophets or preachers (1:11-13).

Understanding these three characteristics of the Jacobite record is crucial in drawing valid inferences from it. For example, the lack of either religious or regal stature among later Jacobite writers does not necessarily mean that the entire Nephite civilization, however wicked (Omni 1:5-7), had fallen into apostasy (see Ludlow 168). Indeed, Jacobite authors quietly contradict this impression, hinting rather that Nephite civilization may have benefited from continuous prophetic leadership: Enos speaks of "exceeding many" unnamed prophets (1:22); Jarom, of men "who have many revelations, . . . mighty men in faith of the Lord" (Jarom 1:4, 7); Amaron, of the Lord's sparing the righteous, proving there was a righteous remnant among the Nephites (Omni 1:7); and Amaleki, of "many preachings and prophesyings" (Omni 1:13). One wonders what sacred experiences the non-Jacobite kings and prophets had, and if these were recorded on Mormon's abridgement of the large plates.

Thus, the Jacobite record does not confirm that Nephite society at large became utterly benighted, but only that Jacob's posterity fell from prominence and, possibly, also from grace. As a family chronicle, the record's spiritual quality varies with the spirituality of each family member; hence, this is the only place I know where a self-professed "wicked man," Omni, writes scripture in a book which, ironically, bears his name.[3] Late Jacobite writers were ordinary men who happened to belong to an extraordinary lineage. Thus, Jacob's posterity became scriptural authors because the plates became genealogy.

The fate of the small plates may have run contrary to Nephi's original expectation. He initially anticipated that the plates "should be handed down from one generation to another, or from one prophet to another, until further commandments of the Lord" (1 Nephi 19:4). When Nephi entrusted the plates to Jacob, he seems to have followed the second principle of succession—that is, prophet to prophet (though, being so much younger than Nephi, Jacob might also qualify as a next generation kinsman). Still, Nephi gave this record not to a son but to his brother, a prophet.

---

[3] The book's title is something of a misnomer. If anything, it should be called the book of Amaleki since he composed the last 19 verses, while the four authors preceding him wrote but 11.

At that point, however, Nephi seems to clarify how the custodianship of the plates was to be determined. He instructed Jacob to keep the plates in the family, handing them down to his seed "from generation to generation" (Jacob 1:3). Hence, Jacob and his posterity down to Amaleki gave the plates not to the preeminent prophet but to a close male relative (usually a son) in the next generation. Filial ties became the main qualification of ownership (and hence authorship) until the plates, by then full (Omni 1:30), were finally entrusted to someone outside the family—Benjamin, a prophet-king, the first such figure to have the plates since Nephi. In the interim, Jacobite authors came to regard their purpose as genealogical. Beginning with Jarom, they inscribed the record "that our genealogy may be kept" (Jarom 1:1; compare Omni 1:1), a purpose never mentioned by Nephi or Jacob.

Yet I do not disparage their dogged resolve to discharge their duty—though their own lives must have seemed pale and even paltry beside those of the heroic first generation. Their authorship could be understood with more sympathy than it is usually afforded. I note that, however embarrassing, each man obediently fulfilled his charge, enrolling his name at the end of the record.[4] I note also that many of Jacob's less distinguished descendants (most conspicuously Omni and Abinadom) are refreshingly frank about their felt weaknesses. Most of us could learn from their humility and unblinking self-honesty. I note further that none of these authors treats the sacred record cynically —not even the avowedly "wicked" Omni. All, except perhaps Chemish, appear to sense the plates' power. The very inadequacy that they express suggests that Jacob's descendants had both read the record and been moved by its power. So it is not entirely fair to dismiss these men as apostate; they are certainly not unregenerate. Their commitment to duty, their humility, their honesty, and their reverence for the sacred—all intimate that Jacob's

---

[4] See John W. Welch's essay on how carefully these writers fulfilled the specific terms of their fathers' charge.

legacy was not entirely dissipated in his posterity. His righteous blood still flowed in their veins, his sensitivity still circulated in their souls.

Jacob's Lexicon

Now let us look at Jacob himself. Even without consulting a concordance, one senses that Jacob's style sets him apart from Nephi. Jacob simply sounds different: he employs a more intimate lexicon and assumes a more diffident posture toward his audience. Nephi "delights," even "glories" in plainness (2 Nephi 31:3; 33:6); he frankly rebukes and frankly forgives his brothers (see 1 Nephi 7:21). Jacob, by contrast, is pained to use "much boldness of speech" in addressing his brethren, especially in the presence of women and children "whose feelings are exceedingly tender and chaste and delicate before God" (Jacob 2:7). (His solicitude for the women reminds us that, as a boy aboard ship, he had been grieved by the afflictions of his mother [1 Nephi 18:19].) He prefaces his temple discourse by admitting that he feels "weighed down with much . . . anxiety for the welfare of your souls":

> Yea, it grieveth my soul and causeth me to shrink with shame before the presence of my Maker. . . . Wherefore, it burdeneth my soul that I should be constrained . . . to admonish you according to your crimes, to enlarge the wounds of those who are already wounded . . . and those who have not been wounded, instead of feasting upon the pleasing word of God have daggers placed to pierce their souls and wound their delicate minds (Jacob 2:3, 6, 9).

This is vintage Jacob: intimate, vivid, vulnerable. A concordance verifies that words about feelings, like "anxiety," "grieve," "tender," occur with disproportionate frequency in his writings (Conkling 3-4).[5] For example, half the book's citations

---

[5] Admittedly, some of these terms occur in Zenos' allegory. As I argue below, however, the emotional content of the allegory is possibly a quality that attracted Jacob to it. Consequently, we may cautiously note the diction of Jacob 5 in a stylistic study of Jacob. Chris Conkling, a college friend, provided a helpful source of word-count tabulation in his unpublished essay on Jacob.

of "anxiety" occur in the book of Jacob, and over two-thirds of the references to "grieve," "tender," and "shame" (or their derivatives) appear in Jacob's writings. He is the only person to use "delicate," "contempt," and "lonesome." Likewise, only Jacob uses "wound" to refer to emotional, not physical, injuries, as in the rest of the Book of Mormon. Similarly, he uses "pierce" or its variants frequently (four of the ten instances) and exclusively in a spiritual sense. Such lexical evidence suggests an author who lives close to his emotions.

Like many sensitive people, Jacob does not preach harsh messages easily. Many times he openly shares his anxiety with his audience, as in his preface to the temple discourse above. He may also betray it covertly in the structure of this sermon against sexual immorality, which disposes first of the relatively easy issue of pride and then, reluctantly, moves to the "grosser crime" of whoredoms (Jacob 2:22-23). This structure suggests a delaying strategy reminiscent of the reluctant prophet motif illustrated by Enoch, Moses, and Jonah.[6]

When Jacob does speak, however, he does so vividly. Notice the concrete diction in the phrase: "instead of *feasting* upon the pleasing word of God [they] have *daggers* placed to *pierce* their souls and wound their delicate minds"; or in his statement: "the *sobbings* of their hearts ascend up to God. . . . Many hearts *died, pierced* with *deep wounds*" (2:9, 35; emphasis added). Strong words for strong feelings: this is the hallmark of Jacob's style, something he may have learned from the "tender" words of his "trembling" father (see 1 Nephi 8:37; 2 Nephi 1:14) and subsequently passed on to his son Enos. Enos' account of his "wrestle" and "hunger" which led to his guilt being "swept"

---

[6] Another way of viewing this structure intrigues me. In most polygamous cultures, concubines are status symbols, signs of wealth. Thus polygamy is intrinsically linked to acquisitiveness. Jacob's denunciations of his brethren for being "lifted up in the pride of your hearts . . . and persecut[ing] your brethren because ye suppose that ye are better than they" may be related to their sinful desire to acquire "many wives and concubines" as root to branch. That is, the Nephite experiment with polygamy is not simply an expression of lasciviousness but an extension of the class differentiation that Jacob denounces so roundly in the first part of his sermon.

away, shows that his father's words had "sunk deep" into the son's style as well as soul (Enos 1:2-4, 6). Like his father, Enos finds concrete, economical language for abstract spiritual experience.

Jacob's emotive language cannot be attributed merely to the sensitive subject matter of the temple discourse, for Jacob rings off silver phrases in all his writing, including his speech in 2 Nephi, separated from the book of Jacob by many chapters and many years. Nevertheless, in both sermons, Jacob consistently speaks of ridding his garments of the people's blood and of the Lord's "all-searching eye" (2 Nephi 9:44; Jacob 1:19; 2:2, 10). Both sermons call upon the people to "awake" lest they become "angels of the devil" (2 Nephi 9:9, 47; Jacob 3:11). In the same verse, Jacob uses the term "reality," closely related to a phrase in Jacob 4, "things as they really are" (Jacob 4:13)—the only such uses of either term in the entire Book of Mormon. These verbal parallels suggest a common author of uncommon sensitivity.

Structurally, Jacob's first sermon also resembles his later writings. It begins, as does his temple speech, with Jacob's hall-mark—an initial expression of anxiety: "mine anxiety is great for you" (2 Nephi 6:3). Then it moves into scriptural quotations, followed by explication and exhortation. This organization compares closely to Jacob's olive-tree discourse, which begins with his prefatory expression of anxiety—"Behold, my beloved brethren, I will unfold this mystery unto you; if I do not, by any means, get shaken from my firmness in the Spirit, and stumble because of my over anxiety for you" (4:18)—followed by scriptural quotation, explication, and exhortation.

Jacob's Exegesis

Significantly, Jacob's scriptural citations from Isaiah and Zenos both treat scattered Israel's preservation. This is one of Jacob's favorite themes, no doubt owing to his own experience as an exile. Jacob's exegesis of the brass plates is consistently concerned with the promises made to scattered Israel. He identifies Isaiah's oracles about Israel on the isles of the sea with the Lehite colony. Note the following comment, expressed in Jacob's characteristically poetic phrasing: "And now, my beloved brethren, . . . let us . . . not hang down our heads, for we are not cast off; nevertheless, we have been driven out of the land of our inheritance; but we have been led to a better land, for the Lord has made the sea our path, and we are upon an isle of the sea" (2 Nephi 10:20). Jacob accentuates Isaiah's eloquent message of comfort and hope (see 2 Nephi 7:1-2; 8:3-12). Few descriptions of God's love in all scripture rival those found in Isaiah. It is to these messages of comfort to scattered Israel that Jacob is particularly drawn.

This, I believe, ought to provide a clue as to how Jacob read Zenos. Unfortunately, discussion of this allegory is often so preoccupied with the world-historical interpretations of Zenos' allegory that we miss the central point Jacob likely had in mind: that God loves and looks after the house of Israel, no matter where its branches or blood are scattered. The allegory is more than a complex puzzle whose solution unlocks world history. The allegory dramatizes God's steadfast love, as a recent *Ensign* article has recognized (Swiss). Thematically, Zenos' allegory ought to take its place beside the parable of the prodigal son, for both make the Lord's mercy movingly memorable.

A key phrase in the allegory of the vineyard, "and it grieveth me that I should lose this tree," is repeated eight times. By means of such formal repetition, called by literary critics "anaphora," the allegory sounds a refrain that celebrates the Lord's long-suffering love. The very recurrence of the line underscores the quality of that divine love—unfailing, persistent, tenacious, resolute. This characterization of the Lord matters as much as, if not more than, the historical details of his plan to redeem Israel. The allegory teaches that the Lord of the vineyard works out his grand design in history. But more than this, it shows us that he weeps over sin: "And it came to pass that the Lord of the vineyard wept, and said unto the servant: What could I have done more for my vineyard" (Jacob 5:41; see Moses 7:28-41).

The Lord of the universe can be "touched with the feeling of our infirmities" (Heb 4:15), for it grieveth him that he should lose any tree of the vineyard. What a remarkable witness: God is not *deus absconditus* but *deus misericors* (or, God is not an absent God, but a feeling God)! I find this allegory one of the most eloquent scriptural testimonies of God's love anywhere. Surely Jacob did too.

Just so we don't miss the point, Jacob tells us what matters most in the allegory. It is not figuring out detailed historical correspondences; it is feeling and seeing "how merciful is our God unto us, for he remembereth the house of Israel . . . and he stretches forth his hands unto them all the day long," and as a result, repenting: "Wherefore, my beloved brethren, I beseech of you in words of soberness that ye would repent, and come with full purpose of heart, and cleave unto God as he cleaveth unto you" (Jacob 6:4-5). This is the neglected undersong of Zenos' allegory.

Jacob's Biography[7]

When Jacob quotes scripture, one senses an intimate link between text and exegete. Jacob must have felt special poignancy in Isaiah's and Zenos' oracles of hope to scattered Israel, for he himself was a displaced person, a pilgrim wandering between two worlds—one dying, the other still trying to be born. I sense this same intimate link between the man and the message elsewhere. Let me list five facts about Jacob's life and suggest how each might correlate with his themes and style.

1. Jacob was born "in the days of [Lehi's] tribulation" (2 Nephi 2:1). He was raised on raw meat rather than milk. Some people are hardened by hardship, but not Jacob. Lehi consecrated Jacob's afflictions for his gain (2 Nephi 2:2). Jacob's sensitive style provides evidence that this patriarchal promise was fulfilled. Long afflictions seem to have softened Jacob's spirit, verifying

---

[7] See Matthews in this volume and also Warner for a good overview of Jacob's life.

the famous Book of Mormon dictum about the value of "opposition in all things"—an aphorism located, significantly, in Jacob's patriarchal blessing (2 Nephi 2:11). We should remember Jacob when we allude to the principle that adversity can have sweet uses. The evidence shows the boy took Lehi's lesson to heart.

2. Jacob is a child of a house divided. He saw a family feud evolve into a more or less permanent state of internecine civil war. Think of what it meant that Jacob was Laman's and Lemuel's brother. The Lamanites were not distant, faceless, nameless enemies; they were his brothers, nephews, and cousins whose names and families he knew. Remembering this helps me read with more sympathy Jacob's sad parting observation: "Many means were devised to reclaim and restore the Lamanites to the knowledge of the truth; but it all was vain, for they delighted in wars and bloodshed, and they had an eternal hatred against us, their brethren" (Jacob 7:24).

"Against us, their brethren"—Jacob uses "brethren" often in his discourses to the Nephites, too. It is his preferred salutation; he employs it some fifty times and almost never addresses his audience directly as "my people," the proprietary term preferred by Nephi (Conkling 4-5). Jacob's mode of address connotes familial intimacy appropriate to a patriarch and priest; Nephi's suggests rule or ownership befitting a king. Jacob's intimate salutation also bespeaks his humility, at the same time reminding us that his immediate audience—those he castigated for whoredoms—were kinsmen. No wonder Jacob felt anxious and pained: both Lamanites and Nephites were relatives.

3. Jacob is the younger brother of a prophet-colonizer. Nephi must have cast a long shadow, and Jacob's writing suggests a man very conscious of this shadow. Nephite kings adopt Nephi's name as a royal title (Jacob 1:11). But more telling of a brother's personal awe may be that Jacob himself chooses to group all righteous family lines (including his own) under the title Nephites (Jacob 1:13-14). Thus Jacob presents Nephi as nonpareil, and himself, implicitly, as subordinate in stature to the founder.

Equally telling of Jacob's awe may be that neither he nor any of his successors appear to have added new plates to those Nephi fashioned. This may indicate lack of resources or technology, of course, though the former seems unlikely as both Jacob and Jarom specifically mention an abundance of gold in the promised land (Jacob 2:12; Jarom 1:8). More likely, it reveals something about the meaning of the plates in the minds of Jacobite authors—ie, they are primarily Nephi's record, a sacred legacy from an incomparable man, to be added to only sparingly by those that follow. Jacob, whose contribution is sublime and considerable, still confesses that his "writing has been small" (Jacob 7:27). One senses an implicit self-comparison to his illustrious older brother. All Jacobite authors seem to suffer from a similar inferiority complex.

Jacob also seems to live in Nephi's shadow because his writing is more limited in historical scope than that of Nephi. This, of course, conforms to Nephi's explicit instruction and example in 2 Nephi. After the death of Lehi, Nephi says very little more about history. Nephi resolves, rather, to write on the small plates only the things of his soul, and so charges his brother Jacob (2 Nephi 4:15; Jacob 1:2-4). Jacob obediently confines himself almost wholly to his ministry: he records sermons, scriptural exegesis, and one story of his priestly conflict with Sherem; he says nothing of the move to the land of Nephi and little of the colonization. The result of Jacob's exclusively religious focus is that he comes across more as a priest and less as a colonizer. Consequently, he seems for readers to live somewhat in Nephi's shadow (whether or not he in fact did).

4. Jacob was visited by Christ. In this respect, he was not a whit behind his brother. Interestingly, it is Nephi who tells us of that experience in a tribute to his younger sibling: "Jacob also has seen him [the Christ] as I have seen him" (2 Nephi 11:3; see 2 Nephi 2:4). Jacob's writings are full of the testimony of Christ. Indeed, he is the first Nephite prophet to whom the name "Christ" is revealed (2 Nephi 10:3). His sermon disclosing the Lord's saving name seems to set the agenda for the rest of 2 Nephi.

Nephi, too, quotes extensively from Isaiah about the scattering and gathering of Israel and concentrates on the "doctrine of Christ" (31:2), and he charges his brother to "touch upon" this topic "as much as it were possible, for Christ's sake," in order to persuade "all men [to] believe in Christ, and view his death, and suffer his cross, and bear the shame of the world" (Jacob 1:4, 8). Jacob amply fulfills this charge. He writes so that his posterity might look upon their first parents "with joy and not with sorrow, neither with contempt, . . . that they may know that we knew of Christ, and we had a hope of his glory many hundred years before his coming" (Jacob 4:3-4). "For why not speak of the atonement of Christ?" Jacob asks (4:12), and speaks of it again and again. Appropriately, the last glimpse we have of Jacob's life concerns his refutation of Sherem, the anti-Christ. Jacob "could not be shaken" (7:5) by Sherem because he had "heard and seen" the Lord (7:12). This sure testimony of Christ underlies all Jacob's writing.

    5. Finally, to end where I began, Jacob was a pilgrim. He is a wilderness writer. He was twice outcast—first from Jerusalem, across the desert and great sea; then, after landfall, from the first settlements to even deeper into the American wilderness (2 Nephi 5:5-6). Like Abraham and wandering Israel, the only security these New World nomads knew lay in their God and his law: eternity was their covering, rock, and salvation (see Abr 2:16). This may help explain why both Nephi and Jacob quote from the brass plates at greater length than any other Book of Mormon prophets. Those plates were living links to a vanished world; they preserved the memory of its sacred tradition.

    How hard it must have seemed to Jacob to forge a new civilization; he didn't even know the old one personally. Yet his lonely lot was like that of Aeneas, legendary founder of Rome, whose melancholy destiny Virgil repeatedly characterizes as burdensome: *"Tantae molis erat Romanam condere gentem"* (1.33)—"it was a thing of such great burden to found the Roman race." So it was with Jacob. Nephite survival must have often seemed perilous; it would have been easy to despair, especially for a naturally anxious man. Time, geographic isolation, and sin could so easily efface sacred tradition; or, if these failed, an enemy might succeed, for the Lamanites were determined to "destroy our records and us, and also all the traditions of our fathers" (Enos 1:14).

Jacob's Valedictions

One feels the cost that the wilderness exacted on Jacob most poignantly in his final farewell. Jacob, like Moroni, writes three farewells: at the end of Jacob 3, 6, and 7. His valediction expresses the accumulated sorrows of a nomadic life: "And also our lives passed away like as it were unto us a dream, we being a lonesome and a solemn people, wanderers, cast out from Jerusalem, born in tribulation, in a wilderness, and hated of our brethren, which caused wars and contentions; wherefore, we did mourn out our days" (Jacob 7:26). By now, it should be clear that the sensitivity, vulnerability, and quiet eloquence of this leave-taking is of a piece not only with the facts of Jacob's life but with his style.

Jacob's tone differs markedly from that of his brother's powerful farewell. Where Jacob ends quietly and in a minor key, Nephi's farewell strikes a dominant chord and is accompanied by timpani rolls and cymbal clashes: "I glory in plainness; I glory in truth; I glory in my Jesus." Nephi is all confidence: "I shall meet many souls spotless at his judgment seat"; "you and I shall stand face to face before his bar." His last sentence reprises Nephi's lifelong commitment to absolute obedience; it could serve as his epitaph: "for thus hath the Lord commanded me, and I must obey" (2 Nephi 33:6, 7, 11, 15). Nephi's farewell never fails to move me.

Jacob's words are no less moving, but in a very different way. Jacob, too, feels assured of personal salvation: he anticipates meeting the reader at the "pleasing" judgment bar (Jacob 6:13). But his farewells are much less sanguine about the salvation of others: "O then, my beloved brethren, repent ye, and enter in at the strait gate, and continue in the way which is narrow, until ye shall obtain eternal life. O be wise; what can I say more? Finally, I bid you farewell, until I shall meet you before the pleasing bar of God, which bar striketh the wicked with awful dread and fear. Amen" (Jacob 6:11-13).

No other Book of Mormon author uses the term "dread." Similarly, no one else uses "lonesome," nor can I imagine any one else capable of the expression "our lives passed away like as it were unto us a dream," or "we did mourn out our days." None are so open about anxiety, none so poetic. No wonder Elder Neal Maxwell called Jacob a poet-prophet (1). Jacob is a poet-prophet whose voice we should learn to recognize, and to love.

BIBLIOGRAPHY

Conkling, Chris. "An Analysis of Jacob, Lehi's Son." Unpublished ms. in possession of the author.

Dryden, John. "Preface to the Fables." *John Dryden: Selected Works*. Ed. William Frost. 2nd ed. San Francisco: Rinehart, 1971.

Jorgensen, Bruce W. "The Dark Way to the Tree: Typological Unity in the Book of Mormon." See *Literature of Belief* 217-31.

Literature of Belief: Sacred Scripture and Religious Experience. Ed. Neal E. Lambert. Provo, UT: Religious Studies Center, 1981.

Ludlow, Daniel H. *A Companion to Your Study of the Book of Mormon*. Salt Lake City: Deseret Book, 1976.

Maxwell, Neal A. *Things As They Really Are*. Salt Lake City: Deseret Book, 1978.

"Nephi and the Exodus." *Ensign* (Apr 1987) 17:64-65.

Nichols, Robert E., Jr. "Beowulf and Nephi: A Literary View of the Book of Mormon." *Dialogue: A Journal of Mormon Thought* (Aut 1969) 4:40-47.

Reynolds, George. *A Complete Concordance to the Book of Mormon.* Ed. Philip C. Reynolds. Salt Lake City: n.p., 1900. Reprint. Salt Lake City: Deseret Book, 1957.

Rust, Richard Dilworth. "All Things Which Have Been Given of God . . . Are the Typifying of Him: Typology in the Book of Mormon." See *Literature of Belief 233-43.*

Shapiro, R. Gary. *An Exhaustive Concordance of the Book of Mormon, Doctrine and Covenants, and Pearl of Great Price.* Salt Lake City: Hawkes, 1977.

Sondrup, Steven P. "The Psalm of Nephi: A Lyric Reading." *BYU Studies* (Sum 1981) 21:357-72.

Swiss, Ralph E. "The Tame and Wild Olive Trees—An Allegory of Our Savior's Love." *Ensign* (Aug 1988) 18:50-52.

Tate, George S. "The Typology of the Exodus Pattern in the Book of Mormon." See *Literature of Belief* 245-62.

Thomas, Robert K. "A Literary Critic Looks at the Book of Mormon." *To the Glory of God: Mormon Essays on Great Issues.* Ed. Truman G. Madsen and Charles D. Tate, Jr. Salt Lake City: Deseret Book, 1972. 149-61.

Virgil. *The Aeneid.* [As translated by the author.]

Warner, C. Terry. "Jacob." *Ensign* (Oct 1976) 6:25-30.

Welch, John W. "The Father's Command to Keep Records in the Small Plates of Nephi." Preliminary report, Foundation for Ancient Research and Mormon Studies. Provo: FARMS, 1984.

Morality and Marriage in the Book of Mormon

16

Rodney Turner

Introduction

*P*resident Ezra Taft Benson has repeatedly stated that the Book of Mormon was written for our day (*The Teachings of Ezra Taft Benson* 58-65; hereafter *TETB*). The most compelling issues confronting our bewildered world were anticipated by the Lord, and they form the inspired content of the Book of Mormon. The winds of opinion blow from every direction. What is ultimately right? What is ultimately just? What ultimately matters? The Book of Mormon answers these questions as it forges the things of time and the things of eternity into one great truth. This truth is the way—the only way—to genuine peace and happiness in this life, and salvation in the life to come.

The need for the Book of Mormon grows by the day as the tempo of our times accelerates toward the prophesied polarization of good and evil (see D&C 1:35-36; 38:11-12). Certainly no generation since the Flood has had a greater need for one particular message in this latter-day scripture: the vital importance of personal morality both before and during marriage. President Benson has said, "The plaguing sin of this generation is sexual immorality" (*TETB* 277; "Cleansing the Inner Vessel" 4). Unchastity and marital infidelity have become virtually pandemic in the Western world. While these sins are by no means new,

Rodney Turner is emeritus professor of Ancient Scripture at Brigham Young University.

historically they have been preponderantly male vices. But no more. Now millions upon millions of females are demanding equality in them, as well as in most everything else, and are joining their male counterparts in such behavior.

Our moral environment is far more polluted than our physical environment. It seems as though good and evil are being homogenized out of existence by a generation largely led by "foolish and blind guides" (Hel 13:29). What was once whispered in shame is now electronically shouted from the housetops as the famous and the foolish appear on television to parade their sins, like so many medals, before laughing, applauding audiences. Every aspect of modern communication seems to have been appropriated by Satan to legitimize the everlastingly illegitimate. It is imperative that Latter-day Saints view these times from a gospel perspective and follow the counsel of our prophet by taking warning from the teachings—and the fate—of an earlier generation of Americans, the Nephites.

Immorality in the Book of Mormon

The Book of Mormon hardly mentions the purity of the marital relationship except in a very general way. Fidelity is simply assumed. While unchastity is cited in connection with other sins, only Jacob, Alma, and Jesus discuss the problem at any length (see Jacob 2:31-33; 3:5-7; Alma 39:3-14; 3 Nephi 12:31-32). In each instance the issue is unchastity on the husbands' part. Wives are mentioned either in connection with concubines or with children, but again, only in general terms. We find a similar situation in the words of Jesus in the Four Gospels. There, the purity of the marital relationship seems to be included with all other human relationships. Being so, it is covered by the two great commandments: love of God and love of neighbor. Certainly one's closest neighbor is one's wife or husband.

The Ten Commandments constituted the basic, general moral code of the Nephites, as it did for the rest of Israel. The law of Moses was reflected in the inspired law of Mosiah—the governing law of the Nephites in times of righteousness (see Mosiah 29:11-15; Alma 11:1; Hel 4:22). Describing the law of Mosiah, Mormon wrote that every man was free to believe as he chose, "but if he murdered he was punished unto death; and if he robbed he was also punished; and if he stole he was also punished; and if he committed adultery he was also punished; yea, for all this wickedness they were punished" (Alma 30:10).

Parenthetically may I add that we, too, have laws against various forms of immorality; but all too often they are written on the wind. An unenforced law has no practical existence; it is only a facade of justice. Worse, not enforcing a law tends to cloud the legitimacy of all laws. For example, the popular argument that capital punishment should be abolished because it does not deter murder is specious. But even if this were the case, the real issue is not deterrence, but justice. If failure to deter crime warrants abolishing a given law, God should revoke the Ten Commandments since countless millions of men and women violate them every day! As yet, however, he hasn't seen fit to do so. Law serves to define the parameters of appropriate behavior. It is not meant to ensure conformity.

But to return to the point. The vast majority of statements on moral behavior in the standard works deal with violations of the law of chastity.[1] Those in the Book of Mormon, unlike some incidents in the Old Testament, are (with one possible exception) never described in any detail. Book of Mormon terminology is even less jarring than some in the Bible. For example, in referring to prostitutes, the Book of Mormon uses the words *harlot* and *harlots* (a total of four times) rather than the harsher Anglo-Saxon biblical term *whore*, which is used in the Book of Mormon only in reference to the great and abominable church, as it is in the book of Revelation.

---

[1] In the Book of Mormon, Jacob and Jesus are the only ones to refer specifically to adultery as such. The last reference is by Christ in his restatement of the Sermon on the Mount (see 3 Nephi 12:27-28, 32).

Abominations

The plural word *whoredoms* (used 27 times) is the general Book of Mormon term for unchastity in all of its forms. *Abominations* is a broader term and covers every thought, deed, and attitude that is offensive to a God who "cannot look upon sin with the least degree of allowance" (Alma 45:16; D&C 1:31). All mankind is guilty of abominations. Whether we call it sin, iniquity, wickedness, evil, or what have you, it is all abomination; it is all reflective of a carnal mind and, therefore, of ungodliness.

Harlotry

It is apparent that to some extent harlotry, or prostitution, existed among the Nephites at certain periods of their history. However, there are only two specific instances actually cited in the Book of Mormon. The first is in connection with king Noah and his priests in the land of Nephi about 150 BC. Mormon writes that king Noah "spent his time in riotous living with his wives and concubines; and so did also his priests spend their time with harlots" (Mosiah 11:14). In confronting the king and his priestly supporters, the prophet Abinadi asked: "Why do ye commit whoredoms and spend your strength with harlots?" (Mosiah 12:29).

The second instance involves Alma's young missionary son Corianton who, while engaged in the ministry, succumbed to the wiles of a popular harlot named Isabel "who did steal away the hearts of many" (Alma 39:4). She appears to have been an outcast from polite Nephite society since her home was in "the land of Siron, among the borders of the Lamanites" (Alma 39:3). This need not mean that she was a Lamanite or that she lived among them. It is more likely that she lived among other harlots in a notorious district of the land. Hence Alma's counsel to Corianton: "Suffer not the devil to lead your heart away again after those wicked harlots" (Alma 39:11).

It is noteworthy that harlotry per se is not mentioned in connection with the Lamanites. Jacob's commendation of them in the late sixth century BC ("Behold, their husbands love their wives, and their wives love their husbands" [Jacob 3:7]) was in sharp contrast to the whoredoms which he accused the Nephites of committing. Spiritually benighted though they were, the early Lamanites had one vital, redeeming virtue: fidelity in marriage. And this virtue rendered them "more righteous" (Jacob 3:5) in God's sight than their enlightened Nephite brethren who had the gospel, the church, and prophets to guide them.

Indeed, it was because of their superior spiritual blessings that the Nephites stood the more condemned. "For of him unto whom much is given much is required; and he who sins against the greater light shall receive the greater condemnation" (D&C 82:3). Because of this principle, no one today faces so severe a judgment as do the Latter-day Saints. The Lord not only judges the sin, but also the spiritual context in which it is committed. This was the basis for the Prophet Joseph Smith's sincere self-characterization: "I do not want you to think that I am very righteous, for I am not, God judges men according to the use they make of the light which He gives them" (*Teachings of the Prophet Joseph Smith* 303; hereafter *TPJS*). Sin is measured against the light in which it is committed. Hence the Lord's condemnation of those early Latter-day Saints who were "walking in darkness at noon-day" (D&C 95:6).

Although the Nephites were repeatedly denounced for their immorality, there is but a single, somewhat ambiguous reference to such misconduct on the part of the Lamanites. In a proclamation by their then-converted king, he admonished (did not accuse) his people to avoid all sins, including adultery (Alma 23:3). Of course, it is very unlikely that all of the Lamanites observed the law of chastity, but it appears that sexual immorality was not one of their dominant, pervasive sins.

Even at the close of the record where Mormon graphically describes the degenerate behavior of both the Nephite and the Lamanite armies during the final battles between those two peoples, it was the Nephites, not the Lamanites, who raped and murdered captive women (see Moroni 9:7-10). Sexual immorality was essentially a Nephite crime and remained so until their final destruction.

Thus, in the Book of Mormon the charge of whoredoms is leveled against the enlightened groups, the Jaredites and the Nephites, but not the Lamanites. And because the early Lamanites kept the commandment against plural marriage, concubinage, and whoredoms, Jacob told the Nephites that "the Lord God will not destroy them; and one day they shall become a blessed people" (Jacob 3:6). While this promise was fulfilled in a measure when the resurrected Redeemer appeared in AD 34, its greater fulfillment awaits his glorious return in these latter days.

The Three Greatest Sins

Obviously some sins are more abominable, more destructive of spirituality, more alienating from the Lord, than others, but all take their toll (see Alma 26:24; 41:11). The three "most abominable," or taking the greatest toll, are identified as such only in the Book of Mormon and only by the prophet Alma. He declared them to be (in order of gravity) denying the Holy Ghost, murder, and sexual immorality.

To deny the Holy Ghost is to deny the undoubtable witness of the third member of the Godhead. It is the ultimate blasphemy. Consequently, as Alma told young Corianton, it is "a sin which is unpardonable" (Alma 39:6). It is unpardonable because it is a total repudiation of pure knowledge, perfect light. The Prophet Joseph Smith said that to commit this sin, a man "must receive the Holy Ghost, have the heavens opened unto him, and know God, and then sin against him" (*TPJS* 358). Thus it is willful rebellion against that rare and priceless truth one has received through the Holy Ghost when the heavens are opened and all doubt concerning the divinity and mission of Jesus Christ disappears (see *TPJS* 357-58).

It is unpardonable rather than unforgiveable because the one committing it is apparently incapable of repenting. Said Joseph Smith: "After a man has sinned against the Holy Ghost, there is no repentance for him" (*TPJS* 357-58). And where there is no repentance, there is no pardon, and where there is no pardon, there is no salvation.[2] To commit this ultimate offense is to become a knowing traitor to God. It is to be an unregenerate, incorrigible liar. "Wo unto the liar, for he shall be thrust down to hell" (2 Nephi 9:34). Such individuals are sons of perdition who, having partaken of the very essence of Lucifer, are sealed up to him as surely as the sons of God are sealed up to Christ. Remaining forever unrepentant, Lucifer and his companions will, following the last judgment, "remain filthy still" (D&C 88:35, 102).

Murder, the deliberate, cold-blooded killing of another without any justification whatsoever, is repentable and, therefore, eventually forgiveable. However, the redemptive blood of Christ is not available to those who, aware of God's law, have maliciously shed the blood of innocence. For such, deliverance comes only after they have personally atoned—in some manner, and for some length of time—for the crime.[3] That is why Alma said, "Whosoever murdereth against the light and knowledge of God, it is not easy for him to obtain forgiveness" (Alma 39:6).[4] No, "it is not easy," but, unlike the sin against the Holy Ghost, it is possible. David had the hope that his soul would not remain in hell (see Ps 16:10; 86:13; *TPJS* 339). In other words, eventually

---

[2] The Doctrine and Covenants draws a distinction between those who obtain eternal life and those who suffer eternal damnation. The latter, which I judge to be sons of perdition, "cannot be redeemed from their spiritual fall, because they repent not" (D&C 29:44; compare 88:32-35).

[3] Speaking of murderers the Prophet said, "Such characters cannot be forgiven, until they have paid the last farthing. The prayers of all the ministers in the world can never close the gates of hell against a murderer" (*TPJS* 189; compare 339, 359).

[4] Note that Alma refers to those who "murdereth against the light and knowledge of God." Those Lamanites who were converted by the sons of Mosiah and repented of the murders they had committed were assured of eternal life because they had lacked a knowledge of God and had murdered in savage ignorance (see Alma 24:9-16). This is an example of the principle that the degree of culpability is relative to the degree of understanding.

David would be saved in spite of his callous murder of his faithful captain, Uriah, with whose wife David had committed adultery. All such repentant murderers are heirs of salvation.

When Corianton became involved with the harlot Isabel, his father Alma, whose own early life had been tarnished with sin (see Mosiah 27:8; Alma 36:5-14), told the errant missionary: "Know ye not, my son, that these things are an abomination in the sight of the Lord; yea, most abominable above all sins save it be the shedding of innocent blood or denying the Holy Ghost?" (Alma 39:5). Unchastity, in any of its expressions, is the third greatest sin because of the spiritual devastation it produces: alienation from the Spirit, the clouding of one's own spiritual identity and sense of worth, and the crippling contamination of those human relationships—marriage and parenthood—which the Lord designed to fulfill and perfect the soul. These losses will prove far more ruinous and lasting than any possible pregnancy or physical disease unless sincere repentance is forthcoming.

Today's hue and cry over AIDS, rather than the gross misconduct that is usually responsible for it, is a perfect example of what Mormon called the "sorrowing of the damned, because the Lord would not always suffer them to take happiness in sin" (Mormon 2:13; see also Hel 13:29). But modern sinners demand that modern science do just that; they claim as their right freedom from consequences, the suspension of the cause-effect principle when it interferes with their desires.

The three sins cited by Alma share a common element: they violate the principle of life (Turner 144-50). The sin against the Holy Ghost makes the perpetrator a knowing, willing accessory to the crucifixion of the Son of God. Such persons are far more guilty of the Lord's death than the high priest Caiaphas and his fellow conspirators who brought it to pass. For with the truths of heaven blazing in their minds they have "crucified him unto themselves and put him to an open shame" (D&C 76:35).

In murder, a living soul is "put asunder" by forcing the spirit to abandon its lawful home. Its mortal probation is cut short and its God-given agency compromised. Ending a life is a prerogative belonging only to God and those whom he authorizes to exercise it in behalf of organized society.

Unchastity tampers with the very fountain of life, the celestial principle which sets the gods apart from all other resurrected beings: the power of endless lives. In one respect, this power makes God God. Thus sexual immorality strikes at his very nature and glory. The power of procreation is a talent (in the sense of Christ's parable), a stewardship temporarily and conditionally granted mortals to provide physical bodies for the spirit children of our divine Parents. If this "talent" is abused or repudiated, the offenders, having "buried" it, may well forfeit it forever. Indeed, of the entire human race, comparitively few will possess this most precious of exalting talents in the life to come.

Thank God for prophets who stand guard over chastity. Thank God for President Spencer W. Kimball who, speaking for all prophets, said: "God is the same yesterday, today, and forever, and his covenants and doctrines are immutable; and when the sun grows cold and the stars no longer shine, the law of chastity will still be basic in God's world and in the Lord's church" (*The Teachings of Spencer W. Kimball* 265).

Plural Marriage

The Book of Mormon has been cited by those who, in the main, do not really believe in it, as an argument against the "notorious" LDS doctrine of plurality of wives. Let us consider the problem in its historical setting.

While no specific information is provided, modern revelation states that plural marriage was practiced by the earliest patriarchs, meaning, presumably, Adam and/or his sons and grandsons, "from the beginning of creation" (D&C 132:38). However, the first identifiable polygynist in the Bible was Lamech, a great-great-great-grandson of Cain. He had two wives, Adah and Zillah (Gen 4:19). They despised him and betrayed his secret murder of his own great-grandfather, Irad. Like Cain, his

fellow murderer, Lamech became a fugitive from justice and a
vagabond in the earth (see Moses 5:42-54).

Jaredite Polygyny

The Jaredites of the Book of Mormon arose a century or so
after the Flood. It is possible, though by no means certain, that
at least some in the early colony were polygynists (the brother of
Jared had 22 sons and daughters [Ether 6:20]). In any event,
polygyny was definitely practiced in the first half of their approximately two-thousand-year-plus history. One of their earlier
kings, Riplakish, was not unlike the later Solomon. He burdened
his people with heavy taxes, built numerous large buildings with
forced labor, had "many wives and concubines . . . [and] did
afflict the people with his whoredoms and abominations" (Ether
10:5-7). Jaredite polygyny was not restricted to royalty. Moroni
recorded that in the final fratricidal war of the Jaredites every man
kept his sword in hand "in the defence of his property and his
own life and of his wives and children" (Ether 14:2).

Old Testament Polygyny

Abraham, who lived about 2000 BC, is the first righteous
polygynist identified in the Old Testament. He had one wife,
Sarah, and at least two concubines, Hagar and Keturah.

A word about concubinage. Concubines were not mis-
tresses or prostitutes, they were lawful wives—usually captive
slaves or foreigners—who had legitimacy but not full honor.
Their children enjoyed no rights of inheritance.[5] It was a case of
social inferiors becoming part of a man's family.

Concubinage reflected the realities of the ancient world. It
was a lesser law for a lesser time. In viewing those times the issue

---

[5] For example, Abraham sent Hagar and her son Ishmael away with no inheritance
(Gen 21:14). Following Sarah's death Abraham married Keturah, by whom he had six sons,
but we read: "And Abraham gave all that he had unto Isaac. But unto the sons of the
concubines, which Abraham had, Abraham gave gifts, and sent them away from Isaac his son,
while he yet lived, eastward, unto the east country" (Gen 25:5-6).

is not what was ideally right or wrong, fair or unfair, but what was workable. If concubinage was a relative evil, it was the lesser of evils; better a concubine than a woman alone, or a harlot. That the Lord justified his servants in having concubines—and he did—is no proof that he viewed the practice as more than a necessary, albeit unfortunate aspect of an imperfect order of things.

The patriarchs who followed Abraham, notably Isaac and Jacob, were also polygynists. The law of Moses (introduced about 1300 BC) acknowledged the legitimacy of the practice (Moses himself had at least two wives [see D&C 132:38]). But polygyny on an extended scale was introduced into Israel by Saul's successor, David (see 2 Sam 5:13). Solomon, his son by Bathsheba, caught the spirit of the practice with a vengeance and acquired seven hundred wives and three hundred concubines. In this Solomon the Wise proved a fool, for "his wives turned away his heart" (1 Kings 11:3). Solomon introduced idolatry into Israel and thereby set the stage for Israel's subsequent bondage and dispersion.

The Nephites and Polygyny

Although the law of Moses permitted wives and concubines, the Lord forbade the practice for the house of Joseph in the Promised Land, in the Americas. This was probably in part because of its historic abuses, but also because the basis for such marriages did not exist in Lehi's colony.

The Nephites did not practice slavery, nor did they take female captives and make wives of some of them as had their Israelitish ancestors even in the days of Moses.[6] As for the many war-produced widows found at times among the Nephites, the

---

[6] The law of Moses specifically permitted Israelites to marry captive women (Num 31:9; Deut 21:11). The Lamanites took women and children as prisoners of war, and on several occasions placed their Nephite captives in virtual servitude (see Mosiah 7:15; 9:12; Alma 58:30).

policy was to care for their temporal needs rather than to marry them (see Mosiah 21:10, 17; Moroni 9:16).

Jacob's Denunciation

Following the death of Nephi (about 540 BC), pride and the "grosser crime" (see Jacob 2:22) of whoredoms appeared for the first time among the Nephites. Certain men "began to grow hard in their hearts, and indulge themselves somewhat in wicked practices, such as like unto David of old desiring many wives and concubines, and also Solomon, his son" (Jacob 1:15).

Jacob, Nephi's younger brother, was instructed by the Lord to denounce this evil in its incipiency. Only some Nephites were actually engaged in polygyny; others probably contemplated doing so, while still others remained "pure in heart." So it was a mixed audience—as such groups usually are—that Jacob addressed. The heart of his message on the subject was as follows:

> This people begin to wax in iniquity; they understand not the scriptures, for they seek to excuse themselves in committing whoredoms, because of the things which were written concerning David, and Solomon his son. [Today, it is Joseph Smith and Brigham Young.]
>
> Behold, David and Solomon truly had many wives and concubines, which thing was abominable before me, saith the Lord.
>
> Wherefore, thus saith the Lord, I have led this people forth out of the land of Jerusalem, by the power of mine arm, that I might raise up unto me a righteous branch from the fruit of the loins of Joseph.
>
> Wherefore, I the Lord God will not suffer that this people shall do like unto them of old.
>
> Wherefore, my brethren, hear me, and hearken to the word of the Lord: For there shall not any man among you have save it be one wife; and concubines he shall have none;
>
> For I, the Lord God, delight in the chastity of women. And whoredoms are an abomination before me; thus saith the Lord of Hosts (Jacob 2:23-28).

Jacob did not proclaim a new doctrine. He told the Nephites: "Ye know that these commandments were given to our father, Lehi; wherefore, ye have known them before" (Jacob 2:34; see also 3:5).

The effort to introduce forbidden practices and to justify them by appealing to scriptural precedents was clearly out of order. It was so then, and it is so now. If ancient scripture does not justify disobedience to the counsel of the Lord's living prophet, how can modern historical examples do so? The Lord's people are bound by the commandments given them through the prophet of their day, not those of an earlier time. They are accountable to the prophets they raise their hands to sustain. President Benson has said, "The living prophet is more important to us than a dead prophet. . . . Beware of those who would pit the dead prophets against the living prophets, for the living prophets always take precedence" ("Fourteen Fundamentals in Following the Prophet" 27). Where obedience is concerned, dead prophets belong to the dead.

Thus Jacob cut to the heart of the matter. What prominent men did and what the Lord approved could be two very different things. Further, no man was justified in deviating from the commandments of the Lord for his time because of the commandments of the Lord to others in another time.

Plural Wives Not Wrong Per Se

In saying that "whoredoms are an abomination before me" (see Jacob 2:28), the Lord was not equating the principle of plural marriage with whoredoms or declaring that all such marriages—including those of Abraham, Isaac, and Jacob—are abominable in his sight. He was denouncing the abuse of a sacred principle, not the principle itself.

But what is abominable to him in any form of marriage is when the relationship is motivated by lust, or when it robs one's wife of her personhood and reduces her to the level of a thing to be used, mistreated, manipulated, or whimsically abandoned. In that regard, some monogamous marriages among us are abominations.

When wives are neglected, subjected to physical or verbal abuse, to emotional trauma, or to humiliating and degrading conduct by their husbands, the spirit of chastity in them is violated. For chastity is more than a sexual matter, it is also a state of mind, heart, and spirit toward one's whole being. The very soul is at issue.

On the part of husbands, the spirit of chastity implies a conscious commitment to the physical, spiritual, and emotional well-being of their wives and of all women. When a woman is rendered a mere object, a piece of chattel, the spirit of chastity leaves her. She does not feel toward herself as she has the right to feel.

For example, Mormon wrote to his son Moroni that certain Nephites had made captives of Lamanite women "and after depriving them of that which was most dear and precious above all things, which is chastity and virtue—And after they had done this thing, they did murder them in a most cruel manner, torturing their bodies even unto death; and after they have done this, they devour their flesh like unto wild beasts, because of the hardness of their hearts; and they do it for a token of bravery" (Moroni 9:9-10).

Such barbarism is probably unparalleled in all history. These Lamanite daughters, though robbed of their physical virginity, died virtuous and innocent in God's eyes. Because, in truth, virtue cannot be taken, it must be willingly given. So these girls were no less chaste and pure of soul because of being violated, but they had been deprived of the spirit of chastity, of their God-given feelings of dignity and worth as human beings. Their own holy of holies in the temples of their spirits had suffered defilement—an "abomination of desolation." It was in this sense that their chastity and virtue were stolen from them. Can anyone doubt that the all-too-prevalent crime of rape is nothing less than a form of spiritual murder? It was this crime—albeit less vicious in degree—that the Lord declared an abomination among the Nephites.

Those who sought to "indulge themselves," as Jacob expressed it, in plural wives were not motivated by a caring love and concern for these women, but rather by pride and lust in their hardened hearts (see Jacob 1:15-16). For was there not a connection between the sin of pride in consequence of their material wealth and their "grosser crime" (see Jacob 2:22) of whoredoms? Not only could they afford wives and concubines, they reasoned, but their very status in society warranted them. Citing the conduct of David and Solomon, who were also wealthy and prominent, was designed to cloak their actions with moral approval.

But the consequences of all such infidelity were vividly described by Jacob: "Ye have broken the hearts of your tender wives, and lost the confidence of your children, because of your bad examples before them, and the sobbings of their hearts ascend up to God against you. And because of the strictness of the word of God, which cometh down against you, many hearts died, pierced with deep wounds" (Jacob 2:35). How many hearts die today because of marital infidelity and insensitivity?

Jacob's message seems to have had the desired effect. Other than the aberrant case of king Noah, polygyny was apparently stamped out for all time among the Nephites. He tells us: "And now I, Jacob, spake many more things unto the people of Nephi, warning them against fornication and lasciviousness, and every kind of sin, telling them the awful consequences of them" (Jacob 3:12).

Nevertheless, Jacob's prophetic warning that unless the Nephites repented the Lamanites "shall scourge you even to destruction" (Jacob 3:3) was fulfilled. In the third century BC, prior to that destruction, king Mosiah led the righteous remnant of the Nephites from the land of Nephi northward to the land of Zarahemla (Omni 1:12-14; compare Jacob 3:4). The fall of the first Nephite civilization suggests that harlotry and other evils—if not polygyny—finally took their toll. Modern prophets have warned of a similar fate for an unrepentant America.

An Apparent Contradiction

Critics have been quick to point out the apparent contradiction between Jacob's denunciation of plural wives and concubines (Jacob 2:23-28) and the subsequent defense of both by Joseph Smith (D&C 132:1, 30, 37-39). How can plural marriage be "abominable" in the Book of Mormon and a righteous principle associated with heaven's highest rewards in the Doctrine and Covenants?

Joseph Smith Knew Moral Law

First, let us grant the Prophet some common sense and at least a modicum of integrity. He was certainly aware of Jacob's teachings in the Book of Mormon (published in 1830) when he first learned of the doctrine of plural marriage (before or in 1831). His initial inquiry of the Lord concerning polygyny in the Old Testament probably came about in connection with his labors on his inspired revision of the Bible—starting with Genesis where the lives of Abraham, Isaac, and Jacob are recorded. This labor began in the summer of 1830.

Secondly, the Prophet was also aware of the moral law of the Church revealed in February 1831 in which the Lord instructed: "Thou shalt love thy wife with all thy heart, and shalt cleave unto her and none else" (D&C 42:22). In March 1831 the Lord added that it was "lawful that he [any man] should have one wife" (D&C 49:16).

Joseph Smith was also aware of God's strong condemnation in August of the same year of adultery among the Saints: "And verily I say unto you, as I have said before, he that looketh on a woman to lust after her, or if any shall commit adultery in their hearts, they shall not have the Spirit, but shall deny the faith and shall fear. Wherefore, I, the Lord, have said that . . . the whoremonger, and the sorcerer, shall have their part in that lake which burneth with fire and brimstone, which is the second death" (D&C 63:16-17). In October he gave Apostle William E.

McLellin a personal revelation which told him the following: "Commit not adultery—a temptation with which thou hast been troubled" (D&C 66:10).

Was Joseph Smith a fool or a hypocrite in all of this? Did he publicly denounce, in the name of Jesus Christ, immoral practices he was privately contemplating? The foregoing pronouncements were made in the same time frame in which he first received the answer to his question on plural marriage in Old Testament times. Thus it was by revelation that Joseph Smith learned that the restriction on the Nephites was neither universal nor absolute.

David and Solomon

Still, it may be argued, in the Book of Mormon God condemns David and Solomon for having "many wives and concubines" (see Jacob 2:24), while in the Doctrine and Covenants he says, "I, the Lord, justified my servants Abraham, Isaac, and Jacob, as also Moses, David and Solomon, my servants, as touching the principle and doctrine of their having many wives and concubines" (D&C 132:1). How can both statements be true?

The answer, I believe, is that in the Book of Mormon the Lord was speaking specifically of two men who had been cited by the Nephites in defense of their own misbehavior. However, in the Doctrine and Covenants, the Lord, speaking generally, alluded to all those polygynists in the Old Testament about whom Joseph had made inquiry, including David and Solomon.

These men were justified in "the principle" of having additional wives given them by authorized servants of God. "Abraham received all things, whatsoever he received, by revelation and commandment" (D&C 132:29). He "received concubines, and they bore him children; and it was accounted unto him for righteousness, because they were given unto him" (D&C 132:37). But such was not always the case with David and Solomon. They committed abominations when they took wives not given them by those holding the sealing power. Their sheer excessiveness and their indifference toward the Lord's duly authorized servants brought them under condemnation.

In Doctrine and Covenants 132, Christ speaks of the "principle and doctrine of [his servants] having many wives and concubines" (v 1). But how many is "many"? Presumably, the prophets cited in verse one had many of each. Yet Abraham had but one wife and two known concubines, and Isaac had but one wife and no concubines insofar as the Old Testament has recorded. Jacob had two wives and two concubines, and Moses had two known wives and no known concubines.[7] David, on the other hand, had a large but unspecified number of wives and concubines. Solomon, as previously noted, had a thousand. Plainly, in referring to "many wives and concubines," the Lord was speaking of a general principle applying only to those he cited.

Insofar as his ancient servants' being justified in taking plural wives, the Lord told Joseph Smith: "In nothing did they sin save in those things which they received not of me" (D&C 132:38). David did not receive Bathsheba from the Lord. His adulterous relationship with her, followed by his murder of her husband, Uriah, cost Israel's king his exaltation. His lawful wives were forfeited and sealed to another unidentified man (D&C 132:39).

Thus, although Jacob denounced Nephite polygynists in the strongest terms, it is clear that he did not make an absolute statement on the subject for all times and all peoples. He knew that plurality of wives was a divine principle, hence the addendum in Jacob 2:30: "For if I will, saith the Lord of Hosts, raise up seed unto me, I will command my people; otherwise they shall hearken unto these things." What "things"? Jacob's teachings on monogamy. How else would the Lord raise up a more numerous people unto himself save it were by magnifying the monogamous principle

---

[7] Since wife and concubine are often used as interchangeable terms, Moses' Ethiopian wife (Num 12:1) was probably a concubine.

of marriage into plurality of wives even as he had done with Abraham? (see Abr 1:2; D&C 132:34). But it was not for the Nephites, or any later individual or group, to presume to expand the principle; the Lord would command. He alone would determine when conditions warranted its introduction and what its manner of implementation would be.

And when he did so, it would not be in a dictum to the world, but to "my people" (Jacob 2:30). They alone, a holy people, would be permitted to perpetuate and expand the doctrine of marriage (whether monogamous or plural) into eternity. For, as stated before, marriage is a celestial talent which can only be retained by celestial men and women. Those who bury it by unworthiness, abuse, or neglect will be saved, but single, worlds without end (see D&C 132:17).

Nor, I believe, will there ever be concubinage again. Those lesser times with their lesser laws are gone forever. Every sealed woman is a full wife with access to every right and blessing enjoyed by her sisters. For the Lord has revealed that the purpose of plural marriage is not to gratify the lusts or ambitions of men, but to magnify celestial women. It is to recognize their divine right to self-fulfillment, worthy husbands, and honorable motherhood; and to thereby raise up a holy posterity to themselves and to their God. Eternal marriage (whichever form) is the only way the immortality and eternal life of man and woman—the endless work of God—can continue (see D&C 132:63; Moses 1:38-39).

Relative Laws

The attempt to circumscribe God's moral sphere of action, to delimit what he can and cannot do, or, as the Prophet Joseph put it, "to set up stakes and set bounds to the works and ways of the Almighty" (*TPJS* 320), is characteristic of Spiritless men and religions. The very diversity in the natures and conditions of people requires diverse application of the laws and commandments leading to salvation. This means that while certain specific commandments may be binding on one people under a given system of law, they are not necessarily binding on another people subject to a different system of law.[8] For example, the spiritual law of Christ (the gospel) was binding on God's people from the time of the antediluvian patriarchs to the time of Joseph, while the carnal law of Moses was not imposed on their descendents until a thousand years after the Flood. Not only this, but changing circumstances within a given system may call for the modification or revocation of a former commandment and the introduction of a new one (see for example, D&C 56:3-4).

Such occurred when the doctrine of plural marriage was introduced by Joseph Smith. In a letter written justifying such marriages, he wrote:

> That which is wrong under one circumstance, may be, and often is, right under another. God said, "Thou shalt not kill;" at another time He said, "Thou shalt utterly destroy." This is the principle on which the government of heaven is conducted—by revelation adapted to the circumstances in which the children of the kingdom are placed. Whatever God requires is right, no matter what it is, although we may not see the reason thereof till long after the events transpire (*TPJS* 256).

If we understand the Prophet's words, we can understand why the Nephites were forbidden to have plural wives and why the early Latter-day Saints were enjoined to do so. The time to "raise up seed unto me" (see Jacob 2:30) came with the Latter-day Saints, not the Nephites. Much of the leadership of the Church has been drawn from just that seed. Many members of the Church today are also products of plural marriage. So the temporary need was met and the commandment suspended. Of course, there are still eternal needs yet to be met, so in due time the Lord will speak again on the subject.

Joseph Smith, the Prophet

If Joseph Smith was a true prophet, and he was, the Church is obliged to accept all that he received from the Lord, both in the

---

[8] Varying but harmonious systems of law are found throughout all organized existence (see D&C 88:37-39).

Book of Mormon and in those revelations which followed. We have no human basis for redefining the meaning, much less determining the validity, of any of the revelations given the Lord's anointed. Yet there are some prominent writers in the Church today—self-appointed ark-steadiers—who have presumed to do just that. But only a new revelation can qualify or set aside another revelation. And we cannot receive revelation for those to whom we are subordinate. The Prophet Joseph stated: "I will inform you that it is contrary to the economy of God for any member of the Church, or any one, to receive instruction for those in authority, higher than themselves" (*TPJS* 21; see also 214-15). Consequently, only a prophet can qualify the words of a previous prophet—and that, only when inspired to do so.

In being commanded to take wives for eternity, the Prophet Joseph Smith was instructed to "do the works of Abraham" (D&C 132:32), not the works of David or Solomon. And because Joseph did the "works of Abraham," he became a son of Abraham and, therefore, an heir of the blessings of Abraham. In receiving the more sure word of prophecy (D&C 131:5), the Prophet was told: "For I am the Lord thy God, and will be with thee even unto the end of the world, and through all eternity; for verily I seal upon you your exaltation, and prepare a throne for you in the kingdom of my Father, with Abraham your father" (D&C 132:49). If Joseph Smith was esteemed by Jesus Christ to be worthy of exaltation, he should be esteemed by every Latter-day Saint to be worthy of his prophetic calling.

Conclusion

In referring to his own record, Nephi wrote: "And it speaketh harshly against sin, according to the plainness of the truth; wherefore, no man will be angry at the words which I have written save he shall be of the spirit of the devil" (2 Nephi 33:5). The Book of Mormon is speaking to us today. Are we listening? It is commanding us. Are we obeying? We cannot plead ignorance or confusion for its message is presented clearly and unmistakably, in the language of virtue. Although it deals at times with unsavory themes, it does not do so in a prurient manner. The impure is treated purely.

Indeed, in discussing problems of immorality, the Book of Mormon is far more discreet than the Old Testament. The Old Testament as we have it is a product of many minds reflecting the religious and cultural character—the ethos—of an ancient people. Much of it was written by unknown chroniclers of Israel's history.[9] Because it recounts in some detail certain rather unsavory events, and contains graphic metaphors by some of the prophets, it has even been accused of being salacious. While the accounts are forthright, they are not salacious; unlike pornography they are not told in a manner to promote prurient thoughts and feelings. In its defense, I quote from Paul who said: "Unto the pure all things are pure: but unto them that are defiled and unbelieving is nothing pure; but even their mind and conscience is defiled" (Titus 1:15).

Actually, specific accounts of immorality are comparatively few in the Old Testament when we recall that it covers a span of four millennia and was written over a period of about nine hundred years. Contrast its ten or so incidents with the steady stream of stories of adultery, rape, and perversion appearing in our news media every day!

Those who gave us the Book of Mormon were clearly sensitive and circumspect in their accounts. This is a testimony of the sensitivity and purity of mind, not only of the original prophets who wrote and abridged it, but also of the prophet who translated it. Joseph Smith was a virtuous man. Out of the abundance of his heart he spoke the sanctifying word of the Lord. The Book of Mormon is not only a witness of the prophetic calling of Joseph, but of his moral character as well. No unclean mind

---

[9] With the qualified exception of the five books of Moses (the Pentateuch) and the 16 books named for the prophets, beginning with Isaiah and ending with Malachi, the authors of the 39 books comprising the Old Testament are completely anonymous.

produced the Book of Mormon or the Doctrine and Covenants or the Pearl of Great Price. I say this because Joseph Smith has been maligned and vilified from the very beginning by enemies both in and out of the Church. Since 1945, biographies and articles on his life, written by supposedly loyal members of the Church, as well as admitted apostates, have been published in ever-increasing numbers. Some of the more sensational—and therefore more popular—contain subtle (and sometimes not too subtle) innuendos that the Prophet's personal moral behavior left much to be desired. This is a demeaning lie.[10] It demeans the Prophet, but more especially it demeans the Lord who raised him up. A holy God does not, and is not obliged to, use unholy prophets to accomplish his righteous purposes.

The life of Joseph Smith is reflected in his writings, both public and private. As he was the first witness of the heavenly origin of the Book of Mormon, so is the Book of Mormon an unassailable witness of the virtue, integrity, and divine appointment of Joseph Smith. Their common testimonies pertaining to the law of chastity flow forth from God, the "fountain of all righteousness" (Ether 12:28). May we all drink from that fountain so that when we stand before the judgment bar of the Almighty we, too, may be found worthy of the eternal blessings of a virtuous life.

---

[10] Brigham Young, who knew Joseph Smith as well as any man during those critical years between 1832 and 1844, said in later years: "I never preached to the world but what the cry was, 'That damned old Joe Smith has done thus and so.' I would tell the people that they did not know him, and I did, and that I knew him to be a good man; and that when they spoke against him, they spoke against as good a man as ever lived" (*JD* 4:77).

BIBLIOGRAPHY

Benson, Ezra Taft. "Cleansing the Inner Vessel." *Ensign* (May 1986) 16:4-7.

———. "Fourteen Fundamentals in Following the Prophet." *1980 Devotional Speeches of the Year*. Provo, UT: Brigham Young Univ, 1980. 26-30.

Journal of Discourses. 26 vols. 1854-86.

The Teachings of Ezra Taft Benson. Salt Lake City: Bookcraft, 1988.

The Teachings of Spencer W. Kimball. Ed. Edward L. Kimball. Salt Lake City: Bookcraft, 1982.

Teachings of the Prophet Joseph Smith. Comp. Joseph Fielding Smith. Salt Lake City: Deseret Book, 1976.

Turner, Rodney. *Woman and the Priesthood.* Salt Lake City: Deseret Book, 1972.

The Testimony of Amaleki   17

Gary R. Whiting

*T*he Book of Mormon is a book of truth and also a book of mystery. God has given this record to all who love the truth. However, he expects each reader to be a diligent seeker of its pages. When the Book of Mormon is explored with the Holy Spirit as the reader's guide, many treasures are discovered and many mysteries are revealed.

There is a key to the study of all scripture and especially to the Book of Mormon. This key is a very simple idea called the "Purpose Principle." It states that everything in the Book of Mormon is there for a reason. God has not placed any "filler" pages in the Book of Mormon. Because everything is there for a purpose, serious students must begin their study by asking God, "Why have these things been included in the scriptures?" In asking questions and searching for answers, we prepare ourselves to allow God to lead us to deeper understanding and increased insight. When we fail to ask questions or look for answers, we leave the Book of Mormon a mystery to us. Those who fail to seek lose many valuable insights into the deep things of God.

The book of Omni is a prime example of a scripture that remains a mystery to many readers of the Book of Mormon, not because it is difficult to understand, but because it is often overlooked. A small book written by five different authors, it covers several hundred years of Nephite history with barely a comment. The first four writers did not write much. The fifth

Gary R. Whiting is an elder in the RLDS Church.

writer is Amaleki, and although he wrote only 17 verses, his contribution to the Book of Mormon is substantial.

Amaleki's work and the book of Omni take on greater significance when we recognize that they are there for a purpose. God arranged for these writings to come to us and promises that they will go to the house of Israel. I will share what I have discovered to be important contributions made by Amaleki. A careful study of these writings will open our eyes to the great things God can do through small means.

An Overview of Amaleki's Record

Amaleki is the last writer on the small plates of Nephi. Approximately the same size as the book of Enos, the record exists as he wrote it, for it was not abridged. Mormon included the small plates of Nephi with his abridgment of the other plates because God commanded him to, though he did not tell Mormon all the reasons why. We now know that one reason is that it covered the same time period as the pages lost by Martin Harris. Therefore, what is written on the small plates is vital to the mission of the Book of Mormon (see D&C 10:38-44).

Amaleki's record in the book of Omni is a very important part of the Book of Mormon because the historical information he includes gives insight into and background for the rest of the Book of Mormon account. He speaks of the Nephite people under king Mosiah, of the people of Zarahemla, and of the Jaredites. In a very few words Amaleki adds to our understanding of each of the three major groups of the Book of Mormon record. He also speaks of another group of people who followed Zeniff, who became their king. This is particularly significant because it is in Zeniff's/Amaleki's record that we see these groups linked together. Many portions of Mosiah, Alma, and Helaman are clearer because of the information presented by Amaleki, who also confirms the book of Ether and Ether's prophecies.

In addition to giving important historical elements, Amaleki presents a strong testimony of the power of God and the gospel of Christ. This alone would make his writings worthy of our study. He shows us how God rescues his people by revelation and feeds them by the preaching of his word. He is shown to be a faithful preacher of the gospel in the short exhortation near the end of his writing.

Amaleki's Background

Amaleki was a descendant of Jacob, the brother of Nephi. That lineage had the responsibility of keeping the records of the Nephites. It appears that Amaleki was the last of this family to keep the plates.

Nephi had been given specific instructions by the Lord concerning what writing should be in these plates.[1] When he grew old and was about to die, he gave the plates to Jacob with equally specific instructions:

> Nephi gave me, Jacob, a commandment concerning the small plates, upon which these things are engraven. And he gave me, Jacob, a commandment that I should write upon these plates a few of the things which I considered to be most precious; that I should not touch, save it were lightly, concerning the history of this people which are called the people of Nephi. For he said that the history of his people should be engraven upon his other plates, and that I should preserve these plates and hand them down unto my seed, from generation to generation. And if there were preaching which was sacred, or revelation which was great, or prophesying, that I should engraven the heads of them upon these plates, and touch upon them as much as it were possible, for Christ's sake, and for the sake of our people (Jacob 1:1-4).

Jacob was obedient and when he passed the plates to his son Enos, he gave him the same kind of commandments concerning the plates. Enos was also obedient (Jacob 7:27), and as he

---

[1] The commandments given to Nephi concerning the plates can be found in 1 Nephi 9:2-5, 1 Nephi 19:1-3, and 2 Nephi 5:29-33. Nephi also records that he was obedient to this command in 2 Nephi 4:14. In two places Nephi states that he will command his seed concerning the keeping of these plates. These commands are given in 1 Nephi 6:3-6 and 1 Nephi 19:4.

passed the plates on to his son Jarom, he counseled him to obey the Lord's commandments regarding the keeping of the record (Jarom 1:1, 2). The plates were subsequently passed on to Omni, Amaron, Chemish, Abinadom and then to Amaleki. All of these men kept the plates according to the commandment that God had first given Nephi.

Amaleki's testimony of obedience shows the importance of keeping all of the commandments of God, even if we feel that we have no great thing to contribute to his work. He grew up with a heritage of obedience, and we have his record today, in large part, because his father and others before him were obedient to the command of God. This is the context in which we should view the writings of Amaleki.

Very little is known about Amaleki the man. From a quick reading of Omni 1:25-26, we know that he had great faith in the Lord Jesus Christ. We also know that he had a brother whom he loved very much. In verse 30 Amaleki mentions this brother who went into the wilderness with Zeniff. There is a sense of sadness in the way he says he has "not since known concerning" his brother and those who went with him. It seems as though Amaleki felt that the expedition was foolish and wished his brother had stayed in the land of Zarahemla.

We have to assume that he had no sons because he says he had no seed to whom he could give custody of the plates. This is why he gave them to king Benjamin. This all tells us that he was born during the life of Mosiah and died sometime during the reign of king Benjamin. We do know he was a man of God, perhaps a prophet, with a gift for writing the things of God.

The Journey to Zarahemla

Amaleki begins his record in Omni 1:12 by describing the migration of a group of Nephites from their homes in the land of Nephi to the land of Zarahemla under the leadership of Mosiah. This was not just an expedition, but it was an escape from conditions and people that posed an immediate danger to the Nephites. The urgency of this move is implied by Amaleki's use of the word *flee*.

It is likely that the Nephites, who had a history of wandering from the ways of the Lord, were in danger of being attacked by the Lamanites. When all other attemps to humble them failed, the Lord let the Lamanites scourge them. God revealed this principle through Jacob (Jacob 3:3, 4) and Amaleki recorded an example of it in action.

Mosiah was warned by the Lord that he must leave the land of Nephi. He took all of the people who would "hearken unto the voice of the Lord" with him into the wilderness (Omni 1:12). During the journey, Mosiah and his people were led by the word of God. Amaleki writes that through "many preachings and prophesyings" (v 13) the people were admonished continually by the word of God. Because of their willingness to obey his word, God led them by the power of his arm into a new land to meet a new people and begin a life where they could again serve him freely.

The People of Zarahemla

When Mosiah and his people came into the new land, they found it populated by a people who had been there for many years. They called themselves the people of Zarahemla, after the man who led them. They are also known as Mulekites because they were descendants of Mulek, who was a son of king Zedekiah in Jerusalem.

By including the story of Zarahemla and his people in his record, Amaleki gives a significant witness of truth. The presence of the Mulekites in the Western Hemisphere is a witness that the Biblical record is prophetically and historically accurate. It shows that the prophecies in Ezekiel 17:22 and 37:16-20 are true. A twig of Judah has been transplanted to the promised land, and the records of Judah (the Bible) and Joseph (the Book of Mormon) have run together and become one book.

Mulek and his followers came from Jerusalem after it had fallen to Nebuchadnezzar, king of Babylon. They had witnessed the fall of mighty Jerusalem to Babylon. This testimony confirmed the many prophecies and visions concerning the destruction of Jerusalem. In particular, their witness confirmed Lehi's and Nephi's prophecy that Jerusalem would be destroyed if her people did not repent of their wickedness. The truth of their testimony had been a point of much disagreement from the earliest days of Lehi's migration. Laman and Lemuel frequently murmured against their father and his prophecies, and succeeding generations of Lamanites continued to speak of the Nephites' "foolish traditions." The Mulekites removed all doubt concerning the truthfulness of Lehi's prophecies (see Hel 8:21) and confirmed the truth of the Book of Mormon. They were also involved in the fulfillment of a third series of prophecies, which will be mentioned later.

Amaleki wrote more about the Mulekites than any other Book of Mormon author. Using his record and the fragments given by others, we see that the Mulekites were essentially contemporary with the Lehites and appeared to have been in the promised land almost as long. Their histories were parallel in many ways. They both had multiplied greatly and had suffered many contentions and wars. Their histories differed dramatically in the matter of records, however. The people of Zarahemla had not brought any records with them from Jerusalem and rejoiced because Mosiah's people had (Omni 1:14). The lack of records had been a stumbling block for the Mulekites, in that without them to stabilize their language it had become corrupt, and they had also lost their religious knowledge and denied the being of their Creator (see Omni 1:17).

Over a period of years, relying only on oral traditions, and coming from a line of kings who generally disregarded the word of the Lord, it is not surprising to find that they had lost their faith in Christ. The Nephites, on the other hand, had records. They knew their heritage and the proper form of religion and belief. Although the Nephites had difficulty obeying the scriptures, they did have the written standard against which they could be measured. The Nephites knew the gospel as well as the history of God's dealings with Israel and the religion of their fathers was preserved.

Zarahemla and his people were not able to communicate with Mosiah because of the language difference. After a period of time the people of Mosiah taught the people of Zarahemla to speak the Nephite language. When they could communicate, the Mulekites shared their oral history with Mosiah. Later they formed an alliance and became one people, and Mosiah was their king. This was evidently more than a political alliance, because by selecting Mosiah they had picked a prophet of God to be their king. This would seem to imply that the Mulekites accepted the Nephites' religious faith as well.

These few words written by Amaleki, describing the union of the Nephites and Mulekites, are very significant as an example of a divine pattern of operation that could be called the "Separation Principle." The end result of every divine call to separation is a gathering. The Nephites were separated from their less righteous brothers in the land of Nephi and gathered with the people of Zarahemla. This resulted in the salvation of both the Nephites and the Mulekites.

The Jaredite Link

After introducing the people of Zarahemla, Amaleki unfolds more jewels of information. After the Mulekites had lived among the Nephites for a period of time and become accustomed to them, they brought a stone tablet to Mosiah with peculiar writing on it. Mosiah interpreted the writing by the power of God. The stone told the story of Coriantumr, in what seems to be the first reference in the Book of Mormon, as we have it, to the Jaredite people.

Coriantumr was the leader of one of two great armies of Jaredites that had fought for years to the total annihilation of the Jaredite people. Coriantumr had eventually killed the leader of the other army and was the sole survivor of the Jaredites. In the beginning of that war, Ether had been told by the Lord to call Coriantumr and his people to repentance with the promise that if they repented Coriantumr would be made king and his people would live. However, if they refused to repent all would be killed except Coriantumr, and he would live only long enough to see another group of people come into the land as had been prophesied earlier (Ether 11:20, 21; 13:21, 22).

There was no repentance and the war dragged on for many more years, but Ether's words were fulfilled and finally only Coriantumr was left alive (Ether 15:29-32). At this point the record of Ether was closed, and we can not tell whether the rest of his words were fulfilled or not. Amaleki finishes the story with the simple statement, "Coriantumr was discovered by the people of Zarahemla" (Omni 1:21), showing the fulfillment of the divine prophecy. Without Amaleki's record, we would not have this evidence.

Coriantumr lived for nine moons (nine months) with the Mulekites and then died. He was buried by these people and thus another part of Ether's prophecy was fulfilled. Once again we find God moving through the writings of Amaleki to confirm the word he had given through another prophet, this time Ether. Amaleki shows us that no word of God is left unfulfilled. As the Lord said through Isaiah, "My word . . . that goeth forth out of my mouth . . . shall not return unto me void, but it shall accomplish that which I please, and it shall prosper in the thing whereto I sent it" (Isa 55:11).

Zeniff and His Followers

Just before he closes his record, Amaleki mentions two groups of people that departed into the wilderness. He is affected personally by this story because his brother is among the second group of these people. Although Amaleki does not give any names, he does give enough detail that we know he is speaking about Zeniff (see Omni 1:27-30). As opposed to the migration of Mosiah and the Nephites out of the land of Nephi, Zeniff's expeditions were not divinely commanded. It was a private desire of men to find the lands of their inheritance, and the expeditions ended in disaster, twice. Amaleki closes his record not knowing what had become of his brother or the others on the second journey. The complete story of these two journeys is told in Mosiah 9-22, but by mentioning it, Amaleki provides yet another link that ties the small plates to the later records of the Nephites.

Amaleki, Witness for Christ

History is seldom personal to us. We may read and understand it, but it rarely concerns us. Amaleki bridges the gaps of time and culture by testifying of the Lord Jesus. He gets personal with each reader as his voice rises "as if from the dust" to speak to each of us about things to which we can relate today, the eternal Christ and the salvation of souls.

Although the record doesn't state this, it is my feeling that Amaleki's purpose in adding the gospel exhortation found in Omni 1:25-26 was that he was nearing the end of his life and was preparing to turn the plates over to king Benjamin. He knew that Jesus Christ was the center of the message written on the small plates and wanted to add his witness. Amaleki knew the Lord Jesus very well. Inspired by the written word and by his family, he sought out the Lord and found him, as all men can. Jesus was real to him and not simply a theoretical Savior. It is from this perception that Amaleki wrote his exhortation. He makes three points in these two verses of scripture, each centering on the Lord Jesus.

First, he calls everyone to come to God, the Holy One of Israel, and then identifies Jesus as the Holy One of Israel. To any Israelite who has studied the Old Testament scriptures, the title

Holy One of Israel would be very familiar. Amaleki has said, in a way that no Israelite should miss, that Jesus is the God of the Old Testament and the Savior of the world. Putting this truth together with qualities and titles associated with the name *Holy One of Israel* in the Old Testament, the house of Israel has another witness of the divinity of Jesus. The Book of Mormon is a special testimony to the Jew, and Amaleki seals this testimony in his declaration of Christ as the Holy One of Israel.

Second, Amaleki says that to serve Christ we must give ourselves as an offering to him. The words of the Apostle Paul to the Romans parallel this idea. Paul wrote, "I beseech you there-fore, brethren, by the mercies of God, that ye present your bodies a living sacrifice, holy, acceptable unto God, which is your reasonable service" (JST Rom 12:1). There is no halfway in the service of Christ. We are called to give ourselves without reserve to the Master. The references by Amaleki and Paul are to the sacrifices of the Old Testament. These offerings were acts of submission to God that revealed the nature of the sacrifice Christ would make in the flesh and also the completeness of the obedience we are to show to God. We live in sacrifice through prayer, fasting, and enduring to the end. Just as the burnt offering was entirely consumed our lives must be consumed by a pas-sionate service of God, given as a daily tribute for the grace of God given through Jesus to us (McConkie 2:116).

Finally, Amaleki calls us to a power-filled belief. He lists some of the gifts of the Holy Spirit and then exhorts us to believe in "all things which are good" (Omni 1:25). He asks us to come to Christ expecting to see such miracles as prophecy, tongues, interpretation of tongues, and the other good gifts of God (Omni 1:25). Through prayer, fasting, study, and obedience, we can develop the faith and discernment required for the exercise of these gifts. Amaleki gives us the key to discerning the good things of God: they will testify of the Lord Jesus. The presence of these gifts glorifies Christ and should humble us. False presentations will testify of selfishness, not sacrifice, and will lead us away from

Christ and the scriptures. Mormon gives additional testimony on this point. He says,

> For behold, the Spirit of Christ is given to every man, that they may know good from evil; wherefore, I show unto you the way to judge; for every thing which inviteth to do good, and to persuade to believe in Christ, is sent forth by the power and gift of Christ; wherefore ye may know with a perfect knowledge it is of God. But whatsoever thing persuadeth men to do evil, and believe not in Christ, and deny him, and serve not God, then ye may know with a perfect knowledge it is of the devil; for after this manner doth the devil work, for he persuadeth no man to do good, no, not one; neither doth his angels; neither do they who subject themselves unto him (Moroni 7:16, 17).

Amaleki makes a powerful plea for all mankind to come to Jesus Christ, for in Christ is redemption and salvation. Every reader is challenged to live wholly for Christ and the house of Israel is specifically called to see Jesus as the Savior. By this testimony, Amaleki joins the testimony of the Old Testament scriptures with the Book of Mormon record.

A testimony like this strikes right to our hearts. As we read it, Amaleki seems to be standing before us, looking into our eyes and asking, "How deep is your love for the Christ? How close are you walking with Jesus?" It is relevant and timeless. Amaleki has given us an eternal testimony of the living Christ.

Conclusion

Although his record is small and is hidden inside a book commonly considered insignificant, Amaleki makes a great contribution to the Book of Mormon. It is plain that he was obedient to the commandments concerning the keeping of the records. He was faithful to his heritage.

His record contributes to the history, prophecy and to the spiritual message of the Book of Mormon. Historically, Amaleki describes the joining of two great nations, the Nephites and Mulekites. He reports the story of the Mulekites and the end of the Jaredites. Because of Amaleki, we know about the life and character of king Benjamin, and we can understand the record of the first chapters of Mosiah more clearly. Prophetically, Amaleki ties the records of the Bible and the Book of Mormon together. The Old Testament scriptures are confirmed and fulfilled. He also confirms the calling of Lehi, Nephi, Jacob, and Ether as faithful prophets of God. Spiritually, Amaleki teaches us to love, worship, and serve the Lord Jesus. He also testifies of the power of the gospel of Christ and its necessity in our lives.

His 17 verses are an excellent example of how to make the most of a small opportunity. We have been blessed by his fine effort. The time spent reading Amaleki's writings is truly a time of joy and learning.

BIBLIOGRAPHY

McConkie, Joseph Fielding and Robert L. Millet. *Doctrinal Commentary on the Book of Mormon.* 4 vols. Salt Lake City: Bookcraft, 1987-.

Subject Index

Harris, Martin, 117
  lost 116 pages of original manuscript,
    62, 217, 296
Haughtiness, 223
Health, 227
Heart, 232
  hardness of, 228
  of spirit body, 227
  pure desires of, 227
"Heart of Heaven," 132, 134, 135, 136
Hebrew language, altered, 59
Helaman, and stripling warriors, 154
  appointed priests and teachers, 80
  commanded to keep records, 66
  obedient, 66
  succeeded Alma, 80
  taught by Alma, 153
Hell, 46
High priests, 40–41
  ancient, compared to bishops today,
    74
  called by Alma, 80
  in Book of Mormon, 80
  in latter days, 75
*Historias del Origen de los Indios de esta
    Provincia de Guatemala* (book).
    See Popol Vuh
Holy Ghost, 105, 111, 148, 197, 236
  assists missionaries, 149
  conferral of, 84
  denial of, 276–77, 278
  gift of, 111
  promptings of, 238
  warmth of, 149
  words of eternal life received through,
    243, 245, 247–48
Holy One of Israel, 304
Hope, 50, 162
  in Jesus Christ, 49, 226, 229
Horticulture, 87
Humility, 146, 224
Hunger, types of, 228
Husbands, effects of immorality on, 285
  immorality in the Book of Mormon,
    47, 272
  responsibilities for wives, 283–84

— I —

Idolatry, forbidden, 115
Immorality, 47, 85, 195, 201, 260, 271,
    278–79
  in Bible, 291–93
  in Book of Mormon, 272–76, 291–93

in latter days, 272
  Nephite crime, 276
Immortality, 11, 195
  See also Eternal life
Incantations, 110
Indians, 125, 137
Inequity. *See* Equity
Infinity, 18
Iniquity, 224
  See also Sin
Inspiration, 112
Intentions, 227
Interpolation, definition, 168
Isaac, authorized to live plural marriage,
    281, 287, 288
Isabel, 274
Isaiah, 42, 44, 45, 196
  quoted by Jacob, 43, 44, 45
  quoted by Nephi, 266
Ishmael, 35, 36, 194, 195
Israel, gathering of, 45, 68, 87, 101, 102,
    170–72
  lost tribes, 97, 99, 100, 101
  scattering of, 45, 87, 98, 99, 101,
    171–72
  tame olive trees a symbol of, 96
  twelve tribes of, 102
Israelites, did not understand atonement,
    122
  hardness of heart, 116
  influenced by foreigners, 109–10
  sacrifices, 115
  worship of, 108, 110
Isthmus of Darien, 130
Ivins, Anthony W., 22, 31
Ixtlilxochitl, Fernando de Alva, 129
Izmachi, 133

— J —

Jacob (Old Testament prophet), 36
  authorized to live plural marriage,
    281, 287, 288
Jacob (son of Lehi), 32–53, 183, 196
  accused of perverting gospel, 178, 180
  appointed by Nephi to speak, 42
  birth, 34–35, 263
  blessed by Lehi, 40, 52, 183
  bold, 43, 44
  book written over period of years, 39
  boyhood account in other records, 36
  called of God, 40, 42
  character description, 33, 43, 44
  child of house divided, 264

chosen in pre-existence, 158
corrected Samaritan woman, 106
covenant of, 107, 108
creator, 11
did will of God, 164
divinity of, 158, 159, 160, 161, 162,
165, 167, 172–73
faith in, 190
forgives sins, 144
fulfilled law of Moses, 41
God of Book of Mormon, 133
God of Old Testament, 304
hope in, 49, 226, 228
light of, 4
names of, 48, 133, 266
on concern for others, 112
on creation, 11
perfect knowledge of, 52
pure love of, 150
received name and power through
God, 164
resurrection, 82
salvation by taking his name upon
us, 165
Savior of world, 304
testimony of, 69, 70, 157, 158
vineyard master, 95
visions of, 40, 43, 51, 159, 160, 162,
183, 197
visit to America, 64, 67, 82, 83,
133–34, 137, 212
worship of the Father through, 163–64
See also God; Holy Ghost
Jews, 97, 98, 99, 100, 101
added to and took from law, 168–69
apostasy among, 157, 165–67
Book of Mormon special testimony
to, 304
cultural differences with Latter-day
Saints, 107
hardness of hearts, 114
spiritual blindness, 116, 120
spiritual deafness, 122
stiffnecked, 167
to be brought back to Jesus Christ,
158, 170
John the Baptist, 197
John the Revelator, 59–60, 197
Joseph of Egypt, 36, 41
writings of, 167
Joseph (son of Lehi), 36
birth, 34–35
consecrated by Nephi, 76, 84
named after Joseph of Egypt, 36
priest and teacher, 76–77, 84

Joy, 242
Judaism, 112
Judges, 78, 80
Judgment, 46, 65, 229, 275

— K —

Keturah, 280
Kimball, Spencer W., on Enos, 145
on guilt, 144–45
on morality, 279
Kindness, 150
Knowledge, 10, 51, 63
cumulative, 8–9
given to man in Garden of Eden,
13–14
perfect, 47, 51, 52
Korihor, 80, 107
struck down, 185, 187

— L —

Laban, 119–20, 197
Labor, trading of, 225
Laman, 36, 78, 197
murmured against Lehi, 300
rebellious, 35
Lamanites, 97, 98, 100, 101, 141
fidelity in marriage, 275
in latter days, 195
potential readers of Book of Mormon,
64
overcame Nephites, 99
records of, 60
sought to destroy Nephite records,
61, 142
women mistreated by Nephites, 284
Lamech, 279–80
Lamoni's father, converted through
prayer, 146
Land, 227
of promise, 222
Languages, difference in spoken vs.
written, 58
difficulty of writing concepts, 57
writing in second, 58
Large plates of Nephi, 209–12
civil and religious record, 211
digested in plates of Mormon,
212–14
strictly civil record, 36, 211, 213
Law, carries penalties, 5
defines parameters of social behavior,
273
definition, 2

Scripture Index

23:6	67	3:16	13
23:10–11	68	4:4	71
26:6	56	4:4–7	62
26:8–12	62	4:6–7	71
27:13–22	176	6:7	136
24:24–26	65	6:20	280
		10:5–7	280
4 Nephi		11:20, 21	302
1:1, 5	83	12:23–24	248
1:2–3	134	12:24	57
1:15–17	134	12:25–26	58
1:15, 17	2	12:28	293
		13:2	136
Mormon		13:2, 15–17	129
1–7	212	13:21, 22	302
1:1–4	209	14:2	280
1:2–4	210	15	129
1:3–4	66	15:26	129
2:2	216	15:29–32	302
2:13	278	15:33	56, 69
2:17	66		
2:17–18	209	Moroni	
2:18	212	2–6	83, 84
3:1–2	210	6:4–9	84
3:17–21	102	7–8	83
5:8–10	61	7:15–19	4
5:9	212	7:16, 17	305
5:12	64	7:44	232
5:13–14	70	8:8, 9	118
6:6	61, 209, 212	8:14	6
8:5	57	8:25–26	148
8:26	235	9:7–10	276
8:35	189	9:9–10	284
9:31	151	9:16	282
9:32–33	214	10	83
9:33–34	59	10:3–5	248
		10:21	248
Ether		10:27	235
1:3	135	10:32	247
1:33	129	10:33	248
1:35	129	10:34	249
3:9–10	13		

DOCTRINE AND COVENANTS

1:19	170	6:26	61
1:24	107, 253	8:2–3	150
1:31	274	9:8	26
1:32	188	10:1	62
1:35–36	271	10:38–44	296
1:38	152	10:40	218
3	36	10:41	211
3:16–19	195	10:63	179
3:19–20	142	18:9	75

PEARL OF GREAT PRICE